A Journal of a Year in the Life of a

BLUE
BADGE
BIRDER

Dedicated to the memory of my late wife, Dorothy, without her love, friendship and support none of this would have been possible.
Also my many friends, both past and present, whose support and encouragement has been so freely given.

Photographic illustrations by Andrew Toman.

BRIAN C. GEORGE

A Journal of a Year in the Life of a

BLUE BADGE BIRDER

First published in Great Britain in 2012 by The Derby Books Publishing Company Limited, 3 The Parker Centre, Derby, DE21 4SZ.

© Brian C. George, 2012

ISBN 978-1-78091-006-2
Printed and bound by CPI Antony Rowe, Chippenham.

Introduction

I have been playing about with the idea of writing a book about birders and birding for some years now, but never really had the time, nor the inclination to put pen to paper in a serious manner.

A little under three years ago my wife, Dorothy, died from cancer, and prior to her death she spoke with me about the book I had always been whittling on about. Dorothy knew she was dying from terminal cancer, and on this one occasion she said to me 'Why don't you write this book you have always talked about, when I am gone you will have time to concentrate your efforts?' This was not the talk I wished to hear at that stage in the proceedings, life without my dear wife was not something I was contemplating, but I did promise I would seriously attempt to do so. What you are about to read is the labour of my efforts.

Books on birds are numerous, many good, equally as many bad. I did not wish to write a book about bird identification, or where to watch birds, others have done this very well, indeed many of their publications are on my bookshelf. My thoughts had always been directed to my love of birds, and the joy and pleasure they had given to me. Since the loss of my dear wife, birds have played an even more important role, they have given me a reason for living. That may sound dramatic, but I shared so many of my experiences with my wife, who loved birds as much as I, that it was inevitable they would become so important to me. When I go birding I can still share the experiences with her.

Since 2008, the year of Dorothy's death, I have written many thousands of words, but few shouted out what I wanted. They may have made interesting reading, but it was not what I wanted to say.

During the last two years I have been affected by 'old age problems', two knee replacements, two dislocated shoulders, a pace maker, and one could go on. I now have great difficulty in walking any distance, so my bird watching has become very much a case of how near can I park my car.

This situation made me think. Bird watching does not always have to be leg work, chasing and walking miles in the pursuit of some rare bird or other, and being disappointed when you arrive to find the bird left 10 minutes ago, a birder's lament! Birds are not train numbers, you tick number one off, now where is number two, they are living creatures, just like us, and they even have personalities: just sit down and watch the birds in your own garden, you will quickly see who is the top dog (or should that be top bird?), no two birds are exactly the same. Just to watch them derives pleasure, at times humourously. I am lucky, I live in a village which possesses a well established rookery, and rooks are regular garden visitors, I do much to encourage them. I can sit for hours just watching them, and it did not take all that long to recognise the top birds.

Surely this is what bird watching is all about, recognise them yes, but watch their behaviour, enjoy their antics, look after them and provide regular food, let them into your life, and above all else, love them.

My idea for this book was now slowly forming. In life today there are many people not physically able to rush around chasing birds, we need to let the birds come to us as much as possible. I have met many people who have said they would love to study birds but are unable to do so due to some physical problem or other, they cannot walk very well or stand for any period of time, welcome to the club. To enjoy birds you do not have to walk all the time, or stand round for hours on end, unless you wish to 'twitch', if that is the case then I am sorry you are on your own, I cannot help you there. However, if you wish to join the happy throng of bird watchers who just love birds, then come along with me.

My aim during the next 12 months is to involve you with the pleasure and satisfaction obtained from just watching birds go about their daily business, and doing so with the minimum of physical effort. Most of my excursions will obviously be on my own patch, you may never be able to visit them, but the whole point of the exercise is the fact you will have just as many spots on your own patch, some you may already know, others you have yet the pleasure of finding. One thing I can assure you is the fact they are out there.

For the beginners to this game, you are probably asking the question, 'This all sounds fine, but how do you find them, how do you get started?' I run a bird study course in Derbyshire, I have over 40 members of varying knowledge levels, always remember no one is born with knowledge, we acquire it. I frequently tell people, we all started off with a blank page. You will almost certainly have a bird watching club in your locality, this may even be a RSPB run one, these are the people who will know much about the area in which you live, and their doors are always open to new members. This information can be gained from you local public library, but if you are fortunate to have a bird study course being run locally, this is probably your best starting point.

It is not easy to completely teach yourself, to have a few experienced birders around is very useful. They will all have made mistakes as they progressed, and learned from it, so you can benefit from all of this.

This book is a diary or catalogue of my birding throughout the current year, 2011. You will, I hope, travel with me to see the many wonders and pleasures birding provides. We will have a few trips round the country, stay at a few nice hotels and enjoy the odd bottle of wine, birding is not all mud and wind. We will meet many a like-minded individual, plus the odd awkward cuss whose neck we would willingly ring, but above all we will meet birds, thousands of them I hope, and with luck the odd rarity too.

On many of our trips we will be accompanied by my daughter Sarah and her friend Martin, plus members of the Rosliston Bird Study Group, much of what will follow is due, in no small account, to their efforts and support. .

As we progress we will talk about books, especially field guides and suitable equipment, so do not rush out and buy any of these until we have had a chance to discuss it, my initial thoughts are to get you involved with the birds, the rest will follow in the fullness of time. I also make reference to the net, it may be a good idea if I provide you with the details so you can use it yourself if you wish. At the time of writing, it is only £25.00 per year. It is www.birdingtoday.co.uk., and I personally find it very good.

So whether, like me you need sticks to walk with, or a chair to keep you mobile, do not let it hold you back, there is still a world out there waiting for discovery, come and join me in seeking it out. It is a decision you will never regret.

The Prologue

2011 is going to come in mild, or so the weather forecasters are claiming, so for once I can prepare my bird food this evening, and just have to put it out in the morning, not to have to thaw out their water bowls etc, will be a positive delight.

Today, New Year's Eve, I went out for an hour or two to survey the local area, and it was local, within about a six mile radius of home, time was rather short, so I did not learn a lot, come the big day I am going to rely on memory and my own knowledge of my patch. Normally, Sarah, Martin and myself would go out together, but today, for a bit of fun we are going to do our own thing, so we have two 'Bird Races' on, Sarah and Martin versus me. We call it fun, but really, underneath it all we would love to pull something over the other, so it is also a bit serious. I also have no wish to impede their efforts due to my mobility, or lack there of. I would normally include the large reservoirs and lakes we have in the county, but due to the very hard weather experienced recently these are still frozen over so waterfowl, the bulk of any Day 1 sightings, are going to be thin on the ground. Fortunately, I do know of one stretch of water which is likely to be open and ice free, and that is the settlement pool for Severn Trent Water over at Coton, near Kingsbury, so a few minutes spent there may help the numbers. This is where knowing your patch comes in useful.

The local rivers the Trent and Tame should also be good for the odd visiting duck, I know already we have had goosander and goldeneye on them both, and geese and swans along their banks, so it should not be all bad. Fields are now clear of snow so the grazers can get at food, this obviously suits the geese and swans, so I shall be a bit disappointed if I do not knock up one or two of those.

I always start my year with an hour or two at home where I hope to get my first 20 or so birds of the year from the comfort of my lounge, accompanied by a coffee or two! Tomorrow will be no different from the past, and with a bit of luck I may get my great spotted woodpecker on the list, that would be rather nice.

While writing this up I have had a thought, at the end of each chapter I will list the map references of the locations I consider to be important, so you can visit them yourselves at your leisure. The only point I would make, if you do, try to visit them at a similar time of the year to my visits, as the birds change with the seasons, and the species I am reporting in January are unlikely to be seen in June as an instance. Some may be residents, the majority are probably not.

That's the end of talk. Get the birds food ready, and we will also fill the inner man, I do have half a bottle of a nice Shiraz to finish off, so first things first. See you in 2011.

Chapter I

January

Idrew back my curtains just before 08.00 hours to welcome in a new year, and my first bird of the year gave me a fly past, well two really, a pair of carrion crows flew by, not a bird I would have considered as a likely number one, that is normally reserved for the blackbird. However, on walking through to the kitchen, the blackbirds were there, running round like headless chickens wondering where their dried fruit was hidden.

I am pleased to say the weather forecasters had it right, no frost, no thawing out to do, just take the covers off the one or two items I had protected from night time marauders, and won't the blackbirds be pleased?

Coffee prepared, now to sit down for an hour and see what nature can provide. It is now almost 08.30 hours and the light is much improved, and the coffee for some reason tastes particularly good.

I have eight feeding stations in the garden, including a slab in the lawn, and I position my chair so I can see all stations clearly, the 'Bird Race' now commences. Let us list, in sequence, the birds I see. Blue tit, robin, jackdaw, rook, magpie, chaffinch, great spotted woodpecker, wood pigeon, starling, long-tailed tit, great tit, collared dove, and at that point my heart almost stops. Sitting on the top of my rowan tree is a single waxwing.

For years both Dorothy and I had dreamed of having our own waxwings in the garden, they are just such a 'buzz' bird, and at long last here one was. Dorothy was not here to share in the event, but it was almost as though she was. I sat spell bound, Sarah was having her shower unfortunately so she was unable to share the occasion. I doubt if the bird was here for more than three minutes before it flew off, but what a three minutes, what a start to a new year and what a bird for day one. I already know my bird of the year for 2011, what ever comes after will not surpass this moment, not for the beauty of the bird nor the emotion of the moment. Back now to my list. Sparrowhawk, Canada goose, needless to say the latter flew over my garden, bullfinch, coal tit, dunnock and finally a fly past of lesser black-backed gulls. 21 in total, not a bad start.

Now for breakfast and the serious work for the day, Kings Bromley lay-by will be my next stop. I have to get there rather smartly, they are having a 'Plastic Duck Race' on the River Trent, a New Year Day event, so the local birds are going to be disturbed somewhat. I must get down there well before the event takes place, I am hoping for two or three nice birds, especially barnacle goose and goosander which have been in regular attendance recently.

The goose flock can be clearly seen well before I arrive at the lay-by, the question is are the barnacle geese still with them? I pull up, the local mallard population promptly run in my direction hoping for bread, which I have not so they are due for disappointment. Studying the geese flock, the barnacle geese are still there, 25 of them, nearby, also grazing are the local wigeon flock, almost in three figures, and the odd moorhen are scurrying about on the water as only they can.

Turning my attention upstream, a solitary greylag goose is on the water with a small contingent of Canada geese, and diving in the water under the footbridge is the drake goosander. Kings Bromley had delivered the goodies, a quick telephone call to Sarah to let her know, she would like the barnacle geese especially. Total now 27.

Next stop Whitemoor Haye, see if I can pick up the whooper swans which are reported from here, on occasion, there are only two, so I am not overly hopeful! Driving there I have a song thrush fly across the road in front of my car, and I arrive at the swan grounds. Mutes are everywhere, a couple of hundred of them or so, now starts the slow process of working my way through every swan in the hope I can find a whooper. After nearly half an hour I draw a blank, if they are here I cannot find them, on now to Whitemoor Haye Lake. The lake is still frozen all over, with just a few gulls standing on the ice, some of these are at least black-headed which provides me with a tick, the others are lesser black-backed, which do not. On now to Stubby Leas, we are after Bewick's swans here, and I am more hopeful of these than I was the whooper.

The swans are still in their field, so once again it is a case of up telescope and work my way through them all, the trouble now is it has started to rain. Just as I start to look at the swans a commotion comes from the hedge behind me. Fieldfare and redwing come hurtling out of the hedge as if the devil is chasing them, and sitting on the top of the hedge is a kestrel, she looks most bemused by it all. Within a split second I had three year ticks.

At least the Bewick's are in double figures, which makes the chances of finding some far easier, and so it turns out. Within minutes I have them, seven of them anyway, and that is more than enough for me. I spend a few minutes enjoying them, they are a very nice swan, the smallest of our three wild swans, although they are still a big bird.

Although I have set no target for today's total, I would like to reach about 50, and the Bewick's has taken us to 34, not bad, although the rain is getting rather persistent, with visibility tumbling.

My next vantage point is to be Coton Lakes, you will remember in my introduction I mentioned the fact these were not frozen over, and could be good for half a dozen birds or so. Driving through Tamworth I pick up tufted duck on the River Tame and as I leave Tamworth I see a mistle thrush sitting out on a telegraph pole. Arriving at Coton the rain is very heavy, not telescope weather unfortunately, I will just have to make do with my binoculars, which are going to be rather limited for birds in the distance, where conditions are very gloomy.

I position myself on the bridge which divides the two expanses of water, it is always nice to be able to look in both directions clearly. There are a large number of birds on the water which is quite understandable, this probably being the only area of open water available to them. I quickly pick out winter great crested grebe, coot, tufted, but we have already had these. Coton is well known for pochard, they are probably the common bird here. Little grebe can be heard calling, and one glides into view, as a cormorant flies overhead. Walking back to my car I spot a buzzard sitting it all out in a bare tree, not the sort of weather for a bird of prey.

Driving home I decided to pop into Middleton Hall, this had not been on my agenda, but as we were passing the door, why not have a couple of minutes looking at the lake. This turned out to be a good decision, although the lake was frozen several gulls were sitting out, and in the only bit of open water a shelduck was swimming. On the ice we had herring gull and common gull, so with the shelduck we knocked up three more species, 45 now.

Nearing home the light started to improve so I thought I would give Whitemoor Haye one last chance and then drive home via Croxall. The Haye was still very quiet, but I did at least pick up a flock of lapwings, nothing hidden among them unfortunately, and driving home via Croxall I added goldeneye, seen as we crossed over the River Tame, and also pheasant. So that was 48. Considering I had hoped for 50, given the conditions of today, 48 was a good attempt.

Mind you, the day was not over yet. As I made myself a cup of coffee two greenfinch came into the garden for their last feed, so we died in the hole, on 49.

Sarah and Martin had not done too badly either, they had 44, including some nice birds, crossbills especially. They had visited Cannock Chase and came across a flock of about 20 crossbills near to the Whitehouse car park, I know where I shall be going tomorrow. They also beat the start of the plastic duck race and saw the barnacle geese, so they were more than happy with their day out.

Sunday came in far brighter than yesterday, there was at least a break or two in the cloud base. Prior to going out, let us see what the garden may have to offer, I was washing up at the time and Sarah was drying up, as a small bird landed on the fat tray, from my angle I could not be sure just what it was but it certainly looked 'warblerish'. Sarah had a better angle than I, and she shouted out 'Blackcap, a female'. That was a nice turn up for the book as they say. Wintering blackcaps are becoming more regular these days, but it is not a bird you anticipate seeing in your own garden at the height of winter. A very nice 50 for me.

Nothing else of interest came into the garden, so I decided to go out earlier than expected and come back for lunch. Driving out of the village I spotted a nice male pied wagtail on a roof, very neat birds they are, and made my way across to the Chase. The Chase was heaving, I have never seen so many cars, I just managed to squeeze mine in at the Whitehouse. Fortunately, most of the visitors were making their ways onto the Chase, for once I was making my way up Marquis Drive, and there were no walkers here.

The only problem here was the sound of passing traffic, when searching for crossbills, sound can be just as important as sight, and just as it became quiet enough to listen along came more cars. I made my way further into the conifer woods in the hope of deadening the back ground noise, initially all to no avail, when a prolonged lull in the traffic occurred. This was my chance to really concentrate, and yes I could hear the chip, chip call of crossbills, but where were they? I spent several minutes looking, but no joy, so I made my way back to my parked car. Here things were much more peaceful than previously, still a full car park, but little or no people. It looked very much as though my crossbills were only going to be an audible record, when as I turned to unlock my car, four birds came chip, chip, chipping over head, I had my crossbills.

What to do next, I still had an hour at my disposal so I thought I would give Blithfield Reservoir a go. I should have known better, the reservoir was fully frozen all over with hardly a bird in sight, so I drove round to the dam. It was still frozen obviously, but you regularly get grey heron on the grassy bank of the dam, which would be another bird to my list. I was in luck, two grey heron were sitting out on the dam wall, and near the sailing club, in a piece of open water, six teal were swimming about.

Once home I quietly made my way into the lounge to have a look up the garden and I was rewarded with a nuthatch on my seed feeder, a nice home coming that one. As I put the kettle on for a cup of coffee I noticed a movement in my border, a quick glance, a wren. The kettle was forgotten as I watched the bird busily ferreting around in the dead plant life, I just hope it found something to take it through the night! I deliberately do not over tidy up in the winter, birds such as wren and dunnock find much food among garden litter.

The wren brought my birding for the day to a conclusion, I have reached 56, much further ahead than I was this time last year when I was recovering from a knee op'.

Sarah and Martin have also had a good day, they are now on 54, just two behind and their top bird today was a Caspian gull. The last day of the holiday is here for Sarah and Martin, what they will do with themselves I do not know, I may go after long-eared owls. Up near to Stoke-on-Trent we have a country park which usually holds one or two wintering long-eared owls, three were reported on New Years Day. Depending upon speed of success, I could then take myself up onto the moors in quest of red grouse, two nice species to chase after, and to tick them off so early in the year would be great.

Park Hall Country Park lies just to the east of Stoke, just off the A520 at Weston Coyney, and is a large reclaimed area from quarrying. Part has been planted with conifer trees, and it is this area the owls prefer as their roost.

Near the Centre is a feeding station, and the birds here are very people tolerant. Fortunately, the feeding station had been stocked up and was very active. At least five bullfinches were busy feeding away, quite unconcerned by my closeness, and a small titmouse kept flicking in and out quite rapidly. I quickly realised this was not one bird, there were three coming in from different directions, these were either willow or marsh tits, or maybe both if I am very lucky.

The differences between these two birds are very small. The willow has a dull black crown and a fairly large black bib, but the main thing we birder's look for is the pale white wing bar, and at this time of the year it should be quite discernable. The marsh tit on the other hand has a glossier black crown with a smaller black bib, and no white in the wing, and these birds certainly had no white in the wings, so marsh tits they were. As if to prove this to be so, one of the birds let out an explosive 'pitchou, pitchou' as a bullfinch came too close, if I had heard that upon my arrival I would not have had spend time studying the plumage of the birds. Regarding these two species, study their calls if you can, they are the most conclusive identification features of the two birds.

Fortunately, the walk down to the conifer plantation is only the matter of a couple of hundred metres or so, the unfortunate thing about it is the fact it is not wheelchair accessible, being just a footpath over a field. I walk with sticks so I am able to negotiate the walk with care.

After just minutes a shout goes up, well not actually a shout, no one wants to frighten a bird off, an owl has been found. We quickly gather round the person who has located the bird, and at almost the top of a conifer sits our prey, a magnificent long-eared owl, and as the bird gazes down at us the ear tufts are very distinct, a superb view. The owl quickly becomes bored with the whole thing, lifts it's head and goes back to sleep, I wonder just how many times this has happened to the bird?

Axe Edge Moor is my destination this lies, more or less, on the borders of three counties, Staffordshire, Derbyshire and Cheshire. A small lane leads off the A53 and links up with the A54, and as you drive along this lane you can see the shooting butts on your left which tells you all you need to know, you are in grouse shooting country, and I will keep my mouth shut on what I think about that!

The turning is signposted to Dale Head and is a single track road, I have to stop at a cattle grid to allow three cars coming towards me to pass. While waiting for the cars to do so I am conscious of a dark bird walking across the open moor, not 30 metres away from me, blimey, a male red grouse is showing wonderfully well, and he has come to see me. What a start, I am very pleased I waited for the advancing cars, without them I may have missed the bird completely. This is birding made easy, but enjoy it, believe me it does not happen very often.

Continuing on my way I had a wonderful half an hour. Driving slowly along the road I saw 14 red grouse in total and heard several more, the distinctive 'go-back, go-back' rang out frequently, hear this and you know you are listening to the red grouse. I know one thing, when Sarah hears about this she will want to come up, since she saw red grouse for the first time last year she fell in love with them, and I do not blame her. After today's birds I am now on 61 for the year, so I am more than happy with that, and not a lot of energy used up in the process, only fuel!

Sarah and Martin have just returned, they too have been up to Derbyshire where they have done well, collecting one or two nice birds, dipper and mandarin especially so. Totalling up, they have crept into the lead, they have reached 62, the race is on!

Wednesday 5 January, is another very damp and gloomy day, just the day for doing as many household chores as possible, but by lunchtime the rain had almost stopped, so I decided to have a little run out. I need to do a bit of reconnaissance for Sarah in the hope we can find her something of interest for our usual Saturday morning excursion. For several years now it has almost become a tradition that we go out together for some local birding, and I do like to try to find her something a bit special or at least different.

Today I am after swans, I called in at Whitemoor Haye to see if I could locate the whooper swan still being reported, which I did not and so on down to Stubby Leas to see if the Bewick's are still about.

Within a few minutes I have my first Bewick's swan, and then locate a few more close by, this is a definite improvement on Whitemoor. These birds have been settled in now for nearly a month, so as long as no major disturbance comes along they should remain for Saturday.

It is now Friday 7 January, the first week of the year is almost over, and today we are back in the midst of winter, a white world with more still falling from a leaden looking sky. The forecasters have hinted it may turn to rain as the morning progresses, let us hope they are right, we have had more than enough snow this winter so far.

When I walked through to my kitchen, on the sunflower feeder is a lovely male reed bunting, a quick call to Sarah, and she is also able to enjoy the bird, a tick for us both. I suppose the bird stayed no longer than a couple of minutes, but that was more than enough time for us both to enjoy him.

Saturday 8 January has arrived with bright, clear skies, quite a change from the drab and gloomy weather so far this year, providing far better birding conditions than experienced yesterday. The only problem is the wind, this looks very strong and may not be of much help with regard to using a telescope, we will just have to wait and see.

Having had a look on the net, nothing else of great interest has been recorded, so swans it will be. The Bewick's are almost guaranteed, so Sarah should have her 'Year Tick', will we be lucky with the whooper, that remains to be seen.

Just as we were about ready to go out we had one of those pleasant little interludes. A goldcrest popped into the garden and started exploring one of my ornamental conifers. I was able to call Sarah in to see the bid, which was a nice male. Last year it took Sarah just over 50 weeks to see her first goldcrest of the year, this year she has managed it in 8 days, such are the vagaries of birding. Incidentally, it was a 'Year Tick' for both of us, and coincidentally our number 65.

Now for Stubby Leas. The swan flock was in attendance and not spread over too large an area which was a good help. It did not take us long to locate the first Bewick's swan, and we quickly found several more, at least 10 birds were visible.

Unlike the swans at Stubby Leas, the Whitemoor flock were well spread over a large area, not making things easy, and several were down the bottom of the meadow where there is a ridge and the birds could only be seen if they raised their heads high. We again spent many minutes looking at these birds, all to no avail, only mutes as far as we could tell. We drove on slowly along the rough lane, here in a field were a dozen or so fieldfare who were catching the sunlight beautifully.

I did not go out again yesterday afternoon as I start a new course at Rosliston on Monday, so I had bits to do in preparation for that. Today, being Sunday, I will have an hour or two's birding, and the great northern diver is still being reported from Carsington and there have also been reports of a duck smew, so Carsington it will be. Incidentally, Blue Badge holders park free at Carsington. It also occurred to me to pop into the information hide as there are usually tree sparrows to be seen on the feeders, and I have not seen any yet this year and you can park quite close to this hide.

I did not have to do any work for the sparrows, they were all over the seed feeders, 14 of them to be precise, sparrows that is, not feeders. Smart little birds tree sparrows, and Carsington is one of the few places where they are guaranteed.

On my way home from Carsington I popped in at Rocester, it should be at least good for both Egyptian geese and red-crested pochard here.

JCB have done a good job here and their waterfowl collection regularly attracts passing wild ducks, which is one of the reasons I like to visit, especially after weather such as we have experienced recently.

It did not take me long to find the two birds I was after, two drake red-crested pochards flew in to join in the melee, and an Egyptian goose was having a stack up with a greylag, and the Egyptian had it's wings fully out showing off a full set of primaries, no argument this was a free-flying specimen.

I had a quick lunch and went onto the net, as well as putting on my three records I obviously had a look at what else had been reported, and down at Croxall five whooper swans had been seen this morning, those were much too near to home to be ignored.

I should only need my binoculars for this visit, so grabbing these I am on my way. I arrive at the spot just as another car pulls up, out of which jumps two birders. We quickly start to scan the swans in the field, there are not many, probably just over 20 in total, and the whoopers soon come into view, six not five. My two new colleagues have telescopes, so they set these up to provide even better views, and one of them mutters 'I have a grey goose here, and I am sure it is a pink-foot'. He asks me to have a look through his 'scope, I do not need an second invite, and I am very pleased to concur with his diagnosis, pink-footed goose it most certainly is. We only have just over 20 birds in this particular field of rape, and three are different species, of which two are cracking birds. That has given me five for the day, I have now reached 70 in total.

Tuesday has come in quite pleasantly and Roy phoned me yesterday evening to let me know he had seen a few golden plover with the lapwing flock at Whitemoor Haye, so I may have a look for them.

I drove on past the Whitemoor Haye Farmhouse to the field Roy had mentioned, and he was at least right about lapwings, a very tidy flock were in the field. Finding a suitable place to park up I started to work my way through the birds. At first it was all lapwings and starlings, then three plump, brownish birds, ran into view, Roy was right about his golden plover. After a few minutes observation I had counted 11.

Still having time available, and the light was still holding up nicely, I drove home via Walton-on-Trent. This turned out to be a good decision. Just past the Walton football pitch two raven came flying overhead, one of them calling loudly, and what a call. Even with my windows closed I could hear the deep, metallic 'krrooap, krrooap' an iconic call from an iconic bird.

Wednesday arrives and I have decided to visit Blithfield Reservoir, there are several places where I can view from the car and secondly I am interested to see if the reservoir has completely thawed. My first stopping place will be the Sailing Club. The reservoir has completely thawed out, but there is hardly a bird in sight, they have obviously not yet received the news.

I will now visit the causeway and see if there is any excitement available from those two view points. As if to put a complete dampener on things down came heavy rain, so I initially pulled into the car park in Watery Lane. A few more duck were visible, the inevitable mallard, eight of them, a wigeon, two tufted and nine more coot, and before I forget, a solitary moorhen was scooting along the shore.

I was about to drive off over to the opposite shore when I noticed six birds flying in, very fast and low, they looked quite elongated, these were no mallards, so I quickly lowered my window. These birds had very distinctive white wing panels and dark heads, female goosanders, I think that is the largest group I have seen this year so far. While watching them vanish down the reservoir I picked up a large gull sitting out on a blue buoy, how I had missed this bird before I do not know, although it may just have flown in, the odd gull was returning to roost.

This bird was big and had a jet black back, no need to work it out, an adult great black-backed gull, a big and mean bird. If it chose to stay put on this buoy, nothing else was likely to chase it off.

Now across the causeway, to see what was on the other side – 'Chickens do that, don't they?' Not a lot, a few more gulls were flying in for the evening roost and the odd cormorant flew past. I did pick up two diving duck just off the causeway which needed a bit of further examination, these turned out to be a pair of goldeneye, and while studying these a flock of small birds flew through, bouncing up and down as though on elastic, were they linnet?

The small birds came zooming back and landed on the waters edge right in front of me, it was my lucky day. They were linnet, and about 50 of them, a very nice tidy flock.

Thursday morning I was having a look on the net and was pleased to note a drake smew had been seen at Chasewater, as I was well up on my chores I decided a trip out this afternoon would be well worth the effort, you do not see smew every day, especially drakes. I must confess I was surprised with this news as Chasewater is nearly dry due to work being carried out of the dam, which sprung a leak last year.

Chores completed, Chasewater here I come. It was as I thought, very little water, but this at least cut down the surface area I had to look through to find my bird. Drake smew are stunning little duck, if you are not familiar with them just have a look at their picture in your field guide. It was some artist who put just two colours together so well.

The light is quite good today and it was not long before I picked up my target, and for once the bird stayed on the surface. Smew are a diving duck and normally they drive you mad as they make frequent dives, usually coming up some considerable distance from where they first dived. Not today, he just sailed across the water putting on a stunning show, if he should stay put I know where I shall be bringing Sarah on Saturday.

While I was enjoying the bird another birder came up, he had picked up the news on his pager, so I was able to put him straight onto the bird. I was very pleased he turned up, he had just left Brownhills after photographing waxwings there, and he was able to give me the exact location. Would you believe it, they were in front of a row of shops right on the A452, the main road through Brownhills, which at this time of the day is bumper to bumper with traffic. These had to be sussed out, Sarah would like the chance of seeing these come the weekend, she could be due for a cracking morning, smew and waxwing within a mile of each other.

I know Brownhills very well so I knew exactly where to stop and park, should conditions allow me, they did not. Traffic was very heavy and due to the numerous pedestrian crossing etc, was moving very slowly, this at least did enable me to study the area well. Approaching the spot where they were last reported I was only moving at about 5mph, and in a tree were my quarry, 12 of them to be factual, totally ignoring the sound and smell of the traffic, and as equally unconcerned with the people walking just a few metres beneath them on the pavement. I just had to drive on, let us hope they remain until Saturday when, hopefully, we can enjoy them fully.

My little journey out this afternoon had turned up trumps, a 'Year Tick' with the smew, and only my second sighting of waxwings this year, you do not grumble with that.

Friday is upon us, the day I usually have to do some reconnaissance work for Sarah, as we are already aware of the smew and waxwings, there is not quite the urgency for me to go out foraging. I have also heard reports that the great grey shrike is again being seen on Cannock Chase. My views last year were all of a rather fleeting manner, I would welcome the opportunity to really have a good look at the bird. We do not have many reports of this bird any more. They used to breed in the UK but they were persecuted by egg collectors and are now just a winter visitor, well visitor is probably an exaggeration, winter vagrant may be nearer the truth. I doubt if I have seen 20 in all my years of birding in the UK, which is why I always welcome the opportunity of seeing one locally.

My best view ever of a great grey shrike was from the Crimea one autumn. Dorothy and I were on a cruise and where we berthed was surrounded by what could be best called an area of waste ground, at first sight not a very impressive welcoming sight to a new country. We had been out for a sight seeing tour in the morning and as the coach drove through this area of waste ground it became suddenly more interesting. It was over grown with a variety of wild flowers and shrubs, so we decided to explore it.

It looked as though man had never set foot in the area, and butterflies and birds were everywhere. Large numbers of wheatear were passing through on their return migration as were various warblers, when, out on the top of an hawthorn bush, not five metres away, popped a great grey shrike. The bird just sat there looking straight at us, almost as though it had never seen man before, and we just stared back at him, Dorothy could not believe what she was looking at. I slowly moved for my camera, which fortunately was not in a case, and raised it to my eyes. I managed to get in about half a dozen shots before the bird moved off, not out of sight, just out of camera range, so we could still enjoy the bird. When ever one talks to me about the Crimea, all I can tell you about is great grey shrikes, very little about the country itself. What a magnificent view, and such a lovely memory too. As it turned out today, our shrike was not so cooperative.

I decide to drive down to Stubby Leas, could the whoopers have joined in with the swan flock here, it is only about a mile away. The swans are still at Stubby Leas, and it does not take long to pick out the Bewick's, but hard as I work, no whoopers. I will now go back to Croxall.

As I had driven along the A513 to Stubby Leas I had noticed a small flock of swans in a field alongside the main road, but I could not stop as I had a large lorry up my tail, so on my return journey I intended finding a suitable parking spot to have a look at these birds. This was not as easy as it may sound, at this time on a Friday afternoon the A513 is a very busy road, but I am in luck, and manage to pull in near a gate into a farmer's field. Winding the window down I start to study the birds, and I am in luck. Two swans raise their heads and I have the jackpot, whoopers they most certainly are, I give Sarah a call and pop home for her, the swans are less then 15 minutes from home.

I shall get to know the A513 at this rate. On my return I find a much more suitable parking spot, less than 100 metres away from the swans, so we move forward, telescope at the ready. I quickly locate two of the birds, focus up and hand over to Sarah. As she is studying them three other birds come into view, we now have five whoopers, these no doubt being the five first seen at Sittle's Farm a day or so ago.

While enjoying the swans Sarah brings my attention to a goose she has located, so I take over the telescope once again. The goose was a pink-footed goose, this just had to be the same bird I first saw a few days ago. These birds had just moved their feeding field by a few hundred metres, and in so doing they had vanished into space as far as reports were concerned. It was rather nice to think we could now put them back on the net for others to enjoy.

Saturday is here, and it is raining, not the start to the morning we wanted. I have been on the net to check out the bird situation, and it looks as though today maybe our last chance for the waxwings in Brownhills. 65 were reported there yesterday afternoon, but the viewer added a proviso 'The berry crop was almost eaten', so this morning may be Sarah's last opportunity for this particular group of birds. The smew was still showing well at Chasewater, and an Iceland gull had put in an appearance, be nice if the gull stays around for a little longer.

From a birding front we have Chasewater to ourselves, so we make our way down to where the edge of the reservoir used to be, here we have a wooden view point where we can set up our telescope. There are a goodly number of gulls in the water, so we concentrate initially on these. Several great black-backed gulls stand out, both by size and colour, herring and lesser black-backed gulls make a nice comparison on size with the great. A large biscuit coloured bird attracts my attention, I point this out to Sarah so we can both concentrate our efforts on this bird, had we located the second winter Iceland gull which had been reported yesterday? After a few minutes, yes we had, and it is only Sarah's second record ever.

Leaving the clutch of gulls alone, time to look for the smew, and by a remarkable coincidence it was roughly in the same area I saw it on Thursday, birding is coming easy today. Two other birders have arrived and they were only too pleased to be put straight onto the smew, unfortunately for them, the Iceland gull had flown off minutes before they arrived.

We drive back through Brownhills to have a look for the waxwings, and what a decision this proved to be. As we slowly drove past the Silver Court we spotted a flock of birds roosting up in a bare tree, and fortunately for us there were parking places right on the spot. We pulled in and Sarah hopped out of the car swiftly, and she chose the right time to do so. Within 30 seconds or so the birds flew off, but we had seen enough, they were most certainly waxwings, about 20 of them, what a magical finish to our morning out.

Sunday has come in far pleasanter than anticipated, rain had been promised but it looks as though it is now not due until after lunch time, that being the case I will have a morning at Croxall Lakes Nature Reserve, I have not really visited the reserve this year yet.

I make my usual stop at the lay-by in Kings Bromley, and this time I am not going to be disappointed, out in the middle of the field is a large white shape, it just has to be the little egret. It is, the bird is back. A nice start to the day. I phone up Sarah to tell her about it, she will no doubt hope to have a quick look later in the day, when she and Martin go out.

Croxall Lakes is quiet, only one car in the car park when I arrive. I drive up to the hide, flushing a male bullfinch in transit, and make my way into the hide. The wind is quite brisk and coming in directly through the hide vents, not the best of birding conditions. A good selection of waterfowl are visible, and the whistling call of the wigeon is much in evidence.

Scanning the far shore, I must admit I was mainly looking for snipe here, I spotted three greyish looking waders, redshank, focusing up I was able to confirm my first thoughts, my second 'Year Tick' of the day. Working my way back I came across another small group of redshank, six this time, so that gave me nine for the day. The sun had actually come out at this point and the birds red legs were very evident.

As I had a few more minutes to spare I had a quick drive to see if the whooper swans are still at Croxall. The swans are still in their field along with the mutes, so let us hope they hang around for some more days.

Tomorrow the Rosliston Bird Study Group has its first field meeting of the term, we are visiting Branston Water Park. A few weeks ago a bittern was reported from there, I have heard nothing about it since, but it at least gives us something to look for.

You do not expect to be birding at 2.30am, but this morning I was awake at that unearthly hour, and while trying to get myself back to sleep, without much success I may add, I heard a sound from out side. I lay still and listened, hooting away, quite close by, was a tawny owl. Being awake no longer mattered, I just lay there for a minute or two listening to the owl go through his repertoire. The owl stopped, and I drifted off to sleep. Not a bad few minutes that!

Monday is nice and dry, with little or no wind, not a bad day for birding. The turnout this morning is very good, 24 plus me, fortunately Roy is one of them so we can split the group into two parts, doing so also provides me with the opportunity of getting to know the newcomers.

Roy leads off and I await any possible latecomers, not that we have any today. I am very impressed with the number of waterfowl visible today, after the recent freeze up I had half expected numbers to be low.

Teal, wigeon, tufted and mallard numbers are good, as are Canada and greylag geese, the odd pochard and both grebes are also showing well. I must admit I am looking for two species in particular, the gadwall and shoveler, I require both of these for my 'Year List', and I know, from talking to some of the group they have never seen either of these two duck previously, so they will also be pleased if we find them.

The weather is brightening up nicely, with the sun coming through, and this shows up the colours of the duck very well, the heads of the drake mallards look superb with either a purple or green sheen showing through, and the drake wigeon are not being out shone either. Panning through the birds I find my first 'target' bird, three nice drake gadwall, we manage to get these in the telescope for all to enjoy, and while we are doing so a small flotilla of gadwall sail past, a nice mixture of ducks and drakes.

Walking further on our other 'target' bird comes into sight, two drake shoveler are sitting out on an island, fully in the sun, and the odd female is swimming about in the water close by. We are able to obtain super views of their large bills, everyone can now fully appreciate where the name shoveler comes from.

We catch up with Roy and his party who are enjoying a couple of bullfinch, and one of my group bring my attention to a bird sitting out on the top of a silver birch, the bird is looking very yellow in the sunlight, they wondered if it was a greenfinch. A quick look soon sorted out what we had, it was in fact a superb male siskin, no wonder it looked so yellow. The bird was a poser, so we all managed to get good views before he flew off.

We have now reached the bottom of the lake so our return journey will take us through some attractive woodland with a feeding station, so we may be lucky here. There is some activity at the station, coal, blue and great tit principally, Roy and a few of his party catch a glimpse of a treecreeper, chaffinch and goldfinch making up the numbers.

Walking on through the woods we come across a nice party of about a dozen long-tailed tits feeding away on the alder, and while enjoying these our attention is caught by a group of small birds feeding away on a silver birch, and doing so most acrobatically, only one bird feeds this way, they have to be redpolls. Sorry long-tails, you have competition here! Fortunately the sun is still out and these birds are showing up very nicely against a blue sky. Now is the time to concentrate, are they all lesser redpoll, or is there another specie hidden among them, such as a mealy redpoll, a few have been reported locally?

Roy, unfortunately, was far in front of us so I could not enlist his aid in working our way through the flock, I briefly explained what I was looking for, and got on with the task in hand. After several minutes, and the odd false alarm, I came to the conclusion they were all lesser redpolls, for many of the group they were a new species, so no one was complaining here. Our first field trip of the new course had turned out very successful, as one of the members said 'The standard has now been set, can you keep it up?'

Due to the return of frosty and cold weather the birds in my garden have been far more attentive. Once again I am being invaded by blackbirds. Long-tailed tit numbers are very good still as they come in regularly, in their usual mob-handed manner, to attack the various fatty foods provided, and my robin is now almost tame as he enjoys the suet pieces put out. If no food should be available it sits on the window sill of my kitchen glaring at me with it's black eyes almost saying 'Come on, where is my food?'

Come Saturday I am hoping to take Sarah across the Park Hall to try for the long-eared owls, she has not seen one of these for over 20 years, so we must have a go for those before they depart back north.

Knowing what we are doing tomorrow, today is not my usual reconnaissance day, so I will just have a lazy drive round Walton and Whitemoor Haye to see what is about, I can also include Croxall for the whooper swans. You never know what lies just around the corner in this game, and my trip out this afternoon has proved that point.

A small party of long-tailed tits were working their way along the hedge, at Walton but little else was to be seen. I was just about to drive off when a small flock of six birds came flying across the football pitch, at first I thought them to be starlings, but as they got closer I realised they were waxwings. I was able to only enjoy these birds for a few seconds as they were just flying through, but I can never see too many of them.

Driving down past the Whitemoor Haye Farm House a large number of birds were feeding in the stubble field opposite, so I found a suitable place to park up, to try to sort this lot out. The majority were lapwing, starling and black-headed gull, but after awhile I picked out a few plump, brownish birds, which were running very quickly over the ground, golden plover behaviour. The stopped their dashing about for a few seconds enabling me to confirm my thoughts, we had seven golden plover, another bird it is nice to see, only my second sighting this year, both at Whitemoor Haye. Driving on a little further a small bird flashed across the road, but fortunately for me it settled right on the top of the hedge, a female reed bunting, and she was well turned out.

Turning round, now for the swans. The small flock could again be seen in fields off the A513, but they had moved a few hundred metres further south, and initially I was unable to park up due to heavy traffic. I drove on, then was able to turn round and in doing so I managed to find a suitable spot to pull off the road. I was much closer to the birds than on my previous visits, and my luck was in today, the five whoopers were the nearest birds to me, probably only 30 metres away. They were not happy with the appearance of my car, their heads were all up glaring in my direction, I had seen all I needed to see, so I drove off, leaving them to settle down once more.

I had only been out for about an hour, so I drove back to Whitemoor Haye to have my last look over the lake, and I was pleased I had done so, two goldeneye, both drakes, were now visible. They gave me four birds to report, not bad for a short journey out locally, and my carbon foot-print was hardy measurable. However, my day was not yet over. Driving back home through Orgreave I had three doves fly across in front of me, stock doves, a 'Year Tick', now that cannot be bad!

Saturday has come in cold and grey, there is a slight possibility of snow later I am told, the most important feature of the weather, as far as we are concerned, is the fact there is little or no wind. It is not funny staring up a conifer, probably 12 metres plus in height, for a long-eared owl, who does not want to be seen in any case, with a wind blowing the tree violently.

As we approached Park Hall I noticed the temperature gauge in the car was dropping steadily. When we started out it read 4 degrees, it now reads zero. Thick frost everywhere, quite picturesque really, but very cold. Fortunately we had brought the right gear with us so once we were togged up I popped into the Visitor Centre to see if any of the wardens were about, two were. They were able to tell us where the long-eared owls had last been seen, and one of them even drew us a little map.

Before starting off down to the conifer plantation we spent some time at the feeding station, you may remember I had bullfinch and marsh tit here when last visiting. We did not have long to wait, birds were coming in and out almost continuously, several bullfinch, probably as many as double figures, then the bird Sarah wanted put in an appearance. A marsh tit landed right on the feeder nearest to us, providing a very good view, and as we were enjoying this bird I had a big surprise, a willow tit came in and landed on the floor after fallen seed. I have never seen a marsh tit and willow tit together in all my years of birding, their natural habitats are totally different, I can only presume that the weather up here has been very bad and food has brought them together.

A very nice start to the days proceedings, can we now get the owl for Sarah? At least we know they are here, finding them is another matter. As we enter the wood we see a small group of birders looking up a tree, and they seem rather enthusiastic, so we approach them. Yes, they have located a long-eared owl, and for once the bird is providing a very good view, so we quickly get onto the bird. Due to the lack of wind, the bird is sitting out quite well, not tucked in hard against the trunk as they do in windy conditions. The bird obviously became aware of our interest and moved slightly, raising his tufts as he did so, there was no mistaking the bird in this pose.

Lunch over, the Chase it is, my destination is to be Penkridge Bank, and I arrive to find it pleasantly quiet from a people front, only four cars parked up. Walking out of the car park I meet a couple with binoculars who inform me they have seen nothing at all, this is not the news I want to hear. I continue on my way and eventually I hear a magpie calling, not very special, but at least life. I finally locate the bird and watch it for a few seconds when the sound of cyclists can be heard, should there be anything at all they will frighten it off, I was not best pleased! As I watched them getting closer, a bird suddenly flew off the ground in front of them, emitting a loud and wild yaffling laugh at it went, a green woodpecker. My thoughts on the cyclists now had to be changed, I very much doubt I would have seen the woodpecker without their interference, so as they passed me by I gave them a cheery wave, that was the very least I could do.

Sunday has dawned dull and miserable, although the temperature is pleasant enough, no overnight frost to contend with. There was little on the bird front reported, so I have decided to have an hour or two over at Blithfield Reservoir, taking in the permissive wheelchair accessible footpath areas the water company has opened up to the general public. This provided hides and feeding stations which are proving very popular with not only the visitors, the wild creatures also appreciate a regular food supply.

I pull in on the car park, which incidentally is free, and make my way along the footpath, I had not gone far when I heard calls from the trees above me. Looking up I saw a nice mixed flock of lesser redpolls and siskins feeding away in the trees, a very nice start. While I was enjoying these birds I heard the call of a woodpecker, and a great spotted woodpecker landed on a tree nearby, where it promptly commenced to hammer away, it was so close it sounded almost like a drill. I waited for a few minutes as I did not wish to disturb the bird, before the bird flew off, the siskins and redpolls had by now vanished from sight and sound.

Tad Bay is very close and I am pleased to say is carrying a goodly supply of water, Blithfield is, after all, a reservoir which supplies our watering needs. Here a large number of water fowl are congregated, and a small diving duck gains my attention. I had at first thought it was a little grebe, but something about it was not quite right, so more concentration is required.

I move slightly, and I was pleased I had, the bird was a female ruddy duck. They used to be a memorable sight, not any more I am afraid, since the decision was taken to eliminate these delightful birds their numbers have plummeted to the extent they are almost a rarity now. It is claimed they interbreed with a rare duck, the white-faced duck in Europe, and as their genes are stronger there is a danger the white-faced duck could become extinct. This is not a decision I agree with, if they want to wipe out the ruddy duck, why do it here, they are not a great migratory species. The fact the white-faced duck is rare is probably down to being almost shot out of existence in France and Spain in any case, and that is nothing to do with the ruddy duck. This bird will not be reported, I have no intention of letting the 'rent-a-gun mob' know she is here.

Time now to visit the feeding station. I have the hide to myself, several titmice are visible, blue, great, coal and long-tailed, the odd pheasant is feeding under the containers on fallen seed etc, and a great spotted woodpecker feeding away on a fat tray, this is almost like being back home. A small dark bird flies across my vision and lands low on the trunk of a silver birch, a quick look and I have a bird I was hoping for, treecreeper, they are one of my favourite birds. I watch it climb up the tree, it's long claws could be clearly seen, and it then proceeded, upside down, along the underside of a branch, what a bird. Unfortunately at that precise moment three magpie came in chattering away loudly, and my treecreeper flew off.

Monday 24 January, the Rosliston Bird Study Group is at Croxall Lakes Nature Reserve, and once again I have a very good turnout, 26, including a new member. The day is grey and cold, but we again escaped an overnight frost, so conditions for the time of the year are not too bad.

The first bird of interest we see is a little egret standing, rather forlornly, on the far shore, for one or two of the group, this is the first time they have seen a little egret, I can assure them it will not be the last. Three goldeneye, two of which are drakes, are showing well, a very attractive duck, and goodly numbers of teal and wigeon are going about their business. A solitary redshank completes the picture.

Time to move over to the East Side but little was to be seen, so we move on to Croxall. The swans were still in their field, and we quickly located the five whoopers, and for a couple of the group, a new bird once again. Time to move over to Whitemoor Haye, here I hope we could locate the solitary pink-footed goose, presuming it is still in among the greylags. A large flock of geese were visible on the far shore. We worked our way through the group of geese to no avail, they were all Canada geese, no grey geese here.

We were just about to drive off down the rough lane to see if the geese were in fields down there when nine curlew came flying across and landed on the shoreline, what a bonus. My favourite bird, and to see nine locally is a very good number indeed, plus the fact they are the first of the year for me. The rough lane was very quiet, just a small flock of goldfinch, always nice to see and a couple of carrion crow in a field, no geese were to be seen. The swan flock was still in the fields, whether the two whooper swans are still among them I do not know, but having already seen the five at Croxall, we did not spend extra time looking.

It was Wednesday before I was able to get in any more birding, and this was going to be a brief ride out, so local patch it was again. I thought I would have a trip out to see the whooper swans again, and then have a concentrated half an hour or so trying to find the corn buntings down at Whitemoor Haye, as I am rather concerned about the latter. The local farmer has being doing a large amount of work in cleaning out his ditches, which he now doubt has every right to do. Unfortunately, as the work had not been carried out for many years, these ditches had become wildlife corridors with untidy hedgerows, these had become home to the corn buntings. Along with the ditch dredging the hedges had also been grubbed up, in the space of a few days the corn buntings habitat had been completely destroyed.

No work was being carried out today, as I slowly made my way round what was left of the hedgerow, with hardly a bird in sight. I decided I would make my way down towards Sittle's Farm, at least there was hedgerow here. As I drove past the entrance to the farm I noticed a flock of birds sitting out in a bare tree in front of the farm. I had to be careful here, you can hardly stare towards a building through binoculars without raising some concern if seen, and it can hardly be termed polite.

As I raised my binoculars the birds took to flight, one or two seemed to have a flash of yellow on them, yellowhammers no doubt, the rest just looked chunky brown jobs, these had to be corn buntings, but where had they flown to? I then realised all the birds had not flown, a small group were still in the tree, would they stay put? They did, and I was delighted to see they were all corn buntings, seven of them in fact. I was thrilled to bits to have located these, they were still in the area, they had just moved on half a mile or so south. I can now report these birds so that other birders will be able to see and enjoy them, but more importantly, can keep their eyes on them for the future.

Saturday is not only our birding morning, it is also the start of the RSPB Garden Bird Watch, when we are asked to spend an hour sometime over this weekend end logging the birds in our own gardens. I have done my stint, between 09.15 and 10.15 hours I enjoyed a coffee and went about my task. I did not see all the species listed but I can not complain, I knocked up 17 species, the largest number at any one time being nine blackbirds, and I did see nuthatch, pied wagtail and carrion crow, which are not the commonest of garden birds.

Today we are off after the corn buntings and the golden plover, whether we will be lucky or not only time will tell. The wigeon flock were evident on the lake, you almost felt they were enjoying today's sunshine, it was a pleasingly bright morning, although cold. The lapwing flock were nowhere to be seen, so we made our way slowly down towards Sittle's Farm. As we approached the micro-light airfield we spotted a large number of lapwings on a field nearby, we managed to find a suitable parking spot, and out with the telescope.

The lapwing numbers were certainly in three figures, so now we had to work our way through them all. We made three passes, no joy, all were lapwings. Sittle's here we come, will it be any better here? The quick answer to that is no. Two house sparrows were all we could find, not that I am knocking them, but we were after more exotic birds.

We drove back via the rough lane. Initially there was little to see until a small flock of birds flew up the lane in front of us. We stopped, and got out of the car to see just what they were. The birds were rather skittish, but Sarah picked up a bright yellow bird in a bush, a quick look confirmed her first thoughts, a nice male yellowhammer, a 'Year Tick' for us both.

We concentrated our efforts on birds further up the lane. The first we were able to identify was a male reed bunting, further yellowhammer and about half a dozen tree sparrow. All in all there must have been about 15 birds in this little flock, a mixture of three very nice birds, the day had brightened up suddenly.

Sunday has come in quite brightly, we only had a very slight frost last night, so what to do with the day? I have decided to visit Cromford in Derbyshire, hawfinch have been reported on a regular basis, plus yesterday, 2 mealy redpoll, both of those would be nice to get acquainted with so early in the year. Cromford is only an hours run from home.

The journey up to Cromford, just 30 miles away was very peaceful, little or no traffic to contend with. I drove onto the Rugby Field car park, which was very busy, and managed to find myself a spot right beneath two large willow trees. A birder was staring up into the trees as I arrived, so I quickly picked up my binoculars and studied the trees. I could not believe my eyes, at the top of one of the trees sat a hawfinch, and I had barely turned my engine off. What a start, to quote my old friend Ivor 'After a start like this there is only one way it can go – down hill'. In all my years of birding this has to be a first. The one bird I wanted today above all others was there, and I was still in my car.I just sat there enjoying it all, I did not want to get out of my car in case I frightened the bird off, but after about three minutes the bird decided enough was enough, and off it flew.

Just as I started to move off in the direction of Cromford church, four small birds landed in the same group of trees and proceeded to feed in upside down mode, these just had to be redpolls. Leaning against my car for support I looked up at the birds, redpolls they most certainly were, but one of them looked different from the rest – we had a mealy redpoll, when compared with three lesser redpolls, it stood out quite differently, on it's own it may not have been so easy. What a start. I had not moved from my car and I had two exceptional 'Year Ticks' in the bag already. Now for Cromford church, here I am hoping to see the dipper, I usually manage to see one from off the river bridge without too much trouble, but today there were two fishermen on the river bank, so it was going to be a question of whether my luck held.

After several minutes nothing had happened so I made my way into the churchyard, sat on a bench round a yew tree and gazed down the river. A few jackdaws were calling from the overhanging cliff, but nothing broke the silence nor caused movement on the river. I was about to move off when two walkers approached along the river bank, as I looked at them a bird flew out of the bank beneath where they walked, landed on the opposite side of the river, with a bob and a curtsy, my dipper. Magnificent little birds with their bold white bib, you cannot mistake one of these no matter how far away they may be. They love fast flowing, clear rivers, such as this the Derwent, and thanks to the walkers, who I do not think had even seen the bird, I had another tick. I just could not believe my luck today, and all with little or no effort. I now had time to enjoy a nice cup of coffee and something to eat, then as I still had time available I would nip across to Bradley to see if I could find the mandarin ducks, that would finish my trip out very nicely.

Bradley is a small village, well a hamlet really just off the A517, north east of Ashbourne. It has this little private lake, well known to the birders of the area, which holds a nice flock of mandarin duck, in the winter they have been known to reach three figures, one will do me today. It is an awkward place to find, but the map reference will be listed at the end of this chapter. It is only by a narrow lane so parking is tight to say the least, and you look for a public footpath at the side of a property called Knoll Lodge. Walk 20 metres or so along this path to find a spot to view the lake.

The lake is frozen solid, ducks, mainly mallard are standing, rather dejectedly, on the ice, but where are the mandarin? Mandarin are tree ducks, so cold ice was not for them. On the far side of the lake the odd bird could be seen perched on the branches of overhanging trees and bushes, just where they should be, not getting cold feet from the ice for these exotic duck. I counted 12 in all, five drakes and seven ducks, and the drake just has to be the most exotic duck we see in this country, just look at them in your field guide, they are impossible to describe, I think you will agree.I am very pleased I made the effort today, four fabulous birds. Tomorrow we are on Cannock Chase, I am hoping to go searching for the great grey shrike, if we are successful there that will be a perfect ending to the month.

The last day of January has come in crisp, clear and cold but the visibility is very good, so we may hopefully get a good mornings birding. We have a very good turnout once again, 28 in total. It was a very pleasant morning for a walk, although not great on the bird front, but we all made our way home happy enough. This walk was about a mile in length, and not wheelchair accessible. The walking is level, but do be cautious, when finished I knew I had done it!

As we were driving home, Audrey who had come with me shouted out, 'Woodpecker', and flying across the road in front of us came a lesser spotted woodpecker, what a bird to finish with. The pity was we only saw the bird for a few seconds before it vanished into the woodland, but we will settle for that any day, it may be our only one of the year. Audrey had picked up the bird of the day.

That ends off the first month of the year. My total has now reached 94, which is a few more than I thought I would obtain, the last few days have been good to me. See you in February.

Map references:
Kings Bromley lay-by: SK 122172.
Whitemoor Haye: SK 179139.
Stubby Leas: SK 188097.
Coton Lakes: SP 212943.
Middleton Hall: SP 193983.
Croxall Lakes Nature Reserve: SK 189139.
Cannock Chase – Whitehouse Car Park: SJ 995162
Blithfield Reservoir – Public Car Park: SK 055236.
Park Hall Country Park: SJ 930449.
Axe Edge Moor: SK 030700.
Carsington Water – Visitor Centre: SK 241516.
JCB Rocester: SK 103393.
Croxall: SK 196137.
Walton-on-Trent Football Pitch: SK 208168.
Chasewater: SK 072040.
Branston Water Park: SK 217210.
Cannock Chase – Penkridge Bank Car Park: SK 001168
Sittles Farm: SK 171121.
Cannock Chase – Cadet Camp Car Park: SJ 998173.
Cromford: SK 300572.
Bradley Lake: SK 223453.

These are not exact locations for the birds, they are just references for the areas so you can visit them – birds do fly!

Chapter II

February

The weather forecast for the next few days does not look good, so I decided to have an hour or two out this afternoon and do my chores tomorrow. As the decision has been made late I can only nip out locally, but that will still be a pleasant start to a new month.

My first stop will be Whitemoor Haye, and the lake is devoid of birds, well not quite, three mallard are visible so I will do my circuit round the rough lane to see what I can find. The farmer is continuing with his ditch clearance work and more and more hedgerow is being pulled out, it is all rather disappointing, the wildlife is going to suffer without a doubt.

A small flock of birds is flitting along what is left of the hedgerow, but they are very wary of my approach. I pick out a couple of yellowhammers, three or four chaffinch but the rest remain a mystery. Driving on I come across the lapwing flock, although I work these rather fastidiously, I can only see lapwing and a few starling.

I complete the circuit with only a kestrel to be added but as I approach the entrance to the landfill site a small group of birds are seen moving along the hedgerow. Stopping, I see they are tree sparrow, seven of them, they have made my trip out worth while.

Now for Walton-on-Trent. Approaching the football pitch I stop to look at a small group of doves in the field, and I was pleased I did so, they turned out to be stock doves, the largest number I have seen this year, there were nine of them. Thursday 3 February I only, literally, had an hour or so available, so one again it was to be very local. It would at least provide me with the chance to have a reconnaissance on behalf of Sarah, so Whitemoor here I come.

The lake was again very quiet, and the ditch cleaning was going on at quite a pace, more hedgerow being dug out in the process. The small bunting/tree sparrow flock was still to be seen in the rough lane, fortunately, the ditch clearance appeared to be only on one side of the lane. Sittle's Farm still had the large mute swan flock, but I could find no other species among these, so the Bewicks's had not moved to join these.

Back at the lake a large number of black-headed gulls had arrived and while going through these I became conscious of six large brown waders on the far shore, curlew. You may remember we had a nice group of these birds at Whitemoor last month, be nice if these hang round until the weekend so that Sarah could enjoy them. Not a bad hour really, nothing new but a few nice birds to enjoy, and that is what birding is really about.

It is now Friday, and they were right about the forecast, a bit of rough weather, gale force winds in the north of up to 90mph, and 60 to 70mph locally, I had to hunt for a couple of my bird feeders which had been blown away. Fortunately they were still in the garden.

Prior to going out this afternoon I have to make my final arrangements for a group visit to Norfolk in March. 14 of us are going, staying for varying times between seven and three days. We are staying at The Pheasant Hotel, a place I know well having stayed here on many an occasion, the most recent being December last year. Four of us are going down for the full week, we leave on Tuesday 15 March, others join us at varying dates. I have all the deposits so these must be sent off today to confirm our booking. That done, Croxall here I come.

During the morning I also had a call from my dear friends Jane and John Hobson who now live in Norfolk. They were interested in my joining them for a few days shortly, they live very near some of Norfolk's choicest birding locations, and by now know their way around. Needless to say I am only too happy to join them, and I await suggested dates.

The wind has not abated, but it has at least become a little brighter, we may not get any rain at the moment.. I intend to call in at Croxall initially to see if the whooper swans are still about, then have a ride round Whitemoor Haye and then into Croxall Lakes NR, hoping for a pleasant couple of hours birding.

The swans are quickly located, all five are still there, so on to Whitemoor. The lake is very quiet and rough due to the wind, with not a curlew in sight. Never mind a trip round the rough lane and then onto Croxall NR. The bunting flock was still evident, there must be at least six yellowhammers among them, which is rather nice.

Parking up at Croxhall I noticed another visitor, he was busily photographing away, he appeared to be interested in seed heads. He was too far away to speak to, we just waved to acknowledge each other, and I went into the hide. Opening up the flaps I nearly got my head blown off, the wind was coming through at gale force. Fortunately the bench is moveable so I was able to retreat back a couple of feet into the hide and this helped to limit the winds force.

Putting up my tripod and 'scope, I started to pan the far shore, here, due to the winds direction, the water was calmer than any where else, and several waterfowl were sitting out in it. As I started to pan through these two white birds appeared on the shore line, two little egrets, a nice start to the afternoon. They were busily feeding away in the shallow water, on what I have no idea, but they were certainly finding something of interest.

A birds call suddenly attracted my attention. The photographer had disturbed a small flock of six curlew who flew across my vision, no doubt the same birds I saw at Whitemoor yesterday, they were obviously commuting between here and there. At the same time as they flew through a flock of redshank took off from the far shore, I had not seen these, nine of them, the curlew had no doubt flushed them. Not a bad first few minutes, can we hope for better things still to come?

I carried on working my way along the far shore, many wigeon and teal were to be seen, the wigeon are probably the flock from Whitemoor Haye lake, the distance is less than a mile between the two lakes. Several groups of mallard, the odd pochard, tufted and Canada goose were to be seen, and three cormorants flew in. I was about to move on when I came across a bird with a very pale front and brown coloured head, the head was tucked in unfortunately so I could not see all of it. I had seen enough to convince myself I had a drake pintail in view, so it was concentration time, this could be my first pintail of the year.

Increasing the magnification on my zoom lens, for several minutes it just sat still, but having studied him closely I was convinced more than ever it was a pintail, the back of the bird was a lovely delicate grey in colour, then came the clincher. The bird raised it's head and started to preen, it had a lovely chocolate brown head and neck with a bright white blaze running down the neck, a drake pintail it most certainly was. Then, as quickly as it had woken up, back to sleep it went. I was not complaining, and should the bird hang about until tomorrow I know someone else who will not be complaining, Sarah. She loves pintail as much as I do, and she will certainly want to see this bird if at all possible.

Saturday, and the windy conditions are continuing, stronger than yesterday in my opinion., and as I sit down typing this, rain starts to fall, not ideal conditions for birding. Fortunately, Croxall Lakes NR has a hide and I can drive right up to the entrance of this, so we should be able to get in a bit of birding come what may.

You may have gathered from reading all of this that I have not been very mobile, most of my birding has been done from near my car, little or no walking, apart from attempts at Branston Water Park and on Cannock Chase. There is a good reason for this, being a Blue Badge holder, walking is not exactly my forte.

I mention this not for sympathy, just to illustrate birding is a hobby which can be pursued by all, irrespective of physical conditions etc., A friend of mine does it from his wheelchair, and he still sees over 200 species each year. In this enlightened age, disability does not mean you cannot get out and enjoy life, many nature reserves have wheelchair access if required, and wheelchair hire is available if needed. It may limit the areas you would like to visit, climbing mountains and the like, but it does concentrate the mind on getting to know the places you can visit. A Blue Badge can also at times be a decided help in getting you closer to the birds. At Snettisham for instance, we shall be visiting here in March when we are in Norfolk. The car park is over a mile from the hides on the reserve, and as part of the walking is over shingle it is not the easiest of walks. Blue Badge holders can drive most of this and park up near to the hides, so even at isolated places such as this, no one is barred. The RSPB are particularly good at helping the 'not so able'.

We have Croxall to ourselves, and the rain is just beginning to fall. We have a large flock of lapwing in the shallows, unfortunately they are all lapwing, there is nothing hidden among them. Three great black-backed gulls are standing among these birds, and by comparison they certainly do look large. Scanning the far shore for the pintail we come across an oystercatcher, a 'Year Tick' for us both, so that is a nice start.

While continuing to look for the pintail a number of swans commence flying in, and Sarah brings my attention to the fact there are whooper swans among them. The swans quickly settle down, and we find there are five whoopers among them. This is a bit of a coincidence, for several weeks now, as you know, we have had five whooper swans with the mute swan flock at Croxall Hall, these just have to be the same birds. When we leave we will drive round to see if the fields at Croxall Hall are empty or not.

Two pairs of goldeneye catch our attention, delightful birds, the drake being a real bobby dazzler. As to be expected with diving duck, they spend as much time under water as on the top. While enjoying these a cormorant flies across, and we are pleased to note this is exhibiting all the elements of being the 'sinensis' race, what we loosely term the Mediterranean race of cormorant, not a common sighting in the UK, another 'Year Tick' for us both.

As we still have time available, we will pop to see if the swans have left Croxall Hall and then drive home via Walton. My assumption regarding the whooper swans looks correct, not a swan in sight at Croxall Hall.

Approaching Walton football pitch, we pull off the road to have a look at the field where I saw the stock doves recently. Initially the field seemed empty, but three grey heads were raised, so we kept our eyes on these as they progressed though the vegetation. Our patience was rewarded, they came out into the open and three stock doves they were, Sarah's third 'Year Tick' of the morning was in the bag.

Sunday 5 February has come in far pleasanter than expected. The strong winds of yesterday have died down somewhat, and after having a look on the net I have decided to visit Carsington Water. The great northern divers are still being reported so I will have another go for those. Carsington also has the advantage of a very nice restaurant, so food will not be a problem.

Sheepwash car park is very busy but I manage to find a car parking spot, and make my way down to the Sheepwash Hide. There is another birder in the hide, and he was able to report that a great northern diver had been seen about half an hour ago, but not by him unfortunately. He was able, however, to point me in the direction of a pair of pintail, and these birds were certainly far more viewable than the one I saw at Croxall a day or so ago. The drake looked simply magnificent.

A nice group of goldeneye were also putting on a good show, nine of them, and wigeon and teal were also showing up well. Scanning the distance a dark bird suddenly surfaced, this bird had a thick neck, could it be the diver. I drew my friends attention to the bird, which promptly dived, needless to say. A good quarter of an hour passed before we had another sighting of the bird, they are not called divers without reason. This time there were two telescopes focused up and we managed to get a much better view, a great northern diver it most certainly was.

My friend drew my attention to a gull which was sitting out on strip of land, he mentioned it looked rather bulkier than the lesser black-backed gulls round it. He was absolutely right and the more I looked at the bird the more I became convinced it could be a yellow-legged gull. My friend, incidentally was from Wales, and yellow-legged gulls are not common place. I mentioned the one or two pointers I always look for at this time of the year. They look a far heavier bird than the herring gull, the head is normally purer white than a winter herring gull, and the mirrors in the black primaries look smaller, and in this bird all of these were apparent. To be absolutely sure we needed to see the birds legs, herring gulls are pink, yellow-legged are obviously yellow. Eventually the bird stood up, and took to flight, yellow legs it most certainly had.

My new friend was now back off to Wales, and I intended to have a few minutes at the Information Hide prior to making my way home. I had the hide to myself and the first birds seen were barnacle geese, counting them, 26, a very nice start. The feeding station was covered with tree sparrow, I counted 14 at one stage, there was no doubt many more in total. Two redshank were feeding along the shoreline, a pair of goldeneye were diving very actively, and a male ruddy duck was also visible. All in all a very nice ending to my trip out. I had two 'Year Ticks', I now stand at 99, saw many nice birds and had an interesting chat with a fellow birder

Monday had dawned and I am out with my Rosliston Bird Study Group. We are at Kingsbury Water Park, well Broomey Croft to be more accurate, just south of the new RSPB reserve at Middleton Hall. It is part of the Kingsbury Water Park which is a very interesting area. Broomey Croft is the birding area and hides have been provided by Warwickshire County Council who own the site. Unfortunately, vandals have been at work and one of the hides is burnt down, what gets into such people I do not know. Entrance by car is £2.50 per vehicle, pedestrians etc enter free. It has public conveniences and a West Midland Bird Club information centre which is manned at weekends and Bank Holidays.

I had heard reports of three smew being seen yesterday in Otter Pool, two of which were drakes, so we decided to make that our first pot of call. It also happens to be the furthest point on the reserve, so we would call in the remaining two hides on our way back.

There were 27 of us today, and the hide was a bit cramped to say the least. We had very nice views of goldeneye, teal, wigeon, pochard, tufted duck and feeding shoveler, but no smew. The shoveler were feeding away in a manner most individual to themselves. In cold weather when food has settled on the bottom, they will congregate in groups and paddle round in a tight circle stirring up food from the bottom. They then sieve this through their large bills, releasing the water and keeping the food particles in their bills. After a while the water settles down once again, so off they go a paddling! For many of my group this was their first experience of feeding shovelers, well winter feeding anyway.

We spent a good hour here enjoying the birds, notching up a cormorant 'sinensis', this was new to many, but no joy with the smew.

On our return journey we called in at the last two hides, the first had nothing new, but at the second hide we were fortunate to locate several snipe, I say fortunate because they were well nigh invisible among the dead vegetation, and it was only if they moved we were able to see them. These were my first snipe of the year and they gave me my 100th 'Year Tick'.

On our journey home we had nice views of buzzard, so that brought today's adventure to a close. I know one thing, I must have walked a mile and a half to-day, and my legs are beginning to tell me something. Incidentally, all the pathways here are wheelchair friendly, and so are the hides with the exception of the last hide, the Sita Hide, which has steps.

Tuesday has dawned lovely and bright. Last night we had a good frost but it is thawing very quickly. I will have a little ride out round Whitemoor Haye this afternoon. I can do all my birding from the car here, so it will give my legs a chance to recover a bit.

The lake at Whitemoor had in excess of 400 Canada geese in attendance, the usual wigeon flock were grazing away quite happily, and pochard numbers were quite good. Driving on down towards the rough lane I notice flashing lights ahead of me, so slowing down as I entered the rough lane I saw hedge trimming work was being carried out, so I stopped at a spot where I could turn my car round, and what a spot I chose.

Right where I stopped a cleaned out ditch ran off at right angles and as I looked a bird flew a short distance down the ditch, before alighting. The ditch is so crisp and clear the bird was in full vision. When it flew I had a quick view of black and white, usually a give away for a green sandpiper, so I lowered my window and raised my binoculars. Darting along the ditch, stabbing into the muddy water with it's longish bill was indeed a green sandpiper, my first of the year. Looking at this bird I could now hardly complain about the cleaning up work the farmer had done. Had the ditch still been overgrown the sandpiper would not have visited it, and I would not be sitting here enjoying the bird.

I watched the bird for a few minutes before realising the hedge trimming tractor was getting rather close, so it was time to turn the car round and move on. As I still had time available to me I decided to drive home via Croxall to see if the swans had returned to their feeding field. They were back in their field, I parked up and had a quick look, the five whooper swans were still with them.

I drove back via Walton, and as I approached the Walton football pitch I drove into the field where Sarah and I saw the stock doves on Saturday. I keep pulling in here because in the past it has been good for partridge, and I have yet to see a partridge this year. Initially the field looks empty but as I was about to call it a day I became aware of some brown shapes moving along the bottom of the hedgerow at the end of the field, eureka, I have my partridge, seven of them, red-legged partridge to be accurate.

Among the various birds seen there had been three crackers, and I had not got out of my car to see any of them, that has got to be comfortable birding don't you think? *Blue Badge Birding* in fact! Tomorrow, I may be going out with my friend Andy Toman to see if we can photograph, we meaning him, the long-eared owls at Park Hall, we just have to await the weather forecast for the day.

I complete my workload far earlier than anticipated, and as the day is rather pleasant I have decided to make a visit to Cannock Chase, calling in at Marquis Drive initially, here I hope to catch up with the brambling, and then, if time, I will pop across to the Shooting Butts for another stab at the shrike.

The feeding station at Marquis Dive is devoid of food and also devoid of birds, a brilliant start to the days proceedings. Walking across I had noticed that seed had been put out on the ground near to the Information Centre and café, and there were birds feeding. As the café is part of the complex, tables and benches are outside, and the birds were feeding quite close to those, so I made my way across and sat down, fortunately the temperature today was about 10c, with little or no wind. I had obviously disturbed the birds on my arrival, but they quickly came back and one, a nuthatch, could not have cared less about me. It's flight path happened to be directly over my head, and it crossed above me at no more than a metre or so, you could actually hear it's wing beats. Great, blue and coal tits were the main visitors with a small party of bullfinch. All of whom seemed totally unconcerned by my closeness to them. After a little while a group of about half a dozen chaffinch flew in, my concentration increased at this stage. Should a brambling be about, chaffinch are the birds it is likely to consort with. Some time passed by, birds were flicking in and out continually, when a bird popped in quietly and I had my bird, it was a nice winter female brambling, my patience had been rewarded. She stayed feeding for two or three minutes, before off she went, showing her white rump as she left. One down, one to go, although, some how, I do not think the shrike will be so accommodating, we will see.

I drove across to the Cadet Huts car park and started to walk across to the Shooting Butts. In transit I met up with a birder I know, he was able to tell me he had seen the bird at about midday, as it was now nearer to 14.00 hours, that did not augur well. This proved to be the case. No shrike although I did see both green and great spotted woodpeckers, so they will have to do, plus I heard a buzzard calling but did not see him.

As I still had some time to spare I drove back home across the causeway of Blithfield Reservoir, apart from the odd gull, mallard and coot there was little else to excite. Driving up the hill from the reservoir I almost put my car through the hedge, well that is a slight exaggeration, but I had the shock of my life. In a paddock of a nearby farm, two large pale birds were stalking about in a very methodical manner, only cranes do this, but these birds were almost white, cranes are a grey bird. These had to be investigated, so I managed to turn my car round and drive back to study the birds. Cranes they most certainly were, but these were two young birds, and they were definitely not the crane we see in the UK. I sat there racking my brains. These birds were about half the size of a full grown crane, but their colour was bothering me. The bills were also relatively short, and then it hit me, they were probably young sandhill cranes, a North American species which take over two years to reach adulthood I believe, which accounts for these young birds looking so small. Obviously they were pets, but I know very few people who would have a bird of this type as a pet, they are hardly canaries. I will have to keep my eye on these to see how they get on, be nice to see them as adult birds that is for sure. And no, before you ask, they are not going on my 'Year List', the brambling is though.

The weather forecast does not look too bad, so after a telephone call with Andy, tomorrow will be Park Hall. As it so happens today is not an early start, Andy is picking me up at 09.15 hours, and Park Hall is a little under an hours drive away. The feeding station, which you will remember my talking about previously is very busy. Once again we have bullfinch in almost double figures and willow tits are flicking in and out, it may be only two of the latter, they are just so active. I suggested to Andy he may like to spend some time here, but he wanted the owls first, which was completely understandable, he has never seen one in the wild.

As we walked down to the wood we heard raven calling and after a little while managed to locate the bird, so that was a nice start. In the woods I made my way to the selected area, and now commenced the neck straining time of gazing at the tops of conifers, many of which are probably 15 to 20 metres high, fortunately there was no wind so they were not swaying about.

After nearly half an hour I located our first bird, and I called Andy across to have a look at his first ever long-eared owl. In turning to summon him across I then found I could not relocate the bird, what a start. I had failed to mark my tree. Andy, fortunately, is a man of patience. It must have taken me a good 10 minutes to find the brute, but at least we did. Unfortunately the view was not the best, you could just about make out the bird was an owl, photography was impossible.

Leaving Andy to enjoy the bird as much as was possible, I carried on searching, believe me, if long-eared owls do not want to be seen, you are in for a struggle. Several more minutes past by, until bingo, I had another one, and this bird was more of a poser, you could see all the bird including the tufts.

Placing a branch at the base of the tree so I did not loose this one, I found Andy and back to the tree we came. This was more like it, so out came his equipment, I went and sat on the bench nearby, and for the next half an hour or so Andy took his pictures. He had got what he wanted, not only having seen the bird for the first time, but actually photographing it as well.

On our way back we had a slight excursion into the Hulme Quarry, this area is of great interest to geologists as well as birders. We birders come here not to admire the geological features but to try to find the little owl which inhabits the quarry. The little owl did not want to be seen today, and was not, but on the return journey we flushed a pair of jay, I was happy enough with these.

Andy was now happy enough to photograph his bullfinches and willow tits. The birds here are very people tolerant, although any dog running loose puts them to flight, which is completely understandable. Andy once again managed to get himself some nice pictures. We finished off with a mug of coffee and a muffin at the Visitor Centre, had a nice chat with the warden, and then made our way home.

Friday has come in very misty. On the bird line someone had reported two merlin at Whitemoor Haye yesterday afternoon, I may well try to see if they are still about. Whitemoor Haye has a very good track record for merlin, although two does sound a little ambitious.

The mist has burned off nicely and we have an almost Spring-like day, the temperature being in double figures, a bit unusual for February, so I will make the best of it while it is still here. Nothing new has been reported during the morning, so Whitemoor Haye it will be.

The lake was quite busy with the usual selection of duck, the far shore had a small flock of greylags grazing away, in company with the wigeon flock. Further along a small flock of lapwing caught my attention, there looked to be a few smaller birds among them. Initially I only located starlings, but then a rotund brownish bird darted into vision, a golden plover. After carefully going through the reminder of the birds I had located seven golden plover, a nice little haul that, I just hope they hang around until tomorrow, Sarah still needs these for her 'Year List'.

I drove on down the rough lane, stopping to view the open ditch where I saw the green sandpiper a day or so ago, no repeat performance today I am afraid. A small flock of finch types were flicking about in the hedgerow, as I carefully approached they took to flight, many had white wing bars so I think it is safe to presume they were all chaffinch.

As I approached the end of the microlight landing strip I stopped to survey an old oak tree, us birders always stop to look at this particular tree, little owl have nested here in the past, and birders are always optimistic. Not today though but stopping to look had done me a favour.

I had hardly started to move when flashing across the lane in front of me came a merlin, all doubts about the merits of yesterdays report were now kicked into touch. This is a wonderful example of how luck plays such an important part in this game of ours.

Today will not be one of my better days I am afraid, if Dorothy had lived on she would have been 72 years old today. Dorothy's favourite flowers were carnations, and Sarah has brought in a nice selection of these to brighten up the home with, and to bring back very happy memories. Memories are wonderful things, be they sad or happy, but the overriding thing is life must go on, our departed loved ones would want it too, of that I am sure.

What Sarah and I will be doing exactly today I am not sure. Yesterday Martin reported in with a nasty cold, and not wishing to spread his germs he stayed at home so we did not see him. Martin is no better so we can now make our arrangements for the day ahead. This morning we will visit the Chase and go to Marquis Drive in the hope we can see a brambling, and then this afternoon we will go across to Whitemoor Haye in the hope we can get something new for Sarah.

As we arrived on the Chase we found it to be heaving with people, a running event was being staged and every car park we passed were full, and as we arrived at the Marquis Drive car park this also looked to be full. Fortunately, there was one space left on the disabled part, so I was very pleased to have my blue badge with me.

We made our way over to the feeding station, this was quite active, bullfinches, chaffinches, titmice of three species and a nice nuthatch, so things were not as poor as I expected. Sarah suddenly mentioned 'Song thrush', and under the bird table a song thrush was busily feeding away. We spent some time here hoping a brambling would put in an appearance, it did not, so we decided we would make our way home, have an earlier lunch than normal, before going across to Whitemoor Haye. Little did we know this was not to be the end of our morning's birding.

Sarah was driving and as we drove through Kings Bromley I noticed a small bird of prey sitting out an a small tree, asking Sarah to slow down, it was a merlin. As Sarah was driving she had been unable to see the bird, so we turned round and drove slowly back. The merlin was still in it's tree and we managed to park up close by. As we looked at the bird it flew off, but not before we had fully identified it, a female merlin.

As we were washing up after lunch we had one of those moments birder's dream of. I noticed a small bird in my rowan tree which I first thought to be a female siskin. Sarah went to get a pair of binoculars, and the bird came lower down the tree providing us with a much better view, It was no siskin, the bird was a lesser redpoll, another 'Year Tick' for Sarah, and the first lesser redpoll I have seen in the garden for over 20 years. The perfect end to an amazing morning.

We park up at the lake, pochard numbers are now well into three figures, a flock of 50 or so Canada geese, probably a hundred or so wigeon are grazing on the grassy bank and while watching these I pick up a small number of large brown birds also feeding on the bank. These are a telescope job, and when we focus up we find they are curlews, seven of them, and another 'Year Tick' for Sarah.

Carrying on looking through the duck, we also find a nice flock of goldeneye, 12 of them in fact, so we spend some time enjoying these delightful diving duck, the majority of which were drakes.

Time now to drive round to see if the swans are still available and then we will drive home via Walton. We first of all called in at Croxall Lakes NR to see if the swans were there, no, it looks as though this flock have decided to move on. We have enjoyed them for over two months so we should not grumble.

Approaching Walton we spotted four brown birds feeding in a field alongside the River Trent, and fortunately we were able to park up quite close to the birds. Red-legged partridge, and another 'Year Tick' for Sarah, five on the day, she will be pleased with that.

Once again we have illustrated just how well you can do locally, the main thing is knowing your patch so you know where to go, and also having that bit of luck as we did with both the merlin and the lesser redpoll.

Sunday has signalled a weather change, light rain is falling with heavier rain promised for later. Martin is still not fully well so Sarah has decided to complete a few of her jobs which leaves me with a free hour or two. Reports locally are sparse, the most interesting spot appears to be Blithfield Reservoir, one or two interesting gulls have been passing through, the only problem is there is no record of what time of the day. They could be evening sightings of birds coming in to the roost, or just birds passing through, all I can do here is take a chance.

The rain slowly increases in tempo as I drive across so conditions are going to be far from good, especially for birds at a distance, and gulls are rarely that close, except where they are fed, but Blithfield is not a park.

I make my way to the dam, the deep end as birders call it, most of the reports included that description. I was rather taken aback by the strength of the wind, the waves were lashing into the dam and few if any birds were to be seen. A small flock of mallards were riding out the waves, a cormorant sat on a large buoy which was swaying quite violently, I think the cormorant was actually enjoying the experience. Two gulls flew through, but no need to get excited, these were black-headed. I did not bother to cross the dam, and as it was locked it saved me the trouble of having to unlock and re-lock the gate in the rain.

Driving across the causeway a couple of cormorants flew over, or it may be more accurate to say were blown over, they did not seen to be quite in control. Parking up on the other side I caught the full blast of the wind,. It made it impossible to even open a car window so I was having to keep my wipers working to get a reasonable view out.

Birds here were very few and far between, a small party of wigeon were grazing the grassy shoreline and a couple of coot were bobbing about like large black corks. I was about to move off as a gull came flying low across the waves in front of me, my first thoughts were another black-headed, but I realised that this bird had white primaries. The water was so grey this fact really stood out, it was none other than a Mediterranean gull, the day became suddenly brighter. I watched it fly past, thanking my luck for being here for these few seconds. I know I keep on saying it, 'The right place at the right time'. The Med' gull needless to say was a 'Year Tick'.

On now round to Blithfield Church to see if there were any woodland birds out today. The odd blue and great tit, a blackbird tossing leaf litter about as it searched for some goodies or other, a robin was attempting to sing, but more interestingly, a raven could be heard croaking away nearby. Although I attempted to locate the bird I could not, but a croaking raven will do any day, you do not mistake this birds call.

In the corner of the wood a nice small patch of snowdrops were fully out, these were quite short so I presume they were in fact our native wild snowdrops, not some foreign import.

As I drove off a buzzard came across, I would like to have said glided across, not today, at best he was driven across, although he did seem to be in more control than the cormorant earlier. On my way home I stopped once again to view the cranes, I am still not sure what species they are, I may have to be cheeky and go and ask.

There has been little on the net locally, well to be more accurate, little I could attempt to see at present, but I have heard whispers of scaup at Croxall Lakes NR, and the whoopers appear to have returned to Croxall itself, both of these areas being suitable for car viewing. Plus the fact the scaup would be a 'Year Tick', always a good reason to make some effort.

The whooper swans were still at Croxall, the rear of Croxall Hall as is their usual repose. The mute swan numbers have reduced somewhat, most of the remaining being family groups, it could well be the fact the other swans have moved off to sort out their territory for the coming breeding season. It will be interesting to see just how long the whooper swans remain, they have quite a trip to make, probably Iceland.

Croxall Lakes was completely deserted, not even dog walkers present, so I had it all to myself. Driving up to the hide I had only to walk a few metres to the hide, which was most welcome, my leg still being most uncomfortable.

The light was very good, and I positioned myself from where I could see most of the lake, and set up my telescope accordingly. After a good half an hours scanning no scaup came to light. I had tufted, pochard, goldeneye, (in poor light any of these could have been mistaken for scaup to the untrained eye), wigeon, teal, shoveler and the inevitable mallard. As I still had some time, down to Whitemoor Haye I popped. Here the lake was far busier, large numbers of tufted and pochard, which I went through with a fine tooth comb, no scaup hidden away here. On the far bank a large mixed flock of Canada and greylag were grazing the shore, and the wigeon flock were enjoying the near shore, and a soaring buzzard completed the scene. Now for the rough lane.

Diving down the rough lane I became conscious of a flock of small birds flicking along in front of me, I picked up a flash or two of yellow. I managed to position myself so I could study them properly, the flock comprised about 20 birds, reed bunting, yellowhammer and seven tree sparrow, the latter species will need to be reported, along with the goldeneye and whooper swans.

Driving home and passing the Whitemoor Haye Farm House, thinking my day was over, I had a very pleasant surprise. Two partridge flew from the verge in front of me and landed just a short distance away in the adjoining field, and they stood out proud. Picking up my binoculars I was delighted to see they were grey partridge, and my first for the year.

Although the weather today was no better I decided I would at least have a ride out and see what I could find from the seclusion of my car, so Whitemoor Haye it will be. You could just about make out the far shore, not that you could identify the birds which were on it, they all just looked black. A few black-headed gulls were on the water nearer in, you could just about make these out, although the noise they were making was as good an identification feature as seeing them clearly would have been.

I had parked up at the entrance to the landfill site, so I could look down onto the lake, and I was very pleased I had done so. A small flock of a dozen or so finches were in the hedge nearby and on closer observation three of these turned out to be corn buntings, that was a nice little bonus. The other birds were goldfinch and chaffinch.

Monday has dawned a very poor morning indeed. Persistent rain, misty and with a decided nip in the air, not a morning for birding, and certainly not a morning for birding over a large expanse of water where it is likely to be both murky and cold. I was heading to Carsington with the Monday group, we are meeting at Sheepwash at 10.15 hours. Just how many people will brave the elements remains to be seen.

I am very surprised with the turnout, 17, plus me, are we all mad? I just hope we have something to see. Roy and Len assure me the mist has lifted slightly, born optimists these two. Mind you the rain had just about stopped, so down to the Sheepwash Hide we go, at least we can all get in it today.

There is only one other birder in the hide, and he is trying his hand at a bit of photography, what his chances are in weather like this I do not know, he has not seen a lot it would appear, but if he has concentrated on his camera work this may not mean a lot. Anyway, we settle ourselves down and commence to stare into the gloom ahead, we do pick up a few duck, tufted, wigeon, teal and the odd mallard, when someone mentions a duck up-ending close by. A quick look and we have our first nice bird of the day, a drake pintail, a new species for some, and we quickly locate the female nearby.

Roy is the next to bring a bird to our attention as he calls me across to have a look through his 'scope. At times I do not know what we would do without Roy, he has again hit the jackpot, a juvenile great northern diver is smack bang in the middle of his lens. Even through the gloom you could see how heavy and large this bird was, it's breast was very pale and the whitish bill was very evident as it preened away. For many it was a dream bird, to see one on a local water was something they never expected, they believed you had to go to Scotland at the very least to hope to see such a bird. I understand from reports they have had up to three at Carsington this year so far, as you will remember this is only my second sighting this year, and the quality of this viewing is definitely superior to my last.

Just prior to Roy bringing the diver to our attention I had been studying a large gull standing out on a nearby spit, I asked Len to have a look at it through his telescope, my initial thoughts being we had a yellow-legged gull, one has been reported regularly and I had one when last here. Len's first comment is the bird does not have yellow legs, so that kicked my initial thoughts into touch, but he agreed with my thoughts that the bird had a very white head, unlike herring gulls at this time of the year. Moving across I had a look through his 'scope, the legs were certainly pinkish, as Roy confirmed, he too had moved onto this bird, but something else caught my attention, the eye looked dark, almost black, in yellow-legged and herring gulls the eye is a bright yellow. Then it hit me, this was a winter, adult, Caspian gull, another variant of the herring gull which is now a full blown species in it's own right.

Most of my friends had never heard of the Caspian gull, and their field guides were not going to show it, unless they were right up to date, so I had to explain a little of what was happening to the 'herring gull clan', so many of the sub-species were being given full status, and this does not make birding any easier, unless you happen to be a gull lover, and funnily enough, not many birders are. It is too darned difficult, although today a little knowledge proved beneficial.

As we were about to move off Roy shouted 'Two gulls with yellow legs flying left', and as though they wished to finish off the morning on a high note, two yellow-legged gulls gave us a fly past. I cannot ever remember having a morning when the only two species of gull seen were rare ones, with not a common gull in sight.

Leaving the hide a small flock of seven goldeneye flew in, that gave us five species for reporting to the net. An unbelievable couple of hours had been spent, in the worst of weather conditions, but the birds had not let us down. Incidentally, if you wish to repeat what we have done today, the Sheepwash Hide is wheelchair friendly, and the journey from the car park is about 300 metres at most.

I was wondering what to do for lunch when Roy and Len mentioned they were going down to Cromford, both would like the chance to see some hawfinches, so I decided to join them. Roy and Len arrived a minute or two prior to my arrival, and had nipped into the toilet block. I got out of my car and looked towards the rugby pitch and saw a small group of birds sitting out at the top of a tall tree, I raised my binoculars, hardly breathing as I did so. Seven hawfinch were sitting out on this tree, nibbling away at the leaf buds. At this point Roy appeared, I shouted 'Roy, get your scope on that lot'. He could not believe what he was looking at, 'We saw them when we arrived, but they looked too big, we thought they were collared doves'. I made some comment about it being a good job I had come along, all in good humour I hasten to add, but we do like to have a crack at each other occasionally.

Len appeared at the end of all this banter, so we just settled down to enjoy the hawfinch. We had the pleasure of their company for a further four or five minutes before they got bored with it all and flew off into the distance.

On Sunday I had spoken with my friend Ivor, he had visited Sittle's Farm last week and had seen the corn bunting flock, you may remember I saw these myself earlier in the year, so I decided to give them a try. We certainly still have corn buntings in the vicinity, I saw some a day or so back, so the ditch clearing has not driven them away completely, which I had feared.

Apart from a solitary chaffinch no other bird was in evidence, so I drove down the lane a little further studying the hedgerow as I went. Nothing doing, so I turned round and returned to Sittle's Farm. Stopping near to the entrance I saw a small flock of birds fly into a bare tree halfway down the drive. Sorting out a suitable viewing point, not wishing to be accused of invading anyone's privacy, I raised my binoculars. My luck was in, corn buntings they were and I had 11 of them, to say I was delighted is putting it mildly. They may not be colourful birds, but to all birder's they are more than a bit special.

Later that afternoon I had cause to visit my local tip and as I drove through Kings Bromley I made my usual call in at the lay-by to see if the little egret was about, it was not. As I drove on I spotted two white shapes on the far river bank which did not look like swans, so I found a spot to pull in to study further. I was pleased I did, instead of one little egret, I now had two. My trip out to the tip was proving to be most successful, I will have to see if there is any more rubbish for removal!

Today is definitely the day to do a bit of birding and when I received a telephone call from an old birding friend, Mike Dix, who was interested in taking his wife Sally to Croxall Lakes NR, and could I join them, my decision of where to go was made up for me.

Sally has never visited Croxall, so Mike jokingly suggested 'What better way for her to see it than in the company of the warden', complimentary bribery can get you anywhere Mike! Birding with Mike can be very interesting. I first met Mike as a novice some 20 years or so ago, he joined a bird study course I was running for Keele University, and he has become a very proficient birder. We often joke he has the best eyes and ears in the business, he can pick up a bird far in the distance before most of us, and he can also hear the softest of calls, a most useful guy to have around! Mike and Sally arrived promptly, so we drove down to the hide on the West Side. Quite a sharp breeze had sprung up and it was coming in straight off the lake, how often do you notice this on a bright day. Mike set up his 'scope and we started to scan the far shore. Mike had previously discussed ringed plover, Croxall being a regular breeding spot for them, and I was able to inform him I had seen none as yet, little did I know this was to be an omen, and a good one to boot.

I located a couple of oystercatcher on the far shore and Mike found us five redshank, there were nice numbers of wigeon and teal to be seen, and a couple of great crested grebe were in display mode, they must have thought Spring was already upon us. The three of us were talking away when I heard a bird call, quickly hushing the proceedings, I turned to Mike, 'I can hear your ringed plover calling, where the devil are they?' As I asked the question four small waders flew in, low across the water in front of us, ringed plover they most certainly were.

Unfortunately the birds did not settle on the lake shore, the water level being very high at present, so they circled round and vanished on the East Side. Here a large amount of work has been done to the River Trent and several gravel islands have been constructed, these being built for birds such as ringed plover to nest, the birds had probably gone to ground there. It was just nice to know they were back.

Now for a few minutes East Side. Mike drew my attention to a wader hidden away in the long vegetation on the side of a scrap, 'I have a snipe' he commented, and swinging round to look through his 'scope I could do little else but concur.

While we were enjoying this a shelduck came gliding in, Sally was particularly impressed by this bird, in today's sunlight it looked exceptionally smart. After a short while another came in to join it, we usually have shelduck breed at Croxall, so today we may have been fortunate in seeing both the first ringed plover and shelduck arrive for the season ahead.

What a difference a day makes. Yesterday was bright and clear, today is grey and miserable, and I do not know what occurred last night, but our cars are covered in a fine yellow dust, have we had a case of 'Sands from the Sahara' once again? You may remember such an occurrence several years ago. Sand or no sand, I am popping into Croxall.

I quickly locate the redshank and oystercatcher from yesterday, the duck species are the same with the exception of a pair of goldeneye, I was not aware of these yesterday. I spend some time really studying the far shore line looking for the ringed plover, all to no avail and was just considering moving off when I heard geese flying in, greylags, and a small flock of seven birds circle the lake as they prepare to land. Studying these I realise one of the geese is smaller than the rest, had we a pink-footed goose among them?

The birds safely land, and the small goose is most certainly a pink-foot at the very least, but the bill colour interests me, had we a bean goose, and not a pink-foot? I now needed the birds to walk out of the water so I could see the colour of their legs, and although they drifted off in the shores direction they were in no hurry to walk out and graze.

Eventually the first of the greylags ventured onto dry ground, and the rest followed suit. My goose was the last to make it, is that not always how it goes, and this bird had pink legs, problem solved, a pink-footed goose it was. A nice bird to get locally.

Before I close for today. Croxall Lakes Nature Reserve is accessible from a public car park, no charge and the main hide is wheelchair friendly with a short ramp and movable seating. The only problem is the fact the hide is about 500 metres from the car park with no facilities for taking a car up to the hide. The pathway up is flat so wheelchair users can get to it as long as they appreciate they may need assistance, unless, of course, they have a motorised chair. It is worth a bit of an effort in my opinion as you can see some very interesting birds, as well as flowers, butterflies and dragonflies in the summer.

Saturday has dawned not very auspiciously, steady rain is falling at present so we hope this passes over within the next hour or so. Our intentions this morning were to visit Croxall Lakes once again, in the hope we can relocate the ringed plover and snipe for Sarah, and then have a little drive round Whitemoor Haye seeking out the corn buntings.

Stopping at Kings Bromley, we were pleased to see the little egret had reappeared, so we spent a few minutes enjoying it. It was feeding very actively in shallow water, and it caught a meal, from a distance it looked like a small eel, but what ever it was it went down easily. Unfortunately this turned out to be our only interesting bird of the morning.

Sunday dawned, and I decide to visit Cannock Chase. I arrive at the Cadet Huts in a very heavy downpour, and cannot get out of my car for nearly 15 minutes, some start this. The rain passes over, now for a walk down toward the shooting butts, not that I will get that far, but from past experience I can obtain quite a sweeping view of the area I am interested in after walking about 400 metres or so. The feeding station at the huts is as busy as ever, titmice and chaffinch principally, with a great spotted woodpecker flying in and out regularly, taking a peanut to a nearby tree where he commenced to hammer it to bits.

Today is the Rosliston Bird Study Group field meeting and we are at Blithfield Reservoir. I had also heard that a great white egret had been reported from Tad Bay yesterday afternoon, and from the permissive footpath you can get a very good view into the bay, especially with a telescope. We set ourselves up at one of the view points which overlook the bay, and set to work. The last reports I had were the bird was roosting up regularly in the willow on the edge of the bay, so this is where we concentrated our initial efforts. We saw many a large area of white, none of which were birds unfortunately, so after awhile we concentrated our efforts on the water, to see what duck we could find.

Due to then damp weather experienced so far this year the reservoir is quite full and this has had the advantage for us birders, of bringing the birds nearer to land. The air was full of the delightful whistling call of wigeon, teal were feeding away in the shallows, with tufted, pochard and mallard scattered far and near. Of the more unusual duck, Roy picked up a nice group of seven pintail, four drakes and three ducks, there were two groups of five of both goosander and goldeneye and two shelduck, among the cormorants there were two 'sinensis, what a good year we are having for these.

We gave up on the egret, and moved off to the first hide and feeding station. Here we had the usual titmice, a nuthatch, great spotted woodpecker several finches and the bird of the morning for many, a pair of siskin. For some of the newcomers to the group this was their first experience of siskin, so they were able to fully enjoy these birds as they were frequent visitors to the feeders.

Having spent so much time looking for the egret, time had by now caught us out, but it had been a most enjoyable morning, even though the weather had not been so pleasant, damp, grey and cold.

February has been a slow month for new species, I have only added 10 to my total which now stands at 109. I am expecting March to greatly improve those figures, especially with my holiday in Norfolk, I could add between 30 and 40 in that week alone if all goes to plan.

Map references:
Cannock Chase – Marquis Drive: SK 006153.
Blithfield Church: SK 044240.
Broomey Croft – Kingsbury Water Park: SP 204970.
Carsington Water – Sheepwash: SK 248528.

Chapter III

March

Mcarch, I am pleased to say, has at least come in dry, and the weather forecast for the week ahead is not too bad. I must be feeling fit today, I have completed all my chores and it is still early afternoon I have a couple of hours available to me, so a trip across to Blithfield Reservoir will not come amiss. I made my way to one of the viewing points, about 300 metres from the car park, here there is a bench where I can at least bird watch in comfort. The pathway to the view point is also wheelchair friendly.

I slowly scanned across the water, in the far distance a nice flock of goosander could be seen, even in the poor light of today the drakes stood out well, the flock actually numbered 13, the largest I have seen this year so far.

Moving further across the water the goldeneye came into view, on this occasion five of them and nearby were six pintail, if the later hang round until the weekend this is where Sarah and I will probably be coming.

Time now to do a bit of work looking for this elusive egret. I spent a further 30 minutes or so working my way through the willow trees in which it is claimed the bird roosts, all to no avail, the only thing white I found was a plastic bag!

While I was doing this another birder came by, who I knew vaguely, he told me the egret seemed to appear late in the afternoon 16.30 hours onwards, depending upon the light conditions and roosted up in the willows, but it was very elusive and mobile. As I was not able to stay that long I decided to move on, I had enjoyed myself for an hour or two so I made my way home quite happily.

Thursday arrived and mid morning Sarah called my attention to a small bird which was on one of our sunflower heart feeders. This brambling is only the third I have ever seen in my own garden, and probably the first for over 20 years, a very nice record.

Not a lot has appeared on the net for today so far, so I will visit Blithfield Reservoir to see if the pintail are still around, Sarah would like one of these, and who knows, the great white egret may put in an appearance.

On the way to Blithfield I drive through the hamlet of Woodmill, I doubt if there are above a dozen properties here, but one of them, Woodmill House Farm, has a very nice pool, I always drive slowly past here just in case, and today I was pleased I did so. Standing on the shoreline was a little egret, and I was able to pull over and have a good look, this one did not fly away.

Today I have brought my telescope so I settle down and start to pan across the reservoir. Goosander numbers are up on a day or so ago, I count 21 today, and the goldeneye numbers have also increased slightly, I now have nine. Swimming close in are eight gadwall, four pairs, and both tufted and pochard are well represented but where are the pintail, the bird I really came for? I thought I had caught a glimpse of one or two among the willow trees which grow out of the water, but I just could not be sure. I spend a further half an hour looking for these birds, but to no avail, if they are still here they are well hidden.

Saturday has come in damp and dismal to say the very least. At one stage we were undecided whether to go out or not, but eventually we thought we would give it a try, and Blithfield it will be. We parked up in the lane to give Tad Bay a quick glance, and why did we bother. The reservoir was shrouded in heavy mist, I would estimate visibility was down to less than 50 metres, for birding almost impossible conditions. To look for a great white egret in this was ridiculous. After a few minutes we gave up and drove round to the Permissive Walks car park to try our luck at the bird hide.

We arrived to find the car park completely deserted, we were the only idiots out this morning, and to make it worse, down came more damp drizzle. Fortunately the feeders were well stocked and we did at least have birds to look at. Four species of titmice, nuthatch, chaffinch, greenfinch, dunnock, a magnificent male pheasant and a pair of great spotted woodpecker. Not a bad little haul considering the conditions of the morning. We stayed in the hide for a good hour, nothing else was added to our list for the day.

I decided to go out in the afternoon so a quick drive round Whitemoor Haye may do the trick. The rain had just about ceased leaving it just a dreary and damp afternoon. Visibility over the lake was at least better than that at Blithfield earlier on, although there was little to see. I still had a little time so I drove home via Walton. Just north of Croxall there is an area known as the Croxall Redwood Plantation, so called for obvious reasons. I pulled in to survey the fields opposite, and a large group of geese were installed there in. At first glance they all looked like Canada, but by now you probably appreciate I never discard the chance to really go though a goose flock. Working through these I located two barnacle geese, so it was well worth the effort and time spent.

Come Sunday I manage to get out by mid morning leaving Sarah and Martin to their own devices, and park up in the lay-by overlooking Tad Bay. It was certainly much clearer than this time 24 hours ago: pochard, tufted, cormorants, great crested grebe could all be clearly seen. I was just about to move on when a birder told me two other birders he had just left and thought they had seen the great white egret fly in 20 or so minutes previously. Although he had stayed with them for several minutes they had no further sightings, something at the very least to keep my eyes open for.

I make my way round to the first viewing area, with not much to report. For some reason I decided to walk up to viewpoint number 2, on the 'Blue Walk', we did not reach this far yesterday.

Sitting down on the bench I scanned the reservoir in front of me, a very broad view can be obtained from here. Goldeneye, five of them and 11 goosander soon came into view, several pochard and tufted were visible on the open water and while going through these a white shape on the far shore caught my attention. This was shrouded through willow, but a white shape it was and it was moving, not a plastic bag job this one. From my angle it could have been a swan, but it did not give the impression of swimming, it seemed to be walking. I just had to get myself a better angle.

Further up the pathway I got to the spot I wanted, and leaning against a tree I again concentrated on the white shape. It was moving ever so slowly, but eventually I got the view I wanted, it was the great white egret, eureka, I had found it. I do not know who the two birders were who thought they had seen it fly in, but they certainly had. I was meant to see this bird I felt sure, why else had I walked further on than originally intended?

I enjoyed the bird for a further five minutes or so before it vanished from sight, I am sure I was in one of the very few places from where this bird could be seen. The right place at the right time syndrome once again.

7 March has dawned a beautiful morning, bright and sunny after a light frost. I am off to Park Hall, long-eared owl hunting, with the Rosliston Bird Study Group. Owls do fascinate people and we have a very good turnout for today's little adventure, 26 hardy souls have made the journey.

We make our way down to the plantation and the area in which I have been fortunate enough to see them on all my previous visits. Several of the group have never seen the bird so I spend some time explaining just what we are looking for and where in the trees it is best to look. Any unusual shape has to be studied intently, the owls are not roosting up for our benefit, so they make life as difficult as possible for us.

Spreading out we start our work, neck breaking work, staring high into the trees above us. Several false alarms are raised, but no success. A good half an hour passes by, and I must confess I was slowly becoming a bit desperate, you cannot bring over 20 people out without finding something for them. After a little while I made my way back to the area where in all my previous sightings had been made, I had already done this area so I approached from a new direction which at least meant I was now looking up the trees from a different angle. From a new angle or not, things did not look any the better and I was beginning to think this morning was not going to be one of my days, then a shape caught my eye. High up, near the crown of a tree, a brown shape could be seen, this was clearly a bird, and there is only one bird it could be. I focused up cleanly, changed my position several times to get the best angle, and there, staring down at me was our quarry, a long-eared owl. I do not remember having spent so much time seeking one out ever before.

Quickly summoning my friends from their various locations we all gathered near the tree in question to study the bird. Even though we knew which tree the bird was roosting in, it was still not easy to pick the bird out. Eventually I managed to get everyone onto the bird. One of my friends suddenly shouted, it's ears are up. We know it is not ears, just tufts of feather, but by seeing these clearly at long last, everyone knew they definitely had a long-eared owl in view, a positive identification. They were happy enough to take my word for it, but they now knew it to be fact.

Time had certainly moved on, over an hour spent in pursuit of the bird, and now half an hour of enjoyment. Along with the owl I doubt we had seen above 10 different species this morning, it is not often I take people out for just one bird, but these are a bit special, and today we had made it.

Just a reminder when visiting Park Hall. The distance to the woods from the Visitor Centre is probably a 500/600 metres round trip at the most, it is walkable with care but is not really wheel chair accessible without careful assistance.

Tuesday looks like another very nice day, so I have decided to change my routine a little, and tomorrow I will do my weekly shop. Today I will do some work round the home and then hopefully have a short trip out this afternoon. I am pleased to say the plan worked, and I am off to Whitemoor Haye and Walton on Trent. My legs are playing me up a little today, so I can at least do all my birding from the car.

The bright weather is still continuing, Thursday has come in very nicely. I had the pleasure of seeing the brambling in my garden again early on, and the woodpecker has been very active, my fat tray is vanishing by the second.

I have a busy day ahead of me, especially this morning. Prior to going on holiday next week there are things I have to do, and I must confess that being on my own means I have all the headache concerned with packing. When Dorothy was around the packing seemed to be done in minutes, now it is days.

By the time I actually got out it was well past 15.00 hours so a quick trip round it will have to be. So a quick run round Whitemoor Haye would be all I could manage, but at the very least it was a change of scenery.

The lake had the usual flock of wigeon grazing the shore line, about 100 Canada geese were on the far shore and the tufted/pochard flock were still in large numbers, it will not be long before these move off, the wigeon along with them. We only see these birds in large numbers during the winter, they are visitors from further north, in some cases from the near Arctic.

Now for a quick drive round the rough lane. The bunting/finch flock are still foraging away along the hedgerow, so I stop and watch these. It is not long before I locate the tree sparrows, it looks like six again, but the yellowhammers seem to have increased in number, I can see at least five males plus the odd female. When I return from my holiday I doubt if this flock will still be in attendance, it may well have split up as the birds seek out their own breeding territories.

Friday is continuing with the fine weather, I most certainly will have a trip out this afternoon, probably go in search of the great grey shrike on the Chase once again. Prior to enjoying myself I have a few things to do and Scott, my lawn man, has just 'phoned in to say he is coming this morning to give my lawns their first cut of the year. Does that mean summer is really here? I doubt it some how!

I have been drawing up my 'Hit List' for the holiday, and if I see them all, which is unlikely, my 'Year List' will increase by 35 species, they do say hope springs eternal! I do like to have something to aim for, it adds to the fun and makes me work a little harder.

On Monday, after our indoor session of the Rosliston Bird Study Group, we are having a meeting to discuss our arrangements for the Norfolk birding trip. Fortunately four of the course members have holidayed with me in Norfolk previously, so we have a lot of experience to draw upon, and then there is my old friend Rob, who is based at *The Pheasant*, he will be able to bring us right up to date with the peak birds.

Scott came, lawns cut, and we have a decided change in the weather, the blue sky has been replaced by dark, heavy cloud, and rain looks very likely, time for a change in my plans I think. I have not heard a lot about Blithfield over the last day or two, apart from the great white egret, so I will have a trip across to see what, if anything, I can locate, also, should the rain come I can bird watch from my car. The rain did come and I saw little.

As things have turned out today, Sarah managed to complete her tasks quite quickly so we have an hour or so at our disposal to pop out this morning, so a quick visit to Croxall is decided upon. There has been a fair movement of ringed plover through the county over the last couple of days, and as I saw four a week or so ago at Croxall, they will have hopefully remained. Sarah has yet to see a ringed plover this year, and this will be our last opportunity of any birding together for a fortnight.

Sarah soon picks up an oystercatcher, and I locate three redshank, so we do have some waders in attendance. Moving further northwards along the shore line I pick up what we have really come out for, a ringed plover. Moving my zoom up to 60x magnification, normally 30x-40x is about the best you can do at this time of the year, I pick up it's yellow bill. Calling Sarah across she can enjoy the bird and chalk up her 'Year Tick'. While she is looking at the bird another plover runs in and the two promptly mate, wonderful, we have at least one breeding pair in residence, and we are only halfway through March. It is always nice to see a bird on your own patch, but to have them breeding is a great bonus.

While all of this is going on I happen to glance out of the side viewing slit in the hide and have a nice surprise – sitting out on the top of a small bush is a magnificent male stonechat, a right corker this one. Stonechat are not known to hide their light under a bushel, and why should they, they are a blaze of colour so flaunt it I say. I quickly called Sarah's attention to the bird, as this was a 'Year Tick' for both of us, and was not anticipated today.

This bird was an exhibitionist if there ever was, it flew to within a few feet of the hide, binoculars were no longer required, and for about four minutes or so we just sat still taking the bird's beauty in. Then, with a flick of it's tail, reminiscent of a robin with whom it is a close relative, it was up and gone. A nice climax to our short excursion, this afternoon I will have a little trip out to Whitemoor Haye.

Whitemoor Haye is very quiet, no people and few birds, so I make my way down to the rough lane area surely there will be something here. I quickly pick up the bunting/finch flock and many of the birds are feeding on the lane verge. I stop and look closely at these, and I am very pleased to see they are mainly tree sparrow, 14 of them in fact, the largest number I have seen here for a long time. What are missing are the yellowhammers, none in sight and only the odd reed bunting, these birds have no doubt paired up and moved off to breed. A few chaffinch were still evident, so to still call it a mixed bunting/finch flock is just about accurate. I have a feeling when I return from Norfolk all these birds will have gone.

Time to drive home, and near the Croxall Redwood Plantation I see two partridge racing across the ground as only partridge can. I am able to stop before they vanish from sight and they were grey partridge. I saw some here a few days ago, I hope that is a good sign they may be breeding in the area, I must keep my eye on these, they are no longer a common bird, I just hope they stay where they are and do not move up nearer the Cotton Shooting area.

Not a bad few hours birding today, and I have five birds which will need to be reported, one of which was a 'Year Tick', this I am sure will be my last before Norfolk.

Sunday has dawned a little more miserable than of late, steady rain is falling, Sarah does inform me that according to the latest Met Report she has seen, the rain will pass over by mid morning. This being the case I will have a trip across to Blithfield Reservoir, sand martins were reported yesterday, be nice to pick up one of those so early in the year.

My first stop point will be from Newton Hurst Lane, just to have a brief view over Tad Bay in case the great white egret is showing itself, needless to say it is not, a grey heron was however. On now to the causeway where the sand martins were reported, unfortunately not today. There were a few duck here, mallard, the odd tufted, but the pick were three goldeneye, a displaying drake with two ducks close by, I hope he was successful, his display alone should have got full results.

As I still have time I will go home via Whitemoor Haye, see if the tree sparrow are still in residence. I parked up on the corner of the lane, and wound down my window to sit and just listen in the hope of picking something up. This turned out to be a good decision. After just a couple of minutes the beautiful song of a skylark could be heard, is there a more English sound than this?

After a minute or so I was able to pick the bird up as it was spiralling high above, the amount of energy this small bird uses in it's display flight song must be vast. I will just sit here and enjoy it, much as I like *The Lark Ascending* by Vaughan Williams, give me the real thing any day.

Tuesday is now here, the start of the Norfolk trip, the party comprising Carmel and Tom Baker, Anne and Colin Foord, Rosemary and Tom Gordon, Jane and John Hobson, Roy Hood, Len Naisbitt, Neil Kelly, Evelyn Syer, Margaret Haywood and yours truly.

The morning was very dull and misty, not at all as we would have liked, and the five of us intend to meet up at Titchwell at 13.30 hours for a quick snack and a couple of hours birding prior to going on to *The Pheasant Hotel*. Things were going very nicely for us until we approached the A5. Here traffic going east was at a standstill, an accident on the M6 south had occurred, and in consequence traffic had been diverted onto the A5, creating a major traffic jam here. As we crawled along we eventually reached Tibtoft, a small hamlet on the A5, here work was being carried out and single lane traffic control was in operation. This combined with the accident on the M6 was the reason for an almost 10 mile traffic jam.

After that we made good time, even managing a stop for coffee etc, and arrived at Titchwell smack on 13.30 hours. We received a telephone call from Margaret, she had been held up by the same jam, but she was running an hour late and hoped to join us about 14.30 hours. The four of us had a quick snack and coffee prior to making our way down to the Island Hide.

The lagoon was full of birds. About 50 avocets were showing well, goodly numbers of dunlin, ruff, black-tailed godwits, golden plover on the wader front. Brent geese were flying in and out frequently, pintail, over 20 of them, were showing very nicely, the commoner waterfowl were in evidence, as were greylag and a flock of over a couple of hundred pink-footed geese. A superb start to our holiday in fact, and while all of this was going on Margaret arrived with the news she had just seen and heard a Cetti's warbler as she walked down, the lucky beggar!

Time to move on, and we arrived at our hotel about 17.00 hours, time to unpack, freshen up and meet up for a pre-dinner drink. Just to whet your appetites, I had a nice salmon darne, washed down by a nice dry white wine. After dinner we made our plans for tomorrow.

Wednesday has dawned, just as unpleasant as yesterday and chillier, with the visibility still very poor, not a day for sea watching that is for sure. I had seen Rob prior to breakfast and he had confirmed the spoonbill and shorelarks are still to be seen and also mentioned that a decent flock of Lapland buntings had been reported at Weybourne, the next village along from Kelling. These were not very easy to locate apparently, but we have to give it a try. We took two cars to Weybourne, paid and parked. It is amazing just how many car parks in Norfolk charge Blue Badge holders.

From Weybourne we proceeded east towards the Coastguard Cottages as they are known locally, in their vicinity the last report of the buntings had been made. As we walked along the cliff many skylarks could be heard, not a morning for cheerful song I would have thought, but the larks seemed happy enough.

From the area round the cottages we scanned the fields, skylarks as previously mentioned, black-headed gulls a plenty, plus the odd carrion crow. As it was getting decidedly colder we turned to return to our cars and head for Salthouse, our next port of call. Approaching the car park a gull caught my attention, it was standing on a metal pole sticking up out of the sea, so I asked John and Tom to put their 'scopes on the bird. Something about this bird did not look right.

John quickly called me across 'I have never seen an herring with a dark tip to the bill, although it has got pinkish legs'. I moved across to study the bird, John was right, whether the bill had a dark red or black tip it was impossible to tell in this light, so I concentrated on other features. The eye was black which contrasted with the persil white head, this had to be a Caspian gull, but I was the only one who had ever seen a Caspian gull previously, and my two were both full adults. I hazarded a guess this was a third winter bird not quite moulted through to adult plumage, but as we were visiting Cley we could have a look in the new book about gulls, this would tell us all we wanted to know. After the lack of buntings this was a nice bit of excitement, a 'Lifer' was in prospect for all but me.

Salthouse was our next stop, here the car park is free I am pleased to say, National Trust. If the snow buntings were still about they would be almost running about your feet. Someone puts seed out for them and it brings these birds in very close, in the far north where they breed, up near the Arctic Circle, people are few and far between, so they show little or no fear. Today, however, there was no seed and no birds, but just as we were about to leave a group of seven turnstone flew in, these too show no fear, so we had wonderful views of these with John's camera clicking away merrily. Driving off we soon stopped again, several small brown jobbies were flitting along the wire fence, meadow pipits, I have never waited so long for my first sighting of this bird.

First things first, use the amenities, order coffee and find the gull book. The ladies ordered the coffees John made his way straight to the books. Out came *Gulls of Europe, Asia and North America* published by Helm, a wonderful book incidentally, mind you at £45.00 so it should be. A Caspian gull it certainly was, and I was pleased to see my diagnosis was correct. Book back on shelf, coffee drunk, now for shorelarks.

To see these birds we had to walk along the East Bank, and I was worried about this. It must be at least 1000 metres to the sea, a 2000 metres round trip, so I told my friends to carry on without me if I found it all too much. This pathway is not suitable for wheelchairs.

My friends were very considerate and we made very slow, if steady progress, towards the sea. Part way along the East Bank we stopped, John had spotted a grey plover in the marsh near by. Nearby was a mound of grass, just the right height to sit on, this plover must have known who was coming. Grey plover are birds we rarely see in Staffordshire, so we spent several minutes getting to grips with this bird, before moving on. Needless to say, the bird was still in it's winter plumage which was a pity, they are one hell of a bird in their summer attire.

Now on for the shorelarks! A birder approached, he had good news, the larks were about 300 metres away, we were in for a treat. Several birders were grouped a little distance away, most with cameras, so John got his ready for action.

The shorelarks were running about on the shingle, about 10 of them, I was looking at more shorelarks in one place than I had ever seen in all my years of birding, and many were males. Their facial markings were showing well with one particularly well advanced, his black 'horns' were visible. Some of the older bird books actually called this bird the horned lark because of these feather erections on the head. Here we probably had the bird of the holiday. John was able to take many photographs and he promised us one each as a souvenir of the occasion.

We drive down to the shore car park for a bit of sea watching but visibility was very poor indeed, anything above 100 metres distance was just a blob in the mist, so although we spent well over an hour seeking, apart from the odd gull close in, we have nothing to report. Back to the Visitor Centre we go, at least parking here is free.

The Visitor Centre is very good. Along the window which overlooks the reserve you have a superb panoramic view, a telescope is usually set up for visitors, and as the centre is set up high off the road the view is unrestricted.

John came up trumps, over the far side of the reserve he had picked up a white shape and closely scrutinising found he had the spoonbill. We quickly moved to the telescope and focused up on the bird. Even at this distance you could see the bird making sideways swipes in the water as it fed. As soon as we mentioned spoonbill most of the other customers joined the queue, including one or two Norfolk Wildlife Trust staff. Another celebratory coffee was called for, we may even have something stronger back at the hotel.

While enjoying our second coffee Margaret spotted the spoonbill had moved to a much more viewable spot, the bird was preening and the spoon-like bill was clearly visible. Back to the telescope, forming an orderly queue, to once again enjoy the bird.

Spoonbills only bred in England last year for the first time in many years; this was only a small colony of eight or nine pairs. Breeding in these numbers has not happened since Queen Victoria was on the throne, with only single incidents occurring. We have all been eagerly awaiting their return.

Jane and John returned home, we will see them again on Friday when they come to stay. The remainder of our party will be arriving tomorrow, but we shall not see them until in the evening. Our little group of five will spend the day at Salthouse and on Cley reserve proper; it has reserved disabled parking and a lift to take you up to the centre proper, so it can be visited by all.

Thursday has come in very pleasantly, the sun is actually trying to break through with visibility improved tremendously. We pop down to the beach car park first for a bit of sea watching. The sea was once again quiet with mainly gulls putting in an appearance, although we did have a particularly good view of a common gull, so we could really study the bird, and a great black-back drifted by. While we were here a large flock, 500 or so, Brent geese came in, their beautiful call echoing in from over the sea. I always think of their call as the soft baying of distance hounds. These birds settled down in the marsh about 50 metres away. There are two races of Brent goose we have each winter in the UK, these were dark bellied from Russia.

Skylarks were plentiful, and I did not blame them for singing today. Groups of oystercatcher could be seen and redshanks came flying past on a regular basis. In a nearby ditch turnstone and ringed plover were feeding away, with little egrets scattered over the area, at least 10 of them.

Time to go to the centre and obtain our permits to visit the hides. The cost here is £4.00, with no concessions for age. They do, however, allow carers in for free, so should you have a companion to push your wheelchair watch they do not charge them. The walk to the hides is along good pathways or board walks so it is very wheelchair friendly.

As we reached the board walk Margaret pointed out a small bird sitting on the fence, only one bird sits out in the open like this, it had to be a stonechat. Focusing up our binoculars we were enjoying the bird when up came it's mate.

We reached the hides, went in the first, and made ourselves comfortable. The birds were much the same as seen at Titchwell a couple of days ago, but the clear light transformed them somewhat. The ruff looked magnificent, their scaly backs showed up well, as did their different coloured legs. Ruff are a nightmare bird at times as their leg colour can vary from grey, yellow to red. Birders often joke, if you cannot tell what the wader is, it is a ruff!

We moved on to the next hide where avocets were plentiful, many were feeding close by and it was interesting to see them moving their up-curved bill sideways as they searched for food, helping us appreciate why the bill is shaped so.

There were only two other people left in the final hide when we entered and they came across to speak to us seeking advice on the waders, they were from Virginia, U.S.A. We spent a very pleasant half hour or so explaining and describing the waders visible and also learned a little about birding in the States.

While in the hide several golden plover flew in and quite a percentage were beginning to look the part. The black on their faces and breast was really showing, and their backs were picking up the golden tint from whence their name comes.

We returned to the Visitor's Centre to view the reserve once again. We had hardly put rear end to anchor as a pair of marsh harrier rose up in the sky and put on a lovely display for us. Magnificent birds, so elegant in flight, and these two were obviously a pair in every sense of the word. Now back to the Pheasant.

The remainder of our party have all arrived safely, and over drinks after dinner we have decided to have a day at Titchwell and return to base via the Choseley Barns, famous for their corn buntings, we hope. And even better the weather is set fine for a few days more.

Titchwell is a combination of lagoons and sea shore, but the sea shore is 1000 metres from the centre, I intended to have a good try at making it. The pathway down to the sea is very good, part firm shale and some board walk, and wheelchairs can be hired from the centre. There were plenty of benches on route so I could always sit down if the need arose.

As we approached the spot where Margaret heard and saw the Cetti's on Tuesday, the bird called as though on cue, and what a call, how so much volume can come from so small a bird I just do not know. We settled down to look for the bird, me grabbing a space on a bench nearby, I had chosen well. A bird darted across an open channel right in front of where I sat, and once in the seclusion of the reeds sang his little heart out, I was the only one to see it.

We decided to move on, we could have another go for the Cetti's on our return. I sent my party on, telling them not to wait for me and followed on slowly, at my own pace. I caught Roy up, he had waited for me as he had located three twite, and he knew this was one of my target birds. They gave very good views and I was pleased to hear all had seen them, and even more pleased the shore was only 100 metres away, I needed to sit down again.

There was a nice selection of birds on the shore, many we had already seen but right out in front of us on the water were four long-tailed duck and a red-breasted merganser, these are birds not to be sniffed at. Out at sea a tidy raft of common scoter were drifting on the tide, with sanderling and bar-tailed godwits near to hand. Roy had found a water pipit and Len had located a chiffchaff. I also think most people had at least a glimpse of the Cettis so we were all happy. Then came the sad blow! I had once again sent my friends on leaving me with just four others and we slowly made our way back towards the centre when Len came running towards us. They had just seen three cranes flying overhead and Len had come to tell us just in case we were in a position to see them. Unfortunately for us, we could not, what a bird to have missed, but that is life. Needless to say my friends were full of it, and who can blame them.

Tomorrow is wader day at Snettisham, but there is no point in arriving much before 16.00 hours, so we decided to call in at Thornham, Hunstanton and Holme on the way. Hunstanton had food available, plus the chance of fulmar, a bird not many of my friends have seen.

The good weather seems to be continuing so off to Thornham we go. This is an area of marsh and mud, you only come here to bird watch or to sail once the tide is in. For once there were very few waders about, Jane and John picked out a spotted redshank which vanished down a muddy creek by the time we all arrived to see it. The odd redshank and godwit put in an appearance and several little egrets could be seen making their way down the numerous muddy channels.

We were just about thinking of moving off when I noticed a pipit flicking in and out of a rowing boat just in front of me. I was separated from my friends so I shouted to draw their attention, and I was pleased I had. Managing to get a very good view from my angle I saw the bird was a rock pipit. Now for Hunstanton.

Parking up on the cliff top, we had hardly got out of the car as a fulmar swept by. The are a wonderful flying machine, frequently mistaken for a gull. They fly on stiff wings with hardly a flap as they just use the currents of air coming up off the cliff faces, minimum effort for maximum effect. They are also a bird not to get to close to. They are tubenoses, and have two tubes directly above their bills which they can send a acidy and fishy substance directly at any one who interferes with them, and it ain't pleasant believe me. It stings like blazes and their aim is good. Now for a quick lunch and on to Holme.

When visiting Holme there are no conveniences, but there is a toilet block at the entrance to the track which leads to Holme Reserve. Take great care in driving along this road, the first part is un-adopted, even though some very posh houses line it, so drive slowly and with care. After about two miles you come to the reserve, there is an entrance fee of £3.00 which on a good day can be quite an investment. You can walk a short distance to the sea and inland there are several hides over looking smallish lagoons, so we initially viewed the sea. Not a lot, and although the tide by now had turned it was still along way out.

Holme possess a sandy beach, and today being Saturday it was being well used, so bird life had to seek peace and quiet elsewhere. As we had time available we made our way to the hides. Here we had avocets, pintails, wigeon, teal, a solitary grey heron and on the numerous small islands snipe could be found. John brought our attention to three buzzards high in the sky which were being dive bombed by a smaller bird, here we had a peregrine falcon out enjoying itself. It may not be able to out muscle a buzzard, but it could certainly out fly one, so for a few minutes we watched all of this before the falcon grew bored and flew off. I can only suppose the buzzards were grateful to get back to enjoying the sun themselves without interference from a smaller upstart.

Time now to move on to Snettisham, for what is in my opinion, the event of the holiday. Shortly we will experience thousands of birds fleeing the incoming tide, we could easily be talking of 100,000 birds or more. It is a sight unique to the Wash, and one no birder should miss, if you only see it once you will take it to the grave with you. The reserve, unfortunately, lies a good mile from the car park, and is not the best of conditions under foot. Blue Badge holders can drive in, you would have great difficulty in making the journey by wheelchair, but if you write to the RSPB at Snettisham explaining your difficulties, they usually provide you with a pass.

Thanks to my badge I was able to drive in, and run a bit of a shuttle service to collect others. The tide was still a way out, but it has a channel close which was filling up rapidly, and once filled this overflows to meet the incoming tide, a piece of very dangerous water, unless you have wings that is.

On the oozing mud, large numbers of birds were enjoying their last feeds prior to the mud being covered by the sea. Close by were knot in their hundreds, the same for dunlin, shelduck were scattered everywhere, and in the distance large flocks of waders were taking to the air as they flew in front of the incoming time. To call this a spectacle does not do it justice, it is mind blowing. How these birds do not collide when flying at speed and in a tight mass I do not know, but they manage it, and as some flew in low over our heads you felt the wind from their wings, there were so many of them.

The further the tide advanced the more birds came in, not only the waders, duck and geese also retreated from the on-surge of water, a flock of pink-foots must have been in four figures with the Brent geese not far behind. Then a miracle occurs, it all goes silent and the birds vanish, they have gone behind us to await the turning tide, when the whole process will be repeated in reverse.

Snettisham is over for us, how do you follow this is the next question. A Sunday in Norfolk can be a very busy time, and with the spell of nice fine weather still continuing, places are likely to be very busy, so we decided to visit two places which were not on our original list, Blakeney and Wells, stopping at Cley Beach for an hour before moving off. We had heard Blakeney was the area that the spoonbill commuted, and Wells where we have a freshwater lake as well as the sea. Hopefully car parking will not be a problem.

The Cley beach car park was completely deserted and so appeared the sea. We decided that I would stay with sea watching and the remainder of the party would make their way to the beach hide, I declined this as the walk was all shingle, and by now my leg was giving me some gyp. So taking a stool from my car, I set up telescope to survey the sea, and through a 'scope it was not quite as deserted as first thought.

Fortunately it was a nice day, very little breeze so looking over the sea was not unpleasant. After a few minutes a small party of kittiwake flew through, I was pleased about this, another 'Year Tick'. Out at sea three duck were flying fast and low over the water, almost clipping the sea with their wings, only one duck flies this fast, they had to be eider. Focusing up I was able to pick out the colour of one of the birds, it was a nice drake eider, the other two brown birds were obviously female, dare I say it, another 'Year Tick', I was beginning to feel pleased I could not walk to the hide! In the distance I could see my friends making their way back and while looking in their direction a small gull flew past, it had very dark underwings, blimey an adult little gull. I was starting to enjoy this sea watching. Now on to Blakeney, my friends incidentally had little to report, my time to gloat I think.

Blakeney was not as bad as expected, car parking was quite easy, so once done we set off on a walk along the old sea wall. There is a waterfowl collection here and I was very interested to see a black swan on the nest. These birds usually nest in late autumn early winter, which compares with spring 'down under', so this early in our year was something new to me.

Wild birds were thin on the ground, a few redshank, oystercatchers and the inevitable black-headed gulls so we started our return journey. At this point a nice flock of Brent geese flew overhead, so that brightened up our morning a little. Now for Wells.

Not everyone was interested in Wells, some were interested in trying Holkham Meals again so only eight of us only made our way. I was pleasantly surprised by the small number of cars parked up. We checked out the lake, mallard, coot and moorhen were all there to see, so we made our way down to the beach by the Lifeboat Station. This is a short walk from the car park and disabled parking is available, again at a price! Here the tide was just starting to come in, although the main channel which fed Wells Harbour was filling up quite rapidly.

A small collection of waders were picked up on the side of this channel, and a nice selection it turned out to be. We had dunlin, sanderling, turnstone and ringed plover, all showing very well, while further out on the mud were oystercatcher, redshank, bar-tailed godwit and curlew, ignoring the black-headed gulls, a very nice selection and all close in, so we sat down to enjoy these.

While doing so I suddenly noticed something was watching us, a seals head was up in the channel and it was staring directly at us, time to get the camera out and Colin and John quickly did so. No sooner did the cameras appear than the seal vanished under the water, to reappear some 20 metres or so down stream, with Colin and John in hot pursuit. The seal was only too pleased to join in the game, as the cameras went in one direction, it would dive and go in the opposite direction. Eventually the seal tired of all this and just lazed on the surface enabling photographs to be taken.

The tide was now coming in at a faster rate, and as at Snettisham, the channel was filling up rapidly. We realised that several seals were coming into the channel on the incoming tide and we now had about a dozen seals to enjoy. Seals here are not uncommon, a large colony breeds on Blakeney Point, and seal viewing trips from nearby Morston Quay are a feature of Norfolk life.

As we still had some time to spare we decided to return to Cley, have a coffee and spend more time looking over the reserve, conditions today were very good for distance viewing, and I would not have to walk, now there's a thought.

My only worry was just how busy Cley Centre would be on a Sunday, fortunately not bad at all, although the window viewing stations were all occupied. Coffee was obtained so we turned our chairs to face the window and stared out. I became conscious of a white bird moving on the ground accompanying a small flock of barnacle geese, and the bird was of a similar size. Earlier in the week Rob had mentioned a Ross's goose had been seen tacked onto the pink-foot flock, these were not pink-foots, but the goose looked the right size to be a Rosse's. I 'rudely' approached a group at the telescope and told them I thought I may have the Rosse's goose, would they mind me using the telescope, at the mention of Rosse's they quickly moved over, and half the inhabitants of the café became interested.

Swinging the 'scope round I focused up on my quarry, red bill, black primaries. A Ross's goose it certainly was. Ross's are a small species of snow goose, which breed in northern America, Canada principally, and are rarely seen this side of the 'pond'. Most are classed as escapees from collections, this one is only the fourth I have ever seen.

A queue was quickly forming behind the telescope so I moved off to enable all those interested to enjoy the bird. Fortunately once you had located the bird you could see it in your binoculars, not as clearly as from the 'scope, but sufficient. I know I have mentioned how well we have done from the centre, I am beginning to think the next time I visit Norfolk I will just park myself here, it would certainly cut out the walking.

Tomorrow is our last day full day and we intend to visit Titchwell again for at least the morning and probably call in at Salthouse Beach for our final stab at the snow bunting. As we are visiting Titchwell Jane and John will have the morning with us.

En route we pass through a small hamlet midway between Burnham Overy Staithe and Burnham Norton, a delightful little spot with a windmill, but unfortunately it does not appear to have a name, well not on my Ordnance Survey map. Here barn owl are a regular sighting and as we pass through this morning we see parked cars and photographers scattered about, an owl must be present. We slow down, and a barn owl can be seen quartering a nearby meadow, by coincidence the second we have seen here this week. We continue on but our accompanying cars pull in, no doubt hoping to take a few photographs.

As we previously had seen barn owl we decided not to turn round, instead we would spend a few minutes at the Choseley Barns trying to locate the corn buntings not seen previously. Our luck was in. As well as several yellowhammer and reed bunting two corn buntings could be seen in a bush by the barns, and very good views they provided, our decision to ignore the owl had turned out right, we had our first corn bunting of the week.

At Titchwell we met up with the rest of the party, photography had not been that successful, although the owl showed well it was all distant. We decided we would make our way to the new hide, I think it is called the Pallinder Hide, which we had not visited previously. This was a walk of about 700 metres with several benches to sit on en route, so once again I declined the use of a wheelchair, and later in the morning this proved to be a very good decision. More of that later.

Walking down the pathway we were again serenaded (or should I say assaulted) by the vociferous Cetti's warbler, who still defied any real visual contact, and the chiffchaff was still calling from a nearby bush. We had wonderful views of ruff and teal were doing their best to join us, they were so close.

After several pauses we made the hide, and very posh it is too. I hate to think how much it cost, but the viewing was very good, it had wind up windows not just bare slits, so you could keep out the wind if needed, not today, there was no wind, so windows opened.

We were much closer to the waders than from the Island Hide, so we had very good views of ruff, dunlin, redshank, black-tailed godwit and golden plover, the latter in their hundreds.

Earlier in the week we had a discussion after dinner regarding spotted redshank, and Colin had shown me some pictures on his camera of a bird believed to be a spotted redshank, taken at Snettisham on Saturday. From the size of the picture in the back of a camera I was not at all happy it was a spotted redshank. For some this could be a 'Lifer', and my opinion was awaited on the matter. Today the problem was resolved. It was Colin who called me over to his telescope, he believed he had a spotted redshank in view, well three of them actually, so I was only too pleased to join him. Spotted redshank he had indeed and as I was studying them a redshank joined in, this was an opportunity too good to miss, so we all spent a few interesting minutes studying the differences between two similar species, and a photograph was no longer required, we all had spotted redshank on our list.

We made our way back to the café slowly, well I and a few friends did, I had told the others to not hang about, especially as some wished to pop up to Choseley in the hope of seeing the corn buntings. I rested on a couple of benches as we moved and I had a first class view of the Cetti's. The bird came out of the undergrowth and sat right out on the top of a twig, calling his little head off, he was so close you could see his throat vibrating and his bill quivering with the effort of his song. This has to be the best view I have ever had of the bird, and only three of us experienced it.

Two cars decided to go corn bunting hunting, the remainder of us decided to visit Cley Beach and Salthouse Beach still hoping for snow buntings. Snow buntings it was not to be, but we did have a bit of fun.

At Cley Tom Gordon called my attention to an unusual looking gull, he mentioned the fact he had never seen one like it, more than a good enough reason to really study the bird. This bird was herring gull size with a pure white head, black eye and a bill which was very dark, almost down to the base. Tom had found himself a second winter

Caspian gull, he was not with us when we had our Caspian at Weybourne, so I spent some time explaining why it was so, and a little of the back ground to this bird, after all it was not in anyone's field guide.

While we were looking at the bird one or two local birders came across to see what all the excitement was about, and Tom spent the next few minutes explaining all about the bird, considering he had never seen one prior to today he did a first class job.

We just had time to pop into Salthouse, and here we had ringed plover and turnstone showing well. We had a chat about the ringed plover where I explained the main differences between them and the little ringed plover. You know by now the differences in leg and bill colour which I use as my main identification features, especially when the birds are at distance. Here it was Evelyn's chance to teach the locals a thing or two. A birder came up to her asking whether we were looking at a little ringed plover, she promptly told him no, and why. Another local put in his place.

Those two little incidents finished the week off nicely, without humour where would we be. It was now a case of back to the hotel, do what packing we could, in preparation for our journeys home tomorrow.

After dinner we sat down and went through our lists for the week, needless to say not every one had seen everything but the group total was 120, my personal total was 110, and included in that total I had 32 'Year Ticks', I was more than happy with that. I will not close the weeks totals yet as Len, Neil and Roy intend to pop into Sculthorpe Moor Nature Reserve in the hope of seeing golden pheasant.

Little did I know then that my week was not yet over. On our journey home Evelyn and I stopped at Thrapston, in Northants, for a coffee break. This lies adjacent to the A14, and time-wise is about halfway home. A little way along the A14 we noticed a large bird of prey circling round in the sky, fortunately the road was quiet so I was able to slow down without causing problems for other motorists. We had the jackpot here, circling above us was a magnificent red kite, totally unexpected, but a real treat never the less. It may not have been seen in Norfolk, but neither of us was worried about that little nicety, this bird was going on our list. I now had 111 and 33 'Year Ticks'.

Later in the evening Roy 'phoned in, they had six more species to add to the list, and yes they did get the golden pheasant, so we closed at 111 for me and 126 for the group, not bad for a group of amateurs!

Back now to home chores and restricted time available, but Sarah and I hope to be able to get out on Friday afternoon to go grouse hunting, you note hunting not shooting at Axe Edge Moor, in Derbyshire.

Today Sarah is doing the driving so I was able to concentrate on the surrounding countryside. Not a lot was to be seen until we turned off the A523 heading towards Dale Head. This lane had cattle grids and just as we crossed these I told Sarah to stop, up on the slope was our prey, two red grouse, and we had not even reached the moor proper, a lovely start to the afternoon. As we drove slowly across the moor we saw several pairs of grouse, they must have paired up, and their beautiful calls were echoing all around us. They are a magical bird, and as Sarah commented, how can anyone shoot them? The dilemma is that without maintenance of these moors by the shooting syndicates, the heather would not be controlled and we would probably have no grouse at all, so is this the price we must pay to see the bird?

We parked up at a spot I usually use if empty and get out of the car to see if we can see any more grouse, two promptly flew up as we opened the car doors. As I got out I was conscious of a golden plover calling, the odd pair breed up here but they are not birds you see very often. Sarah grabbed my arm and pointed, not daring to speak, no more than 20 metres or so away from us a full summer plumaged golden plover walked into the open. If you are not familiar with the bird then just have a look at them in your field guide, they are a knock out! For Sarah it was like a 'Lifer', she had never seen one in this condition before, all her previous sightings had been during the winter. While enjoying this bird a further two walked into sight, these also in their full regalia, a lovely sight, and Sarah's second 'Year tick' of the afternoon.

As we were about to get back in the car a rich, deep croak was heard, raven. Swinging round we saw the bird loafing it's way across the moor with two carrion crow keeping a respectful distance behind it. Sarah has her third tick, she has now broken the 100 for the year mark.

I had hoped to find a meadow pipit for her, as like me, up until last week, this common species had been avoiding us, so we dove off to the Dale Chimney. We parked up and almost before we got out of the car meadow pipits were singing, all we had to do now was locate one. This we did with ease, we found several in fact, so Sarah had the four birds we had come up for, you cannot do better than that.

Saturday morning has come in, still reasonable on the weather front although it is dull, the temperature is fine, but little on the net for us, the good birds are miles away, so Croxall it will be.

As we were about to get into the car we had a very pleasant surprise, from across the road the laughing call of the green woodpecker could be heard. I have not seen nor heard a green woodpecker locally for several years, and this was Sarah's first of the year.

As we cross the River Tame Bridge Sarah shouts 'Martins', and flying across the road in front of us are a small party of sand martins, about a dozen I would guess, we could not stop to check, the A513 is a busy road. For Sarah another 'Tick'.

We made our way onto the reserve, having it all to ourselves, and entered in to the hide. At first there was little to be seen but two medium sized waders flew in, one was a redshank, the white wing bar could be clearly seen and it was shouting it's head off, the other I was not so sure. They both landed in good view, the redshank confirmed now for number two. This was a nice ruff, the first I have seen locally this year, and yet another 'Year Tick' for Sarah, she has had a couple of cracking days.

Sunday has come in grey once again, but it is still warm with little or no wind. I went on the net early but not a lot of interest again locally. I did note a movement of little ringed plover had occurred yesterday in adjoining counties, although none actually in Staffordshire. In view of that it will be Croxall once again, with a short visit to Whitemoor Haye.

At Croxall the car park was empty although a car drove in as I moved off. The main hide was obviously empty so I settled myself in, telescope up and commenced to survey the West Side. Initially nothing was doing until a group of noisy redshank flew in, six of them it turned out to be. At that moment the hide door opened and in walked the other car owner, and it was none other than a friend of mine, Eric Clare, and I had made him walk.

Eric is a top birder much respected locally, we spent a very pleasant hour chatting away, sharing stories and still watching for birds. Two pairs of oystercatcher, two ringed plover and the ruff from yesterday were still showing well. A big surprise was nine shelduck, the largest number of adults I have ever seen here.

Eric was interested in the corn bunting situation down Whitemoor, which I was able to fill him in on, and in return he told me where the little owl was regularly roosting up. I have not seen a little owl this year, now I may have a chance to put that right.

We parted company, Eric did not want a lift back, so off to Whitemoor Haye I went. The owl had been reported in a tree down the rough lane and Eric had been able to tell where exactly the bird normally roosted up during the day, and he was accurate. I did not need my 'scope, binoculars were enough, sitting out was the little owl. The are not much larger than a thrush, just dumpier.

On my journey home I made my usual stop at the Kings Bromley lay-by, four little egret were doing their stuff, a nice end to a pleasant morning, especially as I had not seen Eric for several months.

Tomorrow I am off to Cromford with the Rosliston birders, we hope to see the hawfinch and dipper, I am not too hopeful with the hawfinch as I strongly suspect they may well have paired up by now and moved onto their breeding territories – we will see.

I have now got work to do. On 6 April I commence a new course this one going under the heading 'General Wildlife Studies'. Last year I did a short course on wild flower identification which went down well, so this year we thought we would broaden the subject out and make it a 24 week course. Preparation time is now required.

On Monday the sun was out and it was a very pleasant morning. 21 of us had turned out at Cromford, and with one aim, to try to see the hawfinch which have been reported regularly. I had been delayed somewhat in transit, when I arrived Roy and Len were already studying the trees both in Cromford Wharf itself and those near to the rugby fields. The news was not good, not an hawfinch in sight, a possible had flown over but that was as far as it got. Time now for our walk along the canal as far as the High Peak Junction, I drove round, it was over a two mile walk there and back, and I am just not up to that at present. The old canal towpath is nice and flat, easy walking and certainly wheelchair friendly.

Prior to continuing. When visiting Cromford, park on the rugby fields car park or High Peak, it is free, all the other car parks at Cromford charge, here you are also right by the conveniences and a nice café.

My friends arrived, apart from little grebes they have seen very little, so it was time to do the circuit round the woods and back to the canal, for me the walk went through the car park so I would have a jump off spot. This walk I would estimate being about 1000 metres. The High Peak Junction is famous for it's water voles, not today though, but a good a reason for another visit soon. Dorothy and I have had some magic moments here with the voles, they are very people tolerant.

Proceeding along the towpath for a further 100 metres or so we saw little grebe at the nest, and witnessed a change over, something in all my years of birding I had never seen before. A magic moment.

Prior to turning off by the side of the wood we stopped to admire some truly wild daffodils, not a common sight these days, and whist we were so doing, a shout went up 'Dipper'. We had just crossed over the River Derwent again so making our way back a few paces, the dipper could be clearly seen in the river searching for food. When ever I see a dipper feeding I ask myself the question, just how did this bird adapt to feed in such a way?

The walk alongside the wood was uneventful but as we approached a cottage near the end things livened up. They feed the birds here, and when you feed birds on the edge of a wood all sorts come into your garden, and so it was today. Blue, great and long-tailed tits for starters, robin, blackbird, great spotted woodpecker, treecreeper, nuthatch, blackcap, siskin, and from the woods nearby a chiffchaff could be heard. Not a bad little haul. As we moved on a song thrush commenced to sing his little heart out, what an idyllic sound.

As we neared the car park a buzzard glided across, and this turned out to be the last bird I saw for the stay at Cromford. I was sorry we did not get the hawfinch, but you cannot win them all.

I shall not be doing much birding over the next day or two, I have the local gardener coming in to make some major alterations to my garden. I do not have the time nor the energy to do much gardening, so I am having some labour saving alterations carried out. Alan, the gardener, arrived smack on time, he always does and we discussed my thoughts. He suggested one or two modifications to my original plans, and commenced work.

The month had drawn to it's conclusion, and my 'Year List' has moved onto 145, thanks mainly to Norfolk. April should provide us with a good number as many of the returning migrants will be putting in an appearance. We will see.

Map references:
Woodmill: SK 138208.
Blithfield Reservoir – Causeway, both ends: SK 632239/054236.
Titchwell RSPB Nature Reserve: TF 750436 for Visitor Centre.
Holme Reserve: TF 708448 for Visitor Centre.
Snettisham RSPB Nature Reserve: TF 645335 if walking, TF 658315 if driving.
Thornham Marsh: TF 727443.
Stiffkey Marsh: TF 965439.
Wells Coast Guard Station: TF 915456.
Blakeney Marsh: TG 029444.
Cley Marsh Nature Reserve: TG 055440 for Visitor Centre.
Cley Beach Car Park: TG 049453.
Salthouse Beach Car Park: TG 083443.
Sandringham/Wolferton Triangle: TF 673278.
Weybourne Beach Car Park: TG 111439.
Choseley Barns: TF 758421.
Hunstanton Cliffs: TF 678422.
Holkham Meals/Gap: TF 891447.
Sculthorpe Moor: TF 900306 for Visitor Centre.

Chapter IV

April

I am pleased with my garden re-organisation, Alan was able to improve on my original thoughts and I now have less gardening to attend to, so I am happy. Today being a Friday, I have reconnaissance work to carry out on behalf of Sarah, knowing she would dearly love to get the little owl on her list, I will have a quick round trip to Croxall, Whitemoor and Blithfield Reservoir, the latter in the hope there are a few swallow in.

Sarah had business to attend to in Lichfield this afternoon, so we both left home following each other, and this was fortuitous. Just round the corner on the outskirts of the village is a kennel, or dogs home, and the out buildings have swallows nesting in them annually. As we approached the bend a swallow flew over our two cars, and the way Sarah waved at me she had obviously seen the bird too, our bird was in the bag, and it had come to see us almost.

Now down to Whitemoor for the little owl. Here we had no trouble, the bird was sitting in almost exactly the same spot as seen last, I reckon someone has blue-tacked this bird in position. I just hope it is as easy come tomorrow when Sarah comes to see it!

Off to Blithfield we go, and in transit I had a very pleasant surprise. Driving along the A513, midway between Kings Bromley and Handsacre I spotted a small bird of prey sitting out on a telephone post. Slowing down, fortunately there was no other traffic on the road, I was delighted to see the bird was a female merlin, we have done very well for these locally so far this year, it must be at least my third, sometimes we are lucky to see one.

At Blithfield I made my way to the dam and for the first time in several weeks I drove across the dam to park up in the Angling Club car park. Walking back I surveyed the grassy embankment to the dam, nothing at all, so I drove down the shoreline. Approaching Ten Acre Bay a small flock of wagtails flew across in front of me to land in the adjoining meadow. I took them to be all pied wagtails, but nevertheless I stopped to have a good look at them, as things turned out it was a good job I did. It was a group of four pied wagtails with one white wagtail among them. These two birds cause great confusion when seen separately, and many a mistaken case of identity has taken place. Today, among pied it was a much easier job to sort it out. This group comprised three male and one female pied with the one white wagtail, my second 'Year Tick' of the day.

2 April is a lovely morning, and Whitemoor Haye it will be, as I thought Sarah would like a stab at the little owl, will she be lucky?

When looking in on the net this morning I saw that two Mediterranean gulls had been reported from a ploughed field at Whitemoor Haye yesterday afternoon, they would be nice to see, especially as Sarah has yet to see one this year.

The tractors were busily ploughing the fields and a large number of gulls were following these, picking out a Med' gull was not going to be easy here. We stopped as close as we could to the mass of birds and set up our telescope. The gulls were not going to co-operate that is for sure, they were continually taking to the air as they followed the tractors, we had three of these and the gulls kept changing their allegiance. Finding a Med' gull was getting more and more difficult. We must have spent well over half an hour working these birds, but no joy. Sarah brought my attention to three small birds which had dropped in on us, and swinging the 'scope round these turned out to be linnets, Sarah was delighted, they were a year tick, all of a sudden the Med' gulls had lost their importance.

Time now for a few minutes down the rough lane. The mixed bunting/finch flock had lessened in numbers but it is always nice to check them out, and today it was a good job we did. Once again Sarah came up trumps. She spotted a bird sitting high in a tree so we swung into action, a corn bunting, another 'Year Tick' for her, that was her third over the last couple of days. Unfortunately we dipped on the little owl, that will have to wait for another day.

Sunday arrived and I manage to start out by 10.30 hours, and needless to say I call in at the Kings Bromley lay-by in the hope of seeing the little egrets once again, which I do, well at least one of them. I am then on my way to Wolseley Bridge where Sarah had seen a drake wood duck, what a bird to see, they are only out-rivalled by the mandarin duck, as kingfisher have also been reported here.

A lot of traffic was heading into the Staffordshire Wildlife Trust's HQ so I decided to park up at the adjacent garden centre, and walk into the grounds. The lake soon came into view and it was only the matter of seconds before the drake wood duck swam out. Whether this bird is an escapee or not I do not know, and to be fair I do not worry, just to see so exotic a bird is all I wanted. I will not attempt to describe the bird, no words can, just have a look at it in your field guide, you may need to look for the Carolina wood duck as it was originally called. I sat down and really enjoyed the bird until it got bored with the whole proceedings and swam behind an island, not before I had the chance to tell a couple with a small child just what they had been admiring.

I made my way to the end of the board walk where there is a view point which over looks the River Trent, here from past experience is a good spot for seeing the kingfisher, and I was not the only one who knew this, several photographers were in situ. Fortunately most were standing up so I was able to get a seat. I must have been their lucky token, I had hardly made myself comfortable before the shout went up and darting low over the river came our bird. It perched up in a bush overhanging the river not 20 metres away, well within the range of many of the cameras, which were whirring away. The bird had a fish in it's beak which it stunned on the branch on which it stood, a painful experience for the fish I would think, before flying into it's nesting hole nearby. What a wonderful experience, the unfortunate thing is it was all over in the matter of seconds, we would have all liked it to have lasted longer than that, they do not call the kingfisher the jewel of birds for nothing.

I had become aware of darkening clouds looming overhead, so I decided time to return to my car, I had not brought waterproofs, and I was hardly likely to be able to run back to my car, those days are well and truly over. Nearing the end of the Trust grounds, and just as the fist spots of rain fell I heard a sound that made me stop, rain or no rain, I was listening to the call of a spotted woodpecker, and I did not think it to be the great. I tried to trace the source of the call as a small black and white bird flew off a tree trunk to land towards the top of a nearby tree, it was indeed a lesser, and for several seconds I had a very good view of the bird, before off it went.

I have not been looking forward to today for a few weeks now, I am due back at hospital for a review of my aches and pains, which over the last couple of weeks or so have grown more painful, leaving me struggling to walk any distance. I should have been at Attenborough Nature Reserve with my group today, I have had to leave poor Roy in charge in the hope I may be able to join them later on, this did not materialise.

My apprehension was fully realised. My consultant was very thorough, and she sent me down for an hip X-ray, as she was of the opinion my hip was the probably the cause of most of my problems. Previous consultants had sent me for leg and spine X-rays, which produced very little. I came back from the X-ray department and she showed me the resultant X-ray, even to the layman, I could see what she was saying, an hip-replacement operation was required, and sooner rather than later. She was writing to my doctor and I have to arrange an appointment in a couple of weeks or so. It looks as though my summer is already written off!

After having a late lunch I decided I would pop out to Whitemoor Haye, concentrate the mind on more pleasant things, especially as I saw a report of four scaup at the Haye. I have not seen scaup so far this year, so they are worth a bit of effort.

I should have known better, the scaup were no where in sight. While I was here I would at least have a nosey down the rough lane, and here I at least had something to enjoy. The mixed bunting/finch flock had returned, they obviously had not dispersed as I first thought. Several yellowhammers were still showing brightly, there was the odd reed bunting, several chaffinch and at least 10 tree sparrows, my trip out now came very worth while, and I sat in my car to enjoy them all. A buzzard came gliding over very low which quickly dispersed my birds, so I drove off home.

On Tuesday after a light lunch, and a few chores I found I had an hour or two to spare, and as the day was absolutely glorious, the temperature in my car had registered 21 degrees, I decided to have an hour or so at Blithfield Reservoir. A yellow wagtail had been reported from here, and although no location was provided, on past experience they are usually to be found round the dam, so that would be my destination, see if knowing my patch really worked!

Driving slowly over the dam I flushed a couple of pied wagtails plus a black-headed gull who appeared to have been dozing away in the sun, it's departure was very late. Halfway across the dam another wagtail took to flight, it was some distance in front of me but it certainly looked very yellow, I was convinced I had my quarry. Speeding up a little I drove towards the spot I saw the bird, and as I did I realised I had a car on my tail also crossing the dam. There was no way I could now stop to look for my bird, the dam being single line traffic, so I proceeded to the Angling Club car park, at least with binoculars a yellow wagtail should show up well no matter what distance.

Walking the short distance to the dam I proceeded to scan the dam wall, and after a very short time two specks of yellow appeared on the dam wall, my yellow wagtail was not one, it was two males sitting out there like canaries. At this point another car started to cross the dam. It may do me a favour by pushing the birds along the dam closer towards me. And so it turned out.

The two birds just kept flicking along the dam wall getting ever closer to me, and judging by the pace of the car it was probably another birder enjoying the occasion just as much as I, the car kept on slowing down so the occupier was most certainly studying the birds. Eventually the birds had enough of the game, and flew over the car to vanish behind it. The car drove up, we swopped notes, I knew him vaguely, and like me they were his first yellow wag's of the year. For me they were my 150th 'Year Tick'.

The pleasant April weather is continuing so once I have done my set of morning chores I will pop out again, probably go across to Croxall Lakes to see if the little ringed plover have arrived. Parking right outside the hide has it's attractions at present!

I make my way into the hide as quietly as possible, we have yet to develop a completely sound deadened hide, open the viewing slits and study the lake in front. The two tern rafts are full of gulls, black-headed needless to say, and they are kicking up a commotion, two lesser black-backed gulls are on the water and a pair of great crested grebe are in display mode. There are still a few wigeon on the far shore, it will not be long before they depart and a goodly number of teal are still in attendance. The shelduck numbers seem to have settled in at two pairs, the other shelduck have probably been driven off to seek pastures of their own.

After three or four passes along the shoreline there is little to report. At this point two birders come into the hide, so we now have three pairs of eyes to do the work. These two profess to be beginners at the game, and are only too pleased to have some of the duck pointed out to them, especially a pair of gadwall which were new to them. The lady spots a wader on a nearby scrap, her companion suggested it is a redshank, and swinging round I am able to confirm this, so I move across to allow them to see the bird through my telescope. They are now really able to appreciate the bird.

The lady has located another wader, this time larger than the redshank, her companion expresses the thoughts that it is a curlew. Once again I swing my 'scope round, this is no curlew, instead we have superb black-tailed godwit. When it turns to face us the neck and chest areas are quite red, this bird is almost in full summer plumage. My companions have never seen black-tailed godwits previously, so this was too good an opportunity for them to miss. Focusing up I handed the 'scope over to them, and they were able to enjoy the full beauty of the bird. I know someone else who would like to see this bird, Sarah. At least with the yellow wagtails of yesterday, we now have two birds to chase after.

Friday has come in again most beautifully, even at 08.00 hours it feels warm. We have a clear blue sky and bright sunlight, what more could we ask for. Scott is coming this morning to do some work on my lawns, so once this is completed I hope to get out. A quick check on the net has not come up with anything new, so Blithfield and Croxall it will be.

My first point was the dam, it was here you will remember I saw the yellow wagtails a couple of days ago. I parked up at the Sailing Club car park, and I had only just arrived when another car drove in, I recognised the car as that belonging to my friend Eric Clare, the little owl man of a few days ago. He told me he had seen both yellow wagtails and wheatear on the dam, and he had heard reports of a little ringed plover in Admaston Reach, so that gave me plenty to go for, the last two being 'Year Ticks'. So full of high expectancy over the dam I drove.

I was about halfway over the dam when I saw the first yellow wagtails, two females were catching flies in the dam wall. A little further on a nice male was doing likewise, and it was only a short distance before another male was seen.

As I approached a small grey and black bird hopped up from the verge to land on a fence post, wonderful, I had my wheatear, a female of the species. This was birding made easy, I had not got out of my car to see these birds, they had just come to see me. I parked up, spent a few more minutes enjoying the wheatear, before I drove back across the dam and round to the causeway and Admaston Reach, once again flushing the yellow wagtails in the process.

I parked up in a position from where I could view the expanse of the Reach and swept the shoreline with my binoculars. At first there appeared to be little or nothing to be seen, but a sudden movement right on the waters edge caught my eye, it was a ringed plover alright, but which one? After a short while the one became three, and as I was about to get out of my car and put my telescope up, they started to argue among themselves, with much wing flapping. This gave me just the information I wanted, they had no wing bar, were all little ringed plover. Unfortunately, at this precise moment a fishing boat came in close to the shore and my three birds flew off up the reservoir to vanish from sight.

Time now for Croxall. There were a few more visitors, although none turned out to be birders, so I had the hide to myself. My first concentration was to try to find the black-tailed godwit, this did not work out, if it was here I could not find it. Now to concentrate on the far shore, a job for the telescope. This was not proving to be very successful until I caught a movement, this time it was a ringed plover.

I panned the water for many minutes without picking out anything exceptional when, as I was working my way through the gulls, I picked up a bird with a black cap, focusing up I had a tern, and once it showed me the bill colour I knew I had my first common tern of the year, it was a red bill with a black tip. My third 'Year Tick' of the afternoon, this could not have been better had I planned it. Sarah now has the prospect of four 'Year Ticks' come the morning.

We had made a slight change to out venues, yesterday I learned that both wheatear and white wagtail had been reported at Whitemoor Haye so we will go after these rather than the common tern, white wagtails are a little more unusual. On all my recent visits Blithfield has been very quiet from a birding point of view, very few, if any, birders being present, although some nice birds have been seen, will we be lucky today?

We drove slowly across the dam, but birds were very thin on the ground, a pied wagtail, carrion crow and two linnet were all we managed. A slow journey back was no better, two bird I almost thought were bankers had vanished out of sight. Nothing else for it, the causeway here we come, were the little ringed plovers going to be more accommodating?

We parked up on the western side of the causeway, Sarah got out of the car promptly, and on the waters edge in Admaston Reach were our quarry, two superb little ringed plover, the previous gloom was swept away in a moment. Up telescope and we could enjoy these fully, the yellow eye ring was even visible at this distance, no possible error here. Now on to Whitemoor Haye.

At the Haye we met a couple for friends, they had not seen our birds, but they had seen the little owl in it's oak tree, so we had something to fall back on, Sarah has yet to see a little owl this year. We drove slowly round the circuit, a lot of ploughing and planting of potatoes has gone on this year, but at least the soil is clear and black, the two birds we were after should show up quite easily on this back ground, but they did not.

We arrived near to the little owl's tree, set up the 'scope, the owl is notorious difficult to find. I must have spent nearly a quarter of an hour studying, so I handed over to Sarah, could younger eyes resolve the difficulty, within minutes they had. We enjoyed the bird for a minute or two before it again vanished from sight.

Anyway, Sarah has her bird, and it has given her two 'Year Ticks', so she has no complaints. It just goes to illustrate the essence of birding, you can go out full of high expectancy based on either information received or ground work previously carried out, to fall flat on your face, or on the other hand see a bird which never entered your realms of probability. Never expect, just enjoy what you do see.

I intend to have a quiet weekend now. My leg is giving me much gyp, so as I have a field meeting on Monday with my Rosliston group I will rest it up in the hope I can get through the morning. Since I learned about my required hip-replacement I think my leg has come out in sympathy, I am getting pains from areas I never had pains before, but keep on smiling.

Our field meeting on the Chase did not produce much, a singing blackcap and a passing raven were the only birds of note. When I arranged this meeting I was unaware of just how early the school holidays were starting this year, and because of this the Chase was rather busy to say the least. I managed to walk some of the way with my group before sending them on to the Stepping Stones, not that they saw any more than I. It was so quiet, well that is on the bird front, there was plenty of noise from children enjoying themselves, and why not.

On the way home from my weekly food shop, while driving through Rangemoor, I saw my first house martin of the year. Also, I managed to have a drive out in the afternoon for an hour to Whitemoor and this proved to be pleasantly productive. The lake was again very quiet so I took my customary ride round the rough lane. A few tree sparrows were still in residence along with the yellowhammers, and the little owl was sitting out in his tree. As I turned the corner I picked up a splash of bright yellow on the ploughed field, so I quickly stopped. By the time I had raised my binoculars this splash of yellow had turned into two, two superb male yellow wagtails were strutting their stuff. Against the rich brown of the ploughed field they really stood out, a gorgeous little bird. As I was about to drive off a movement nearby caught my attention, at first I thought it to be a pied wagtail, but as it came more fully into view I realised it was a white wagtail. No complaints here, it is only my second of the year, Sarah would have loved these two birds.

The next day dawned and at Blithfield I headed to the dam. There was no sailing today and only the odd fishing boat was on the water so I almost had the place to myself. As I drove across the dam I flushed a yellow wagtail, but it vanished as if by magic, mind you the grassy embankment is covered with dandelions so picking out a yellow bird is not that easy, especially when driving! I crossed the dam without any further excitement, so I turned round to repeat the process.

I had hardly commenced to move when a small bird popped up onto a fence post, this just had to be a wheatear, and so it was, a smart female of the species. I was able to stop and study her for some time before she grew tired and flew off down the embankment I slowly made my way over the dam and I was about halfway over when four birds flicked up from out of the grass verge, three male and one female yellow wagtails, the mass of flying insects on the ground was all they were interested in.

While putting my observations on the net I was pleased to see someone had reported a greenshank from Whitemoor Haye this afternoon, I just hope it hangs around long enough for me to have a go for it come tomorrow, I have yet to see a greenshank this year.

Pulling up at the lake I spent several minutes surveying the scene, and all to no avail, not a sign of a greenshank anywhere so home I go. Approaching Yoxall I decided to pop down Meadow Lane, an area much loved by Dorothy, and I must confess I had made very few visits since she died. Too many memories I am afraid. Down the lane is a wooded area known as Yoxall Meadows Woods, a recently planted area as part of the National Forest, and Dorothy and I have spent many an happy hour walking here, enjoying the birds, butterflies, flowers and just sitting to watch the River Trent flow by.

There is only room for one car to park up at the entrance, and today it was vacant. As I got out of the car I was serenaded by a willow warbler, and this moment brought back the memories. The last time I had been here was prior to Dorothy being diagnosed with cancer, we had experienced exactly the same thing, a willow warbler singing it's little heart out to us both, and here it was being repeated. I just stood leaning against the gate, with a tear running down my face, it was as if Dorothy was here with me, or could it be her singing to me, I do not know. This little bundle of feathers, weighing in at just a few grams, had released an avalanche of emotion in my heart, and I was just so happy to be here sharing it with him, even though I had a damp face. I know one thing, this will not be my last trip down to the Yoxall Meadows Woods, I should not have stayed away for so long.

This little fellow was not only putting on a vocal show, it was coming down low in the bushes to seek out flies and was providing me with wonderful views, my first for the year.

I just stayed put leaning against the gate soaking up the atmosphere. A blackcap could be heard, as could robin and blackbird, the hedge was full of blackthorn blossom, and even a small area of hawthorn was showing colour, an idyllic scene and for me charged full of emotion.

On Friday there were a few interesting reports locally. The greenshank I failed to find was again reported from Whitemoor Haye late yesterday afternoon, but more interestingly one was reported from Croxall Lakes along with a ruff and two green sandpiper, they will have to be checked out. The first hobby and cuckoo of the season have been reported from the Chase, and yellow wagtails are everywhere, it must be the best year we have had for many a year.

Saturday has dawned bright and beautiful, with only a slight breeze, an almost perfect day for a bit of birding. I have been on the net, there is nothing new to report so we will concentrate on Croxall Lakes. Yesterday I drew a blank at Blithfield but Croxall produced a common tern and two green sandpipers, still no sign of the greenshank which keeps being reported. The little owl was also in his tree, so should we have time we will spend a little time seeking him out, ending up, hopefully, with the willow warbler. Sarah has three possible 'Year Ticks', four should the greenshank put in an appearance.

Once again Croxall is very quiet, no cars parked up so we look as though we have the place to ourselves. Setting up the telescope I start to scan the far shore, two pairs of oystercatchers, the mute swan appears to be sitting on her nest and two ringed plover are dashing backwards and forwards along the shoreline. Moving closer in I manage to locate the common tern, Sarah's first tick of the morning. The tern is very accommodating, just sitting out on the mud preening, the red bill with the black tip is very noticeable at this distance making identification positive, Sarah keeps the 'scope and studies all the birds close in.

We decide to have walk on the East Side. Nothing to add here I am afraid, just greylag geese, so back to the hide we go, and as events proved this was a wise move. Sarah had hardly sat down when she pointed to the shore close in, two green sandpiper were strutting their stuff right on the waters edge and you did not need to use your telescope to see these birds, you hardly needed your binoculars they were so close. Ringed and little ringed plover were also rushing about wildly on the mud, accompanied by redshank, a very nice finish to our morning at Croxall. Now for the Yoxall Meadows Woods, and the willow warbler.

We had hardly got out of our car before the willow warbler struck up and serenaded us with his beautiful liquid notes, summer definitely has arrived. Unlike my previous experience the warbler did not show itself, but Sarah was more than happy with an audible record for this one, she recognised it's song quite easily.

On Sunday I am doing a 'Bird Walk' for the Staffordshire Wildlife Trust at Croxall, it is again a glorious morning, but where are the bird watchers? Only one has turned up, a real disappointment, anyway, birding we go. The ringed plover are still as active as they were yesterday, the little especially so, I do not know where they get their energy from. Redshank numbers are almost in double figures and the common tern is still present, but hard as we work the green sandpiper are not to be seen.

While we are studying the birds a friend of mine comes into the hide, Neil Kelly, a member of the Rosliston Bird Study Group and a good birder. He had walked up from the car park and in transit had heard both whitethroat and sedge warbler, we will have to pick these up on our return journey, both would be 'Year Ticks' for me. The other birder, Alan, was most interested in trying to locate these, so should we be fortunate that would be a nice ending to our morning.

The sedge warbler was no problem, he was right where Neil said he would be, and he was blasting forth with vigour. You could certainly hear him although he was proving very difficult to see as he was singing from a large, dense, bramble patch. Just as we were about to give up on seeing him he sat out right on the top of a tall bramble so a clear view was finally obtained, and a tick was in the bag. Now would the whitethroat be as accommodating? The short, sharp answer to that is no, but he too did at least sing. His brief, staccato song could be clearly heard from a very dense patch of vegetation, but unlike the sedge warbler he was not coming up for air, but I will take an audible any time, so into the bag goes another 'Year Tick', and a perfect end to a lovely morning.

Monday has dawned very pleasantly, a very good morning for a bit of birding I would think. April has been a very good month so far with temperatures way above average, we will no doubt suffer for it later on, so let us enjoy it while we have it.

Chasewater, for some reason, is never one of the most popular places we visit with the Rosliston group, and today we only have 17 members, will their tolerance be rewarded? Sheila is the first to locate something of interest, she has found a gull behaving in an unusual manner. I move across to her telescope as quickly as I can, which is not very fast I must add. She has hit the jackpot, her gull is a little gull, a second year bird, and once we have focused up accurately the bird provides us with a very good view.

We all spent some time studying the bird, for many it was a 'Lifer', you do not see many this far in land, it is only my second sighting of the year and the previous one was from Norfolk. While enjoying the gull a ringed plover scurries past, and a black-headed gull lands close by which provides us with a nice exercise in comparison, you could really see the difference in size when they are so close. You soon realise why it is called the little gull!

Sheila is working well today, she now has a little ringed plover in her scope, and on this one the yellow eye ring could be clearly seen. While studying the plover a small brown bird is located just behind, partly hidden in newly growing vegetation. I spend some time trying to locate the bird, and I was very pleased to have done so, our bird was none other than a female whinchat, a bit special to say the least, and totally unexpected, Chasewater was proving to be a gold mine.

Last night, just as Martin was about to leave, Sarah brought my attention to a bird calling, so I popped outside to have a listen. In the stillness of the night a crisp, clear, 'klee-vit, klee-vit, klee-vit' could be heard, a female tawny owl was calling. I could not hear the male so she was not responding to him, she had probably been disturbed by a marauding fox and was just interested in driving it off.

Tomorrow I will have to do my usual bit of reconnaissance work for Sarah. I cannot wait until Friday this week as my car is going in for it's service and M.O.T. There have been a few reports of black terns moving through, both Sarah and I would like to get that one on our lists, and wood warblers have been reported from the Chase, the wood warblers have been heard singing from the car park at Seven Springs. That would be highly convenient, little or no walking, and I can spend some time at Blithfield for the terns.

The car park at Seven Springs is quite busy, children can be heard splashing away in the springs, thoroughly enjoying themselves by the sound of things. I shall be making my away from this as I intend to walk a little along the pathway, I shall not make the Stepping Stones as this is about a mile distance, but after about a quarter of a mile the area opens up and is ideal for tree pipit, one of my target birds for the day.

As I move away from the car park I can hear blackcap singing and from the woodland chaffinch are letting forth. Forking right for the track towards the Stepping Stones I hear something a bit different from the blackcap. So I pause to listen more intently, and I realise I am listening to a garden warbler, my fist of the year. Their song is very similar to that of the blackcap, more melodious and of a longer duration I find. The blackcap belts it's song out, having almost the quality of a nightingale with it's power. Up north they actually call the bird the northern nightingale because of this power, nightingales rarely reach so far north. The garden warbler on the other hand is much sweeter, almost like comparing a song thrush with a blackbird. Having heard the blackcap only minutes ago certainly helps with splitting these two.

Moving on I find a suitable spot to sit down, so I can just listen to the birds singing away. The afternoon is not the best time for bird song as birds are busy feeding but one can only try. Chaffinch are certainly busy and a blackbird is still doing his stuff, and then I hear the sound I really came out for, a wood warbler. A repetitive 'Tiuh, tiuh, tiuh, tiuh, tiuh' echoes out from the top of a nearby oak tree, can I locate the bird. I move my location to get nearer to the tree and once again sit down to study the tree tops. After awhile a movement right at the top of an oak tree catches my attention, the bird will not stay still as it darts from twig to twig, by it's behaviour the bird is obviously a warbler, but which?

I am in luck, the bird flies out onto a bare twig, and shows a large amount of yellow in it's plumage, I most certainly have my wood warbler, and then, as if to confirm my observation, it again burst into song. At this point another birder appears in view, I am able to show him where the wood warbler was last seen, and in return he is able to inform me of where he last encountered the tee pipit. The tree pipit is about 200 metres further down the track so I should be able to make that without too much difficulty.

Progressing slowly I hear further blackcap, thought I heard a redstart but could not be sure, and as I rounded a bend the song of the tree pipit could be clearly heard. It is difficult to describe the song of a tree pipit, but I will try. The bird usually rises vertically from it's chosen song post, usually the top of tree, with rapid wing beats, and then parachutes back down to it's original perch, uttering a series of delightful trills as it progresses downwards. Quite distinctive really, they start off accelerated, slowing down as they approach their perch. I could not see my bird today, but it's song was more than satisfactory, and it saved me additional walking, so I was not complaining.

Friday has turned out far better than first thought. My car was collected at 08.30 hours and I was told my car was the only vehicle in for work so I should have it back by early afternoon, and so I had time to give it a little run and do a bit of birding. Sarah is very busy at present so we may only manage an hour or so tomorrow morning, so I thought a quick visit down to Croxall was called for, do a bit of reconnaissance for her.

Croxall was as busy as I have seen it recently, it is of course, Good Friday and a lovely day to boot, so most of the visitors were family groups. As I was closing the gate I heard a sound I have been waiting for, a reed warbler was calling from the adjacent reed bed, wonderful, they are back for another season. Sarah will be pleased with this one, as so am I, another 'Year Tick'.

I stop on the corner, the sedge warbler was still chuntering away from his bramble patch, and the whitethroat could be heard in the background, three 'Year Ticks' here for Sarah, even though they may all have to be audible records.

The hide was empty so I had this to myself, obviously not many of the visitors were birders. On the far shore eight shelduck were sitting out, the oystercatcher was still on it's nest among the gulls and the common tern numbers were up to about a dozen. In the distance two 'ringed plover types' were running along the shore, but as I had not brought my telescope there was no way I would identify these unless they flew, which they did not.

A small flock of swallows flew across low over the water, hawking flies which were rather plentiful to say the least, and a green woodpeckers called briefly from the railway embankment. Not a bad little collection of birds in just an hour or so, let us hope we can repeat it again on the 'morrow.

As I thought, we are only able to have a short trip out today, so Croxall it will obviously be. On the way through we stopped at the Kings Bromley lay-by in the hope we could pick up a little egret, we failed for the egret but we had a bit of luck, three house martins came flying down stream.

The reed warbler was singing away loudly as I opened the gate at Croxall, another tick for Sarah, and we were fortunate enough to actually see the bird fly across, so this was a visual record. Two other birders were studying a bird further up the track, so we approached carefully. It was in the area where I saw the sedge warbler recently, but they were not looking at a sedge, instead they had a grasshopper warbler in their 'scope. We quickly had a peep, and for once the bird was showing well. Normally grasshopper warblers are heard and rarely seen. I have great difficulty in hearing them, so my records of them are few and far between these days. Their pitch is now outside my hearing range. I could see this birds bill quivering away as it sang, but to me no sound was being emitted.

A group of birders came rushing up the track, I knew them vaguely, 'Was the ouzel still about?' they shouted to me. I told them I was not aware of the bird, apparently the bird had been seen an hour or so ago, from the West Side hide. A ring ouzel would be a bit special to say the least, Sarah has never seen one, so she could be on a 'Lifer', so up to the hide we drove. After a few minutes about a dozen birders had assembled, all intent on trying to locate the ring ouzel. While we were doing this a sudden burst of song came from out of a nearby bramble patch, a sedge warbler was letting rip, another tick for Sarah, she is having a good morning.

Working the far shore a sandpiper dashed through my 'scope, I quickly followed the bird and once it stopped rushing about I got the view I wanted, it was a common sandpiper.

We spent a further 10 minutes or so looking for the ouzel, all to no avail, it looked like the bird had moved on, so it was time for us to move off.

Our birding, however, was not over. As we drove towards Kings Bromley we noticed two birds having a tussle in the sky, and we were able to slow down to look at them, we had a raven and peregrine falcon harassing each other, a wonderful sight. For Sarah the peregrine was yet another 'Year Tick', her sixth of the day, she has not had such a good day for a few weeks now.

Easter Sunday is now with us, and many of the local birding spots are also much loved by the tourist at Bank Holidays and can become very busy, so I will probably re-visit Croxall Lakes. Looking in on the bird reports this morning I also noticed the ring ouzel had been seen again, this time early afternoon, so another attempt after him would not go amiss. Plus the fact the Rosliston Bird Study Group are visiting Croxall on Monday morning, so it will not hurt to check out a few things for them, especially the grasshopper warbler.

Croxall is again very busy, I doubt if you would get another car on the car park, the ring ouzel is certainly the bird of the moment locally. I just manage to open the gate as there is a car parked directly in front of it, and drive in. A group of birders are standing on the corner from where we saw the grasshopper warbler yesterday, and stopping to talk to them I was informed the bird could be heard well, but was not showing itself. I was able to tell them where it was seen mostly yesterday and left them to it.

Parking at the hide there were about a dozen birders in attendance, many of whom I knew, and I gathered the bird had been seen quite frequently and from a specific area, very useful information.

The two ringed plover were still dashing about on the far shore line, the sedge was singing away from the nearby bramble patch and a colourful male reed bunting was feeding near to the hide. A flock of sand martin were feeding low over the water, today was a very cloudy day which no doubt had forced flying insects down lower, and the martins were making the most of it. The oystercatchers were very vociferous and active, and several redshank were actively feeding along the far shore.

I must have been in the hide for over half an hour when a blackish bird flicked down onto the ground I was studying, this just had to be my quarry, but the bird would not stay still nor come out into clearer ground, it was now a question of patience. After a couple of minutes my patience was rewarded, out popped a male ring ouzel, his white courgette clearly visible, and as he was now moving quite slowly I was able to get the 'scope trained upon him.

The bird was an absolute cracker, in prime nick. The yellow bill could be clearly seen through the 'scope, the white courgette stood out brightly, and the silvery-grey margins to the feathers on the wing were clear and distinct. No mistaking this bird. It is probably only the fourth of fifth ouzel I have seen this century, and my first for the county since the nineties, they are no longer a common bird, hence the amount of interest being shown here today. I intended to enjoy this bird so I spent a further hour spotting him intermittently, but he certainly had his favoured hunting ground, so it was no problem just waiting for him to re-appear.

As I still had time to spare I drove off down Whitemoor Haye. The lake was very quiet so a trip down the rough lane would finish my afternoon off. I stopped near the little owl tree, but nothing was visible today. The tree was almost in full leaf, so finding this little fellow was no longer going to be easy. Parking up on the corner I spotted a small bird on the top of an hawthorn tree, a nice corn bunting, so even though the farmer has desiccated the hedgerows, the bunting had obviously found somewhere suitable. Well done them. I was just about to drive off when a small, pale bird flicked over the hedge and dropped in on the other side. A quick look, a cracking male wheatear, what a bird to finish off with. Time to go home, a very contented man!

Easter Monday is another glorious day, are we having our summer in April this year, trust not. I have a good turnout for the bird group, 22 of us, so let us hope we can find something of interest for them.

The grasshopper warbler is still calling away from his bramble patch, or so I am told! Birders who have been here earlier tell me they saw the bird displaying earlier, so that is a good sign, there is obviously a pair in residence, this may be a new breeding record for Croxall.

We make our way up to the hide and on getting out of our cars we are greeted by a cuckoo calling from over East Side, a very nice welcome indeed, my first cuckoo of the year.

I point out to my colleagues the area from where I saw the ring ouzel yesterday, and then comes our first disappointment of the morning. About 20 metres or so away from the spot two anglers are set up with their equipment spread all over the place, they had obviously been here for sometime, and would have driven the ouzel away.

The two ring plovers were still actively going about their business and while watching these a pair of little ringed plover came into view, a nice opportunity to study them both and point out the differences. They were quite close so we could see beak and leg colour, plus the fact the yellow eye ring of the little ringed was also clearly visible.

The common terns were still drifting about, no attempt to breed at present, they just seem happy with the sun and food supply, and several were bathing, quite energetically so. As we had plenty of time at our disposal today, we made our way under the railway line and over to the East Side. As we came out through the bridge a little egret took off from the scrape in front of us and flew off down the river, it's yellow feet clearly illuminated in the bright sunlight, no mistaking this fellow.

The rooks from the nearby rookery were in good voice, judging by the sound from the youngsters they must be well developed. A buzzard chose this moment to fly over the rookery, and with a burst of guttural sound, about 20 or so birds flew up to chase the poor buzzard away, he had no choice but to retreat. The rooks returned to their nests in victory, some almost performing victory rolls in celebration.

We now decided to have some time down Whitemoor Haye, my friends were interested in the opportunity of seeing wheatear, which as you know, I saw yesterday. Stopping at the corner where I saw the wheatear yesterday, we were delighted to see two family parties of lapwing, both of whom had young birds in attendance, just lovely small balls of yellow and brown fluff, we did hope they survive the next few weeks.

It seemed only minutes when the shout 'Wheatear' went up. Just a few metres away in the field a pair of wheatear popped into view. It was rather nice to see both a male and female bird together, I very much doubt they are a breeding pair at present, the chances of their breeding here are slim indeed.

Time had caught up with us, so we said our fond farewells and made or respective ways home. I was fortunate in the direction I took as I saw two grey partridge legging it off down the lane in front of me, I slowed down for a few minutes as I watched them, they certainly can motor. I think they realised they were no longer being followed and stalked off into a nearby field at a far more leisurely pace. I was happy enough with that, a nice bird to end the morning on.

Sarah is still on holiday today, so once we have completed our daily chores we will pop over to Cannock Chase, we would both like the opportunity of seeing the redstart and pied flycatcher reported from near to the Stepping Stones. We park up at the Punchbowl car park, and there are not many other visitors today, so it should at least be quiet and peaceful, a useful pre-requisite for the study of woodland birds, your ears are so important in tracking these birds down.

Walking up towards Brocton Coppice we hear several willow warbler singing away, plus the inevitable chaffinch, but the bird we are hoping to hear today, the chiffchaff, are remarkably quiet, not a sound.

Turning at the bottom of Brocton Coppice towards the Stepping Stones we hear the laughing call of a green woodpecker. A song thrush was giving it some 'wellie' from the top of a nearby tree, a delightful sound this, and a buzzard flew silently overhead. We located the bird box where it is reported the pied flycatcher has shown much interest, and settle down to wait.

After half an hour or so we had seen nothing near to the box, so we decided to stroll down as far as the Stepping Stones, only a short distance away. Sarah called my attention to a bird sitting out on a tall silver birch, I am pleased she did. It was none other than a tree pipit. It is the first I have seen this year, my only record was an audible a few days ago, you may remember it, near to Seven Springs.

As we got nearer to the Stepping Stones we picked up a treecreeper creeping up an old oak. Watching the bird we saw it walk in behind a large piece of bark, it no doubt had it's nest here. Although we waited several minutes for it's reappearance, it did not, so we just walked on wishing it the best of luck.

We turned back at the Stepping Stones with nothing else to report. On the return journey I stopped, I had just heard a wood warbler singing, so I called Sarah back. Although we waited for several minutes the bird was not going to perform a repeat.

The afternoon had turned out rather disappointing really, I had secretly hoped for about six 'Year Ticks' for Sarah, plus three for myself, instead Sarah had one, me none. I always say nothing is ever guaranteed in birding, and there is always tomorrow.

Wednesday has dawned slightly more grey and chilly compared with recent days, but it is still very pleasant and should be a nice morning for a bit of birding. Numbers are low today with several being away on holiday, just three course members plus yours truly.

We slowly made our way down towards the Greenheart Lake, here I was hoping we would see reed warblers, a few pairs breed here most years. As we walked down we were serenaded by willow warbler, blackcap and chiffchaff, blackbirds were also in good voice, and plenty of them. As we rounded a corner we had one of those amusing incidents. A blackbird and a song thrush were sitting at the top of a tree, not a metre apart, both singing their little hearts out. It reminded me of the popular song 'Any song you can sing, I can sing better, I can sing any song better than you. No you can't, yes I can'. As far as I was concerned today's little competition was a draw, they both sang beautifully.

We walked on with a smile on our faces. Nearing the Greenheart Lake we noticed the pathway across the lake was fenced off, this was a pity, but as we neared the lake we could see why. A notice on the entrance told us the pathway was closed, a mute swan was nesting right on the edge of the pathway so they obviously did not want the bird disturbed, plus the fact an angry protective swan could be a dangerous animal.

Walking round the edge of the lake we soon heard what we were coming for, a reed warbler burst forth, putting on a virtuoso performance. As we stopped to listen we realised another reed warbler was also doing his stuff from a little further along the reed bed. A few goldfinch were also feeding actively on the reed seed heads, a lovely splash of colour they made. A reed bunting was not going to be outdone, as he added his refrain to the general bird sound being experienced. While we were soaking all of this up a scratchy little song came from a nearby bramble patch, a whitethroat was joining in, not that he was much competition, but nice to hear all the same. After awhile he popped out of the brambles so we could see him, and the name whitethroat became obvious to all.

We moved on towards the smaller pond, the Flight Pond as it is known. Here we had coot with young, little gingery coloured balls of feather as they bobbed on the water following mom. A little grebe was trilling away from the reed bed, not that we could see him, and a female mallard swam past with eight ducklings in tow. A very idyllic scene in fact. While this was all going on a small black and white bird caught my attention as it flew into a nearby willow tree. This started an adrenaline rush, could this have been a pied flycatcher, remember we were after one of these yesterday.

I quickly brought this to the attention of my colleagues so we could concentrate on the tree. It was not long before I found what I wanted, and yes, it was a pied. What a lovely surprise, such a superb bird for us to find. I have never been aware of their being seen or reported from Rosliston, so we have a probable first for the location. A very nice record, and one which will have to be reported.

On returning home I managed to get my chores accomplished quite quickly so I had an hour or two at my disposal, so a trip down to Whitemoor Haye would not go amiss, I also needed to call in at my bird food supplier to stock up on both peanuts and sunflower hearts.

The lake at Whitemoor was very quiet, a few tufted, the odd mallard and half a dozen greylags were all I could see, so down to the rough lane. Driving down a buzzard glided slowly across, for once not being chased by rooks and crows. Slowly driving down the rough lane I flushed a couple of yellowhammer plus the odd chaffinch before arriving on the corner, here I stopped and got out of the car. I had hardly raised my binoculars to my eyes before a wheatear popped up, in exactly the same spot we saw them on Monday. Today we only had one, the male, and he was totally oblivious to my presence. I was able to spend several minutes enjoying the bird before the call of a whitethroat caught my attention.

Turning to look in the direction the sound had come from, a whitethroat was sitting out on the top of some dead docs singing his scratchy little song, just as the one had at Rosliston this morning. I hope this one is in territory as it could be a useful bird to bring Sarah down to see.

Thursday is now upon us, and another nice day we have in prospect. Tomorrow, of course, is the Royal Wedding, so I think it is safe to presume tomorrow will be a quiet day on the roads, so I may go a bit further afield. Blithfield here I come. As usual my first port of call will be the dam, and I drove across slowly but have only two pied wagtails to report, so I proceeded down to Ten Acre Bay. The domestic geese were still present, seven of them, along with half a dozen greylags, should these interbreed we will have quite a mixture, Heinz 57s as I tag them.

Parking up I study the bay and two swallows catch my attention, they are busily flying in and out of an angler's shelter, probably nesting in there, but one of the birds keeps flying low over the grass chasing something off. After a short while I realise the swallow is harassing a wheatear, why he should I do not know, the wheatear is no danger to the swallow. Eventually the wheatear has had enough and it flies off leaving the swallow to get on with what ever it was doing prior to arriving on the scene. It was a nice few minutes studying bird's behaviour, which is what true bird watching is all about.

When entering the wheatear on the net I was very interested to note that at Tittesworth Reservoir, in North Staffs, both wood sandpiper and greenshank have been reported over the last couple of days or so. It has all the facilities, a nice café and it is wheelchair friendly, so hopefully I will be introducing you to a new location.

The royal wedding is upon us, let us hope they have a lovely day, there is talk of over one million people being in London to witness the event, I think it is a fact no country in the world can stage an event of this magnitude with the skill we do. As I was not invited I will have my day out birding, and as nothing new has arrived on the scene Tittesworth it will be. As I expected, it was not overly busy, many people no doubt have stayed at home to watch the wedding. Although it is a pay and display car park, Blue Badge holders park for free, and you can park anywhere you chose, not just in the disabled spots.

From where I parked it was only about 100 metres to the causeway, an ideal location. There were no other birders in sight, which is not a good sign when two decent birds have been recently reported, so I was going to have to do all the work on my own. Walking out onto the causeway I had a surprise, the wind was blowing across very strongly and there was no shelter from it, but fortunately it was coming from the north so I was able to turn my back to it as the birds had been reported from the southern side of the causeway.

Late yesterday both birds had been reported from the small island just off the causeway, so this is where I initially started my work. The island has quite a mound upon it so only a little over half the island can be seen from any one location. I commenced with just my binoculars, it was going to be very difficult to hold a telescope and tripod still in this wind. There were not many birds on the island, a few tufted riding out the waves, the odd lapwing running about on the island and two, rather sleepy looking, oystercatcher just sitting out.

I moved my position so I could view another part of the island. Not a lot to report from here, a couple of Canada geese put their heads up, and two mallard were dozing away on then waters edge. Moving further round I caught sight of a small wader dashing along the waters edge, this was too small to be what I was after, and so it turned out, it was a little ringed plover. Time to move over to the northern side of the causeway and full face into the wind.

I tried my 'scope, but it was useless, I could not hold it still. Things over this side were more active as part of the shoreline was out of the wind. Three pairs of shelduck, a lovely drake goosander, a few grey heron, more lapwing and oystercatcher and two further little ringed plover, but still no sight of the birds I had come for.

This small area of water is over looked by a bird hide, the East Hide as it is known, and the wind seemed to be coming directly from behind the hide, so I decided to walk round and do some studying from the comfort of the hide, my prognosis of the winds direction was smack on. I settle myself down, opened up a viewing vent, and sorted out my telescope. I was not able to add much more to the birds previously mentioned, apart from a few swallows and sand martins, but at least I was out of the wind.

I was about to move on to get a bit of lunch when a bird of prey came dashing across the water, it was flying at speed, which was hardly surprising the wind was right up it's tail so to speak. The shape of the bird, and it's manner of flight was suggestive of a falcon, and the bird was rapidly vanishing into the distance, when the bird made a stoop at a passing martin. This was just what I wanted, the bird was an hobby, and for a second or two it closed it's wings as it attempted to catch the martin, and what a sight it was. The martin lived to fight another day, the hobby missed and it had to carry on with it's hunting. A lovely turn up this turned out to be, I may not have seen the birds I hoped for, but the hobby was a 'Year Tick', so who's complaining?

I would now visit Swallow Moss and have nice drive over the Staffordshire Moorlands in the hope of seeing a red grouse or two. I have not seen a Staffordshire red grouse for a year or two, most of my red grouse days have been on Axe Edge Moor just over the county boundary into Derbyshire.

Turning off at The Winking Man inn I made my way slowly across the Upper Hulme Ranges, no red flag was flying today so there was no need to duck the flak. I pulled in at a suitable spot, turned my engine off and lowered my window. The wind I am pleased to say was coming from the other side of my car, these little facts can be very important when you use your car as a bird hide. For several minutes all I saw were the odd linnet and meadow pipit, but then I heard what I had hoped for, a string of 'go-back, go-back, go-back's' rang out, and about 30 metres away up came the head of a red grouse. It held it's head right back as it called away, and a short while later up came another head, we had a pair here, the male was calling and the female responded by showing herself. It did not last long before they both flew off over a rise and were gone for ever. I was happy, I had my Staffordshire red grouse.

Driving on towards Swallow Moss, I was near to Oxbatch at the time, when I saw a small bird of prey dashing across the heather at zero feet, this just had to be a merlin. I was able to stop, no other cars on the road luckily, and a male merlin flashed across in front of me only metres away. The Moss was very quiet and here we were sheltered quite nicely from the wind. This spot was a well known place for black grouse a few years ago and you rarely came here without finding several birders already in residence. Unfortunately the black grouse have long since gone, I am sure most of us only call in for a bit of nostalgia. Today, however, I was in for a bit of a surprise, no not black grouse, but I did have a lovely view of a male wheatear, I have not seen one in this location for some years. They are a moorland breeding species and there are several spots where I go to see them, but it is rather nice to see one totally unexpected.

The last day of April has come in bright and clear, and we managed to get out very promptly, and went straight down to the lake at Whitemoor Haye, and hit the jackpot immediately, three Arctic terns were flying over the lake. The birds were very close, which is rather nice especially when you are looking at minor detail to confirm your identification. One bird flew in almost head high and we could clearly see the bill was bright red, no black tip, the tip would have meant the birds were common tern, not Arctic. Arctic terns are our longest migratory species, each autumn they will journey from the northern limits of the UK to the South Pacific, off the coast of Australia. Just how many miles they fly in a lifetime cannot be imagined, but it certainly puts 'man in space' into the correct perspective, and the tern only has muscle power to drive it on!

We notice a couple of ladies studying these birds from a little further down the lane, and realise we know them well, Joyce Bradley and Nicola Corfield, we have had many happy hours birding together. We confirmed they had seen the terns, and drove down to the corner of the rough lane with them, they too were after the whitethroats and wheatears which have been seen here recently.

Parking up on the corner we found the wind to be particularly strong, this was not going to be very good for small birds, although we could hear the odd skylark. The scratchy notes of a whitethroat could just about be picked up, but trying to locate it proved impossible. Wheatears were nowhere to be seen, our bird had probably moved off on his northern migration.

Joyce's experience proved useful, she had picked up the song of a corn bunting and wind or no wind, the bird was sitting out on the top of a nearby hawthorn bush, always a nice bird to see. We spent a further 20 minutes or so searching for the whitethroat, all to no avail, and Sarah had just got into the car to drive off when I picked up a bird of prey in flight over the micro-light airfield. I quickly called Sarah from out of the car, this bird was a hobby, a first of the year for Sarah. The four of us had very nice views as the bird flew across our line of vision, it was also only my second of the year.

Turning to say goodbye to our friends I noticed three birds in flight, these were swifts, another nice bird to pick up, 'Year Ticks' for all of us it turned out. I was very pleased we had not driven off earlier needless to say.

Time now to move off, Sarah and I wanted another few minutes at the lake and we also wished to spend some time near the Alrewas National Memorial Arboretum at a spot where we usually manage to record lesser whitethroat, they have started returning in recent weeks.

We parked up on the corner of the small coppice near the lake, and the first bird we heard calling was a chiffchaff, I had forgotten Sarah had not heard one of these this year, she now had her fourth 'Year Tick' of the day. The terns were still sporting themselves over the lake. So we enjoyed them for a few more minutes before moving off to the arboretum.

We managed to park up on the corner of the lane and walked down the old roadway, now very much overgrown, no car had been down here for many a year. The first bird we heard was a whitethroat, calling very loudly from the middle of a bramble patch, he was not going to be seen, but Sarah was happy with an audible.

Walking further on I stopped, a wooden rattle-like sound was coming from a bush, had we a lesser whitethroat, it sounded very much like it. Sarah suddenly pointed, high up in the bush sat our quarry. It's white throat was vibrating with the passion of it all, a cracking view, and a wonderful finale to our morning's birding. Sarah had picked up six 'Year Ticks', and I had three. As I shall not be going out this afternoon I close for the month on 171, not bad for just four months work, and apart from my week in Norfolk, most of the birds were local.

We will wait to see what May brings in.

Map references:
Cannock Chase – Seven Springs: SK 006205.
The Punchbowl: SJ 985207.
The Stepping Stones: SJ 987201.
Whitemoor Haye – corner of the rough lane: SK 175128.
Yoxall Meadows Woods: SK 139176.
Wolseley Bridge – HQ of the Staffordshire Wildlife Trust: SK 023204.
Tittesworth Reservoir – Visitor Centre: SJ 995602.
Upper Hulme Ranges: SK 035630. This is a very broad reference as the ranges cover a
    very wide area. Just park up where ever you can on the road side.
Oxbatch: SK 040618.
Swallow Moss: SK 078088.
Rosliston Forestry Centre: SK 244175
Alrewas National Memorial Arboretum: SK 183145.

Chapter V

May

Anew month is upon us, and it has come in very pleasantly. I cannot remember such a dry April ever, the only problem is rain has to come at some time, and when it does come I just hope it knows when to stop.

Today I have decided to make a trip across the county boundary, and visit Foremark Reservoir in Derbyshire. I have not visited Foremark this year so far, I usually visit during the wintertime as you can see some very interesting gulls here. My reason for a visit today is to try to find the turtle dove which has been reported from the Carver's Rocks area, turtle dove are not common birds in our part of the world.

I am able to park on the A514, at the old entrance to the reservoir, which is handy for the area I wish to visit. This entrance is not really suitable for wheelchairs, unless you have someone with you who can lift the chair over the gate. Once over the road surface is very good, being the old road surface to the car park which is no longer used by the public.

If you wish to go into the reservoir proper, you need to take the entrance at the northern end of the reservoir. Here you have to pay to enter, cost currently £2.50, and as you pay to get the entrance barrier raised there is no 'discount' for Blue Badge holders. The car park has an information centre, all facilities, with a nice view over the reservoir, and most of the footpaths are wheelchair friendly.

Today, however, we are in for free, having walked in. The Carver's Rocks nature reserve is only a short distance from the entrance, 300 metres or so, and the walk up to it is most pleasant. I am being serenaded by blackcap, garden warbler, robin, blackbird, willow warbler and chiffchaff, quite a 'dawn chorus' in fact, but not the bird I have come to see, no turtle doves purring away.

As I still had time before lunch I decided to drive back via Whitemoor Haye, the greenshank had again been reported, and these birds are beginning to bug me.

I arrived at Whitemoor Haye to find the lake very quiet, a few geese on the far bank and the odd tufted duck on the water, the only wader visible being a solitary oystercatcher. I was about to give up when I noticed two greyish shapes running along the far shoreline. I quickly followed these and eventually got the view I wanted, my greenshank at last, they were not a myth. They were very distant, but the light was good, and they were behaving exactly as they should, wading right up to their bellies in the water. I could now go home, satisfied at last, my morning out had been well worth the effort.

I prepared myself a light lunch and went onto the net to report my greenshank sightings and while doing so I was surprised to see a wood sandpiper had been seen at Croxall during the morning, along with both black-tailed and bar-tailed godwits. I promptly decided I would be going out again.

The car park at Croxall is quite busy, and quite a few of the cars have birding stickers on the windows, and a couple of the cars I am familiar with, friends of mine, Julian and Eric are obviously here. My two friends were in the hide, but the news regarding the wood sandpiper was not good, apparently the bird had flown off mid morning along with the black-tailed godwits. There were, however, still two bar-tailed in view, so I settled down to enjoy these. Both were in an advanced plumage state and were looking quite red, almost like two overgrown robins!

On Monday I was back at Croxall bright and early for the Rosliston group, although I was not the first, several were already waiting, so I opened up and waved them through.

I drove up to the hide and was promptly called over to a telescope by Peter Tyson, had he a ruff in his scope. It was indeed a ruff, or to be more precise, a reeve, as it was the female of the species. I was again asked to have a look at another bird, here they had a godwit, the question was which one? The view was not particularly good so I can understand their hesitancy, but it turned slightly and the legs could be clearly seen, this one was a black-tailed godwit. The legs are quite important with our two commoner godwits. On the black-tailed the thigh is rather long, making the bird look taller when standing, on the bar-tailed the thigh is probably half the length, making the bird look shorter. There are differences with bill shape and plumage etc, but a lot of these are only really noticeable if you have the two species close to each other, the leg length on the other hand I feel is the real clincher.

We decided to have a drive back down the track to an area where we could hear both reed and sedge warbler, I little realised just how good this small area of ground would be. We were hardly out of our cars before the sedge warbler started up, and this bird gave us it's full repertoire, even showing himself in the process. From this spot we were absolutely amazed by the variety of warblers to be heard. Whitethroat appeared to be everywhere, blackcap and garden warbler were singing in direct competition to each other, a chiffchaff was calling from the railway embankment with a willow warbler directly behind us.

Earlier on I had been talking to my colleagues about the differences between the songs of our two whitethroats, the whitethroat sings a scratchy little ditty, the lesser whitethroats song is more like an old football supporters rattle. One of my party said she believed she could hear a lesser, so we all became quiet. After a few seconds the sound of a lesser whitethroat burst forth, and I swung round saying, 'There it is, a lesser whitethroat is calling'. One or two of my 'so-called friends' burst into laughter, Jeff Hoffman had in his hand a mobile telephone from which a lesser whitethroat could be heard calling. The cheeky blighter, I was going to call him something else but ladies were present, had recorded some bird calls, one of which was the lesser whitethroat. He did at least have the decency to acknowledge I had got it right!

As we had sometime left a few of us decided to pop down to Whitemoor Haye to have a quick look for the greenshank, for one or two this would be a 'Lifer'. After the morning we had had I suppose it was inevitable we would go out on a high. Tucked right in the nearest corner of the lake to where we were standing was a greenshank, 30 metres away at the most, and from this distance you could easily see where the name greenshank comes from. What a superb way to finish off the morning, and as if to celebrate three buzzards came circling overhead, they too were enjoying the day.

I have just had a quick look on the net and I see a dotterel has been reported. I have only ever seen four dotterel in my life, and only two of those were on mainland UK, I most certainly will have to have a try for this bird.

I have drawn a blank, no sign at all of the dotterel, mind you I may have gleaned a bit of information regarding the bird, it would appear the recent sightings have all been in the evening, after 18.00 hours. From this it would appear the bird flies off during the day, no doubt to feed, and returns to Whitemoor Haye to roost up for the night. Not much help to me as I was over the Haye early afternoon.

I spent some time while down the rough lane listening for quail. Over the last few years we have had quail breed here, and as I have seen reports of the odd bird back in the Midlands, I must keep my eyes and ears open. Quail are our smallest game bird, and return to the UK each summer to breed. They are a difficult bird to see, so most of us birders listen out for them. They have an unusual call which is best described as 'wet my lips', 'wet my lips', repeated four or five times. Sarah came up with a more up-dated version of this, she described the sound as that produced by a coffee percolator. Today, however, nothing was heard, bubbling coffee or other wise.

On Saturday Sarah and I had Blithfield to ourselves, I located three smaller terns, and these were flying very low over the surface of the reservoir, these just had to be black terns, so I drew Sarah's attention to them. They were very much located over one stretch of water so I was able to get the 'scope on them, black tern they most certainly were, Sarah had her first tick of the day.

We enjoyed these birds for a few minutes, terns are so graceful, before moving off to Whitemoor Haye, and the prospect of garganey. We had the Haye to ourselves. We quickly picked up a greenshank and a redshank. A mallard with seven ducklings came paddling across and on the far shore two oystercatcher were standing out, but on the water there was very little. We worked the area for many minutes but no garganey came into sight, the most exciting duck we saw was a gadwall. So onto Croxall. Needless to say we parked up right by the hide and made our way indoors. Sarah very quickly picked up a large wader and I was able to get the 'scope onto it smartish, this bird was certainly a godwit, but it had it's head tucked in and was standing in water up to it's belly, we needed it to move or at least become more active. After a few minutes the bird stretched it's wings, that was all I needed, it had a white wing bar which signified the bird was a black-tailed not bar-tailed godwit. There was a lot of activity on the scrape, we had four adult ringed plover with three young, two family parties here, a lapwing had four young, two little ringed plover were chasing each other around in a frenzy, nine oystercatcher were spread over the area, and we had at least 10 common tern. Not a bad little collection, and from outside the hide a sedge warbler and whitethroat could be heard singing.

As we still had time we decided to go back to Whitemoor Haye for one last look for garganey. The greenshank numbers had now increased to three, the redshank was still accompanying the greenshanks, and along the shoreline was a magnificent yellow wagtail, always a delight to the eyes.

Sarah then called my attention to three birds she had seen on a grassy slope some distance away, this was a telescope job. Focusing up they were three mistle thrushes, an adult with two young. Sarah was delighted with this find, I had forgotten she had yet to see a mistle, so she now had her four ticks for the day. Not quite the selection we had hoped for, but she certainly was not complaining.

Time now for home. I am being taken out for dinner this evening, it is my birthday next week so we are starting the celebrations a little early, and I am all for that.

Tomorrow, we are off to Bempton Cliffs by coach for a day with the sea birds. Bempton is one of the best sea colony sites in England, boasting the largest mainland colony of gannets anywhere in the UK, and these birds are a magnificent sight. There are also large colonies of kittiwake, razorbill and guillemot, plus the most well known and much loved of all British birds – puffins.

Puffins are instantly recognised by almost everyone, but how many people have ever seen one? Due to climate change we are in real danger of losing the puffin as an English breeding species. The principal food of the puffin is sand eels, and due to the increase in water temperature, sand eels are moving further ever northward, with the effect puffin are having to follow their food supply.

We departed from Barton Marina smack on time, 08.00 hours, and proceeded on our journey to Bempton. Although we may have left on time our journey time was very slow due to various accidents on both the A38 and the M1 and the coach driver was becoming very concerned with his tachometre reading. We stopped at Flamborough so he could have his regulated rest from driving. North Landing is not a bad place to visit in it's own right. Everything you hope to see at Bempton will be seen here, it is just the difference in numbers. Here they are in their hundreds, Bempton in their tens of thousands. We quickly picked up guillemot, razorbill, puffin, gannet, kittiwake and fulmar, so the six sea birds of the area were quickly put to bed. Tree and house sparrow were seen in nice numbers and skylark could be heard singing from the cliff tops. The car park is a charge car park and this includes Blue Badge holders, but the charges currently are not great. They start as low as 50p for one hour. You can view from the car park or sit on benches which are close by. Access to the bay beneath is not good, but is not necessary to go down for the bird watching, it is perfectly satisfactory from the cliff tops.. There are toilets and various eating establishments locally, so most needs are accounted for.

The Visitor Centre at Bempton is accessible to wheelchair users. From the centre, there is a short 1:10 descent leading to a gentle, sloping 0.9m-wide, rolled limestone path. The nearest viewpoint is 250 metres away and provides good views of the breeding sea birds. The furthest viewpoint is 900 metres away from the Visitor Centre. There are toilet facilities and refreshments can be purchases. Dogs must be on a lead at all times, both for their own safety as well as that of the numerous ground nesting birds. Entrance is free, none RSPB members have a car parking fee to pay, members do not.

Before you reach the cliff tops you become aware of the number of birds present as birds soar away high over the top of the cliffs and the noise levels build up almost to a crescendo, especially that of the kittiwakes. You quickly realise you are now seeing a sea bird city where thousands of birds appear each summer to raise their broods.

As well as the sea birds previously mentioned at North Landing, here you will see large numbers of doves. The birds you see are mainly feral pigeons, whose ancestors, the rock dove once graced these cliffs. Rock doves were the forerunners of domestic pigeons, thousands of these have returned to the wild and bred with the rock dove to such an extent many ornithologists believe pure rock doves are now extinct. As you will have noticed, earlier in this paragraph I used the word 'mainly', and I did this deliberately. Many of the doves you will see here look pure rock dove, their colour, their markings, everything about them screams rock dove, so I personally enter both rock dove and feral pigeon on my list, and hang what any purist wishes to claim.

You certainly have no reason to walk far along these cliffs, birds are everywhere, nesting on the steep cliff sides, flying past you at only a few metres distance, you can almost 'shake hands' with the gannets. This is just a grand occasion, one all bird watchers should experience at least once a year.

Bempton is not all about sea birds, the grassy slopes above the cliffs are home to many other interesting species, so at times it does pay to turn your back to the sea, and look inland. Grasshopper warbler have been reported, but owing to my hearing difficulties with this bird I shall not get too enthusiastic, but skylark are singing away most pleasantly and the odd meadow pipit and linnet can be seen flitting about.

While studying a couple of pipits my attention is drawn to a small, dumpy looking bird, standing out on a fence post. Moving to obtain a clearer view this bird turns out to be a corn bunting, a bird which does very well on these grassy slopes, and as we enjoy this bird another small bird pops up on a nearby post, a delightful male stonechat, always a lovely bird to see.

Tomorrow is my birthday, when I become 78 years young, so I will have a day out birding to celebrate the occasion. I will probably go up to Blacktoft, an RSPB reserve in East Yorkshire, lying at the confluence of the Rivers Ouse and Trent on the southern side of the Humber. This is one of my favourite RSPB reserves, it is compact and easy to get round, and if driving conditions are favourable, I can complete the journey in about an hour and a half. It is also home to bittern and bearded tit.

The reserve has several hides, all wheelchair accessible, although the Ousefleet Hide can be a bit difficult after wet weather as the pathway is grassy. The pathways to the other hides are all firm and good. The distances between these hides is very small and the pathway is flat. Entrance is free to RSPB members, none members have to pay an entrance fee, currently adults pay £3.00, car parking is free, and there is a Blue Badge area closer to the first hide. There are toilets, and cold and warm drinks can be obtained between 9.00 hours and 16.00 hours most days. It boasts the second largest tidal reedbed in the UK, and as well as the two species mentioned above it is also home to avocet and marsh harrier, so you have four very special birds in prospect.

Most of the activity appeared to be coming from the Marshland Hide so I will start off my day from there. As I approached the hide the yelping calls of the avocets could be heard, they are rarely quiet at this time of the year, especially as some, by now, may have young, and the parents are always keeping an eye on their offspring, not without just cause.

It is not often I can say this at Blacktoft, but I had the hide completely to myself, so I was able to sort out for myself the best vantage point for looking over the lagoon. Avocet numbers were very good, at least 40 birds were evident, and at quick count produced 11 fluffy youngsters running about. This probably meant at least six pairs had already hatched off their broods, and looking round there were at least 20 birds who appeared to be sitting on their nests.

On the far side of the lagoon a nice party of godwits were feeding away, up to their bellies in water. Concentrating on these birds I noted their powerful and heavy bills, black-tailed these had to be, and some were looking nice and red as they were moving into their summer plumage state. There was little else on the lagoon, coot, greylags, mallard and a couple of shoveler, so time to move on. I called in at the Xerox Hide, this again was empty of people. Not a lot happening here, black-headed gulls were nesting on the islands, a few more duck species were to be seen, and in the distance a marsh harrier could be seen quartering the reed beds, a female.

The weather was now taking a decided turn for the worst, dark grey clouds were drifting across so I decided to make my way to the Singleton Hide, the furthest hide to the east, this is usually very good for the harriers. Today we were not going to be disappointed. At one point I had five harriers up, two males and three females, and as they drifted over the reed beds various duck came hurtling out to escape their attention. Two of these did surprise me a little. They crash-landed onto the open water in front of the hide, two superb drake wigeon, and they were their in all their beauty. I have often wondered if they have started to breed here at Blacktoft, as they had no females with them. Any sitting female would have remained tight until the very last moment, relying on her camouflage to keep her and her nest safe. The sky was getting darker by the minute, so I decided to move off and try to get back to my parked car before the heavens opened up. They did so I cut my losses and left for home.

I had only reached Whitgift where flying low across a field came a bird of prey, obviously a falcon by it's shape and speed. I was able to stop and watch the bird fly across the lane in front of me, it was a male hobby, and for a few seconds I had a superb view of the bird, before it was gone. Incidentally, when this way do stop and have a look at the church at Whitgift, study the clock face carefully, and see if you can see the 'deliberate mistake'. I will not tell you what it is, let us just see how observant you are!

As I drove further south conditions improved nicely, so as I now had time to spare I thought I would pop into Whitemoor Haye for half an hour to see if I could locate the quail. The only problem was the wind once again, it was blowing quite strongly and the noise as it progressed through the hedge was not good for quail listening. A quail's call is quite soft at the best of times, with this background noise it was not going to be easy. I must have spent over 10 minutes listening away before I got what I had come for.

Saturday has dawned with a very showery look about it, with spots of rain falling as I speak. As soon as we got out of the car at the Haye the screeching of swifts could be heard, and many of them were flying in, low over the lake, searching out food, their numbers were, I think, well into three figures. While enjoying the swifts, a small white bird flew among them, a little tern. This was completely unexpected, and certainly made up for dipping out on the quail later as far as Sarah was concerned, a 'Year Tick' for both of us.

We arrived at Croxall and settled down for a bit of study. As with Whitemoor Haye, swift were very active, and among them the odd hirundine could be seen, in fact we had all three, house martin, sand martin and swallow. The water levels were even higher than yesterday, so it did not look a good day for waders. I located a redshank on the far shore, along with a few oystercatcher, and while looking at these Sarah drew my attention to a wader working the near shore, a very dark bird according to Sarah. I quickly swung round to where she was indicating, and she had hit the jackpot, her bird was a spotted redshank, her first for the year. This bird had no doubt been brought down with the heavy weather last night.

We now had three birds to put on the net, quail, well for me at least, and for both of us little tern and spotted redshank, not a bad little haul. While making my entries I noticed a black-throated diver had been showing well during the morning, so that makes up my mind for me, Shustoke here I come. I have not visited Shustoke for over 50 years, the last time was when Dorothy and I were courting and we used to do a lot of cycling. Dorothy lived in south Birmingham at the time and we used to cycle quite a lot in Warwickshire.

According to the net the diver was last reported as being seen from the disabled car park area, and I quickly located this. Car parking looks free, there was no mention of fees apparent, so although the disabled area was only good for half a dozen cars or so, there looked adequate parking not far away.

I found a spot out of the wind and proceeded to work my way round the reservoir. At the western end of the reservoir several great crested grebe could be seen, no divers among these unfortunately, and several Canada geese, along with mallards could be picked out. I worked my way down the far shore, the northern bank, the reservoir lies east to west, very little was to be found here although a small group of waders flew through at speed, they did not settle, but I saw enough to presume them to be dunlin.

Now for the eastern end. The water near to the shore here was quite calm, obviously the artificial banking of the reservoir was serving as a nice wind break here, and it was far easier to obtain better views of the birds. Once again great crested grebes could be found, tufted duck, a couple of pochard and a number of gadwall could be seen swimming about, and in the back ground a largish black and white bird drifted into view – this just had to be the diver. I moved my position slightly for a clearer view, and a juvenile black-throated diver it most certainly was. Juvenile black-throated have one very clear identification feature at distance, and that is their white sides and flanks, which show up well. This bird was a good 100 metres away so bill shape and forehead shapes are not too distinct, I go for their white sides and flanks every time.

As I had time I called in at the Handsacre Flashes, they are old subsidence pools, nicely reed fringed with areas of rough vegetation, and has from time to time seen the occasional top bird, a black-winged stilt being it's best. Today I was after both reed and sedge warbler, and I was not going to be disappointed. I had hardly parked up my car by the gate and wound down my window before I was assailed by several reed warblers and a single sedge, all trying to out do each other, both in the variety of their song as well as in volume.

It is now Monday morning and the Rosliston Bird Study Group are off to pastures new. We are visiting Whisby Nature Park in Lincolnshire. This reserve has a very good reputation for nightingale and turtle dove

I must confess I was immediately impressed with the place and I had not even got through the door. Car parking was £1.00, Blue Badge holders free with their parking right in front of the building. The centre itself, which is called the Whisby Natural World Centre, is as impressing a building as it is in name. It boast a fine shop, café/restaurant, entrance to the reserve is free, the toilets, needless to say, are wheelchair accessible, as are all the hides, and the site is covered with five waymarked trails which are principally compacted limestone, or limestone and grass, highly suitable for wheelchairs. Incidentally, electric wheelchairs can be hired, but more about that later.

We approach the northern shore of Coot Lake. Parallel with the walk lies a railway line which cuts the reserve in half almost, and as we walked along the pathway we could hear both blackcap and garden warbler singing away, very melodious I might add, but not nightingale quality. Neil stops us, and points across the railway line, a nightingale has just started up, but he only utters a few notes before stopping. We moved on, and just at the end of the lake another nightingale started up, and this one intended to be heard. We moved closer to the source of the sound, and just stood there spell bound by the exquisite tones coming from this little bird, unfortunately he was in a dense tangle of vegetation and could not be found. As the bird continued in song I went and sat on a nearby bench, my leg was really beginning to let me know, and we were only halfway round the walk.

Here I had one of those moments which are so infuriating. The bench over looked the end of Coot Lake, so I was looking over the lake at the same time as I was listening to the nightingale, and while doing so a dove flew past me, at speed, a turtle dove, and before I could draw any ones attention to the bird it had vanished from sight, a five second job this one had turned out to be. Fine for me, not so fine for my 12 companions, especially if it turns out to be our only sighting.

As we arrived at the junction in the pathway next to the level crossing, another nightingale burst into song, and if we thought the other one was good, this bird was on a different planet, and fortunately for me, another bench stood right here. The bird was singing from out of a large willow tree, and he was providing us with his full vocabulary, every note inch perfect, and Roy and Len almost simultaneously shouted, 'Got it'. Sure enough they had, and we were able to get all our telescopes onto the bird very quickly. You could see almost every movement the bird made, it's quivering bill as the music poured out, it's vibrating throat, tail flicking, here you could see the red on it's tail, the bright black eye in the head as it raised it head to help the music flow. What a performance, no wonder both poets and musicians have waxed lyrical over this bird, they may no longer sing in Barclay Square, but they certainly do at Whisby! This was a virtuoso performance, I doubt if I have ever enjoyed one so much. The bird must have sang for over 10 minutes before it stopped, and flew off. Our lunch had had to wait a little longer than we first thought, but no one was complaining.

We still had an hour an half available, so we decided to visit the hides round the Grebe Walk, another 1.3 miler, there was no way I could attempt this, hence my comments about electrical wheelchairs, had they one available for hire, yes they had, and the cost was only £2.00 but I would recommend booking in advance as they only have 2 available. I have been wheeled about in chairs on occasion, this is my first attempt at self propulsion.

I must admit I thoroughly enjoyed this 1.3 miles. We again heard nightingales, further garden warbler and blackcap, and chiffchaff and willow warbler were not going to be out done. There were several common terns flying over Grebe Lake, one or two of whom looked as though they were attempting to breed on the tern rafts, we saw our first great crested grebe of the day, and the only real disappointment was no return visit from the turtle dove.

Roll on next Monday, the day I have my appointment with the consultant. My leg at present is giving me hell, whether the walking I did yesterday was far too much, it probably was, I do not know, all I know is how I am suffering. Life, however, has to go on, so I completed my weekly shop as usual, did my normal Tuesday house work on return and decided to have an hour or so out birding. Prior to doing so I had a sudden thought.

I write about all these spots I have locally from where I can bird watch easily, many directly from my car, and others in close proximity to my car, and you may be beginning to wonder how on earth can you find such places in your own locality. I have already mentioned joining your local branch of the RSPB, or checking up on your local bird watching club, most counties have one, or even checking to see if bird study courses are run locally. These are very useful centres for information as well as guidance.

Another thing you can do, and you can do this completely on your own or with friends, is to suss out these places for yourself. I can already hear you asking just how, so let me make a suggestion. First of all buy an Ordnance Survey of your area, preferably a Landranger Map, a 1:50 000 scale, and on this map locate your own home, this need not be exact, a few hundred metres out will not cause any problem. With a compass, draw yourself a circle 12in diametre on the map, and every where in this circle will be no more than 5 miles or so away from your own home.

This done, study the circle closely looking particularly for water and woodland, these being prime areas for birds. Then check just how closely road, lanes, and public footpaths are to these locations. For those which are close, it is just then a question of driving out to really study the landscape. As with where I live, it is remarkable just how many of these prime locations are bordered by roadway or pathways, and with regard to the roads and lanes just how close you can park your car, with the benefit of little or no walking. When studying your map look closely at the contour lines, the wider they are apart the more level the terrain.

Keep you eye on what the local farmer or land owner is up to. Should he be planting grain crops this may be beneficial to land birds such as partridge or skylark, and during the winter invite in flocks of lapwing and golden plover. If the fields should become water logged waders and waterfowl will call in for breakfast so to speak, these in turn attracting the odd bird of prey. Fields being ploughed always attract gulls, corvids and numerous small passerines, linnets, meadow pipits, thrushes in winter etc., Any stretch of water, and this need not necessarily be large will have coot and moorhen breeding upon it, and if it is large enough mute swan, grebes, and mallards will nest, and in the water side vegetation warblers such as reed and sedge will appear in summer, and reed buntings will almost be resident.

Woodlands are home to a vast array of birds, titmice, warblers in summer, birds of prey, corvids, owls, finches, the list is endless, as long as these are deciduous woodlands and not conifer. The latter are no where as near as productive.

That is more than enough for starters, you will quickly realise your local area has many other type of habitats, marshland, bog, waste land, parks and not forgetting your own and your neighbours gardens. All of these will attract their own range of species, and remember you are still only five miles from home at the most. So give it a try, you will find out spots near home you did not know existed.

Anyway, back to birding. At Croxall a lapwing was on the scrape with quite a large chick, and an additional ringed plover, this one being close enough for identification purposes. As I started to move off I noticed a small bird move behind the plover. There are not many waders smaller than a plover, some similar in size such as sanderling, but this bird was decidedly smaller, and I had not brought my 'scope. This bird had to be a stint, but which one?

I opened my door slowly and quietly so I could get a more comfortable view of the bird, time for fine detail. You may remember I mentioned the fact that several Temminck's stints had been reported passing through the country, be nice if this proved to be one of those, I have not seen a Temminck's for some time.

This bird was quite stocky for it's size, giving an impression of being a powerful little bird, and was a brownish-buff in colour, especially the upper parts, and as it walked clear of stones on the scrape it had decidedly shortish legs, no thigh was visible, and the legs were pale, almost clay-coloured. This was the clincher to me, it had to be a Temminck's, little stint's legs are longer and black. A superb sighting, Temminck's are quite rare really, I have probably only seen a dozen or so in my life in the UK.

Friday dawned nice and bright but as the morning progressed it became cloudy and a bit more breezy, not that this will stop me from visiting Croxall this afternoon, this is the main advantage with having hides. Whether the news of the Temminck's stint yesterday will bring in the birders I do not know, it is probably the first for Staffordshire this year. By coincidence I note a little stint has appeared at Doxey Marsh this morning, both of our stints seen in the county within 24 hours of each other is some sort of record I would think.

Arriving at Croxall I am very surprised to find only one car in the car park, and I know this car so we do have at least one other birder here. While we were talking a movement on the scrape outside caught our attentions, and we both could not believe our luck, it was a sanderling. It was a nicely marked bird, nearly in it's full summer plumage, and it was providing stomping views. Sanderling are birds of passage to us in the Midlands, this one would be moving further north very soon.

I was contemplating moving off when I thought I would do as I did yesterday, I was now the only person here so I was not going to disturb anyone, so I slowly drove a little further up my side of the lake, parking up much as yesterday afternoon. The sanderling was still visible from here, as were a couple of lapwing, when a movement on the water caught my attention. Quickly focusing up I found I was looking at two dunlin, both in best summer plumage and sporting their black bellies. Viewing from my car was proving to be most beneficial, so I just sat back and enjoyed these two birds, another one for Sarah tomorrow.

The more birding I do from the confines of my car makes me realise just how good a hide they can become. As long as you do not make any excessive engine noise, do not open and close doors, make all movements within the car slowly and carefully, the birds just seem to ignore you. One thing I have learned is to have everything you need to hand, no leaning over to the back seat which will distract a bird, and do not poke your telescope or camera through open windows, this will instantly frighten the birds off, and always keep your hands within the confines of the car. If you do want the windows open, do so in advance, the noise of an electric window can be heard 'miles' away.

Once again Croxall is quiet, just a couple of dog walkers, so we have the hide to ourselves. We had hardly settled in when we picked up a nice little group of waders on the scrape, quickly focusing up my 'scope I realised we had hit the jackpot as far as Sarah's hit list was concerned. On a spit were eight dunlin, a single sanderling and five ringed plover, all standing there waiting to be seen.

Now would we be so lucky for the quail? As we drove past the entrance to the micro-light airfield a game bird flew up off the road and landed in the potato field at the side, I shouted Sarah to stop, it looked like a partridge to me, not a young pheasant, as Sarah had thought. Sarah was the first to relocate the bird, 'It's got a red head Dad' she said, this could only mean one thing, we had a male grey partridge, and would you believe it, another 'Year Tick' for her. We made our way on to quail country.

Sarah brought my attention to another bird singing, in a nearby sapling a corn bunting was joining in. The occasional sound of the quail could be heard but it was difficult to pick it up against the background of other birds' song. I could actually hear a female calling, but could not draw Sarah onto the call. Finally, we did it, a male burst out with 'Wet my lips, wet my lips, wet my lips', or in Sarah's case her coffee percolator was bubbling nicely.

While I was trying to make my mind up on where to go on Sunday I received a telephone call from my friend Ivor, and he made my mind up for me. On Thursday, Ivor, along with two other friends of mine, John and Len, had spent a day on the Moorlands, they had invited me to join them, but I knew there would be too much walking involved so I had to decline their offer. Ivor had 'phoned to tell me they had a great day and Tittesworth was particularly good, especially for spotted flycatcher, pied flycatcher, redstart and grey wagtail. Three of those would be 'Year Ticks' for me, and I have only seen one pied flycatcher, and knowing where the birds had been seen there was little or no walking as long as I was lucky with car parking.

The area I wished to visit first was the wooded river valley which feeds the north easterly arm of the reservoir, the River Churnet in fact. Today was a day for binoculars, telescopes are not much use among thick trees. I started to walk along the river and made my way through a gap in the hedge which led into the original car park and here, within seconds of arriving, I had my first 'Year Tick'. Sitting out on a branch of a tree sat a spotted flycatcher, I did not even need my binoculars, I could not believe my luck, what a start to my morning. I enjoyed the bird for a few minutes before it dashed off in hot pursuit of some small flying insect. Back to the river.

It must have been a good quarter of an hour later before I heard the redstart, his soft song was coming from high in a tree nearby, and because of the thick leaves it was doing it's level best not to be seen. I must have spent some three or four minutes studying this tree before I caught a flicker of movement, another minute or two and I finally had my quarry, a male redstart, who just flicked his tail and vanished once again. I turned to retrace my footsteps as down came the rain.

I made my way across the lane to have a look along the river from the river bridge, and here I found two more birds. A pied flycatcher had just come out of his nest box so I concentrated my efforts in that direction, and it was not long before I was rewarded, the male came back and went straight into the box. It was obviously taking in food, whether this was just for it's mate or for young I do not know.

A flash of yellow on the river caught my eye, focusing up I was delighted to see I had two grey wagtails, a pair, the flash of yellow had been the male. This bird is a 'Year Tick' for me, and I just cannot believe it has taken me almost a full five months to catch up with this bird. Most years I see them very early on, they normally breed along my local river, not this year, we are rather concerned about this bird after the very hard winter recently experienced. A nice end to my trip out.

I thought I would spend a little time talking about optical equipment, it is about time we had a serious look at the subject. With binoculars and telescopes the sky is the limit almost in what you can spend, and as silly as it may sound, the most expensive need not necessarily be the best for you, other considerations have to be taken into account. The first question to ask yourself is how often will you use your equipment? If, like me, it is almost every day then price does not really enter into the equation, £1,000 spread over 50 years continuous use is minimal, but £1,000 for one hour a week is slightly different. It is important you make up your mind on how much you have to spend, it is very easy to go over budget once you are let loose. My advice is to go to your supplier and tell him at the onset you have 'X' to spend and you are quite happy to buy second hand, also if you can, tell him the size you are interested in. This will help in selecting a range for you to try.

So where do you go? If you look in any bird magazine you will find a host of people selling optical equipment, most of these are very good so choosing one fairly local should present no problem. The main thing is to select one who covers a range of manufacturers, and also one who deals in second hand equipment as well. Some birders are like crazy motorists who must have the latest model as soon as it comes out, so there is a very good turnover in second hand product, and this can be the way to buy quality, both my latest binoculars and telescope were second hand. Most of the quality manufacturers guarantee their equipment for many years so buying second hand is not a problem, and all the reputable suppliers will guarantee their sales in any case. Just remember one thing, they are only waterproof is they say so, damp proof does not mean a thing, and believe me you will bird watch in rain – unfortunately.

When selecting your binoculars consider what you are using them. This may sound rather obvious, you want to look at birds, but where will most of your birding be done? If, like me, you are to spend much time viewing over long distances, i.e. the coast, reservoirs, open moor etc., you will need a pair with a decent magnification, a minimum of 8x, or as in my case, 10x, so look at 8x40 or 10x40 or similar. I personally use a 10x42, and I find these cover most eventualities, when they do not my telescope comes into operation. One thing I am always careful of is 'zoom' binoculars. I do not like them and I have yet to find a pair which justify the cost.

Weight is also important. When walking for a few hours with a pair of binoculars bouncing away on your chest, it as amazing how heavy and hard they become as the day progresses. Another point is comfort, can you hold them easily and use the full freedom of you fingers to operate them? Some binoculars are mighty uncomfortable depending upon the size of your own hands, so always try as many pairs as you can.

Now telescopes. Much of what I have already said about binoculars applies to telescopes, the principal difference being cost, telescopes are, in the main, more costly than binoculars, so once again try as many as you can. Another consideration with telescopes is the fact there are many different types. The major detail to remember is that your optical lens, the big one, should be at least 60mm in diametre.

Another big consideration is the type of view you require, by this I am referring to the viewing lens. Most telescopes now take interchangeable lenses, so you can either buy with a fixed magnification or a zoom, I would suggest you go straight in for a zoom. The only reason you need at telescope is to view birds at distance, and sometime distance really does mean distance, you could be watching a flock of gulls over the sea at over half a miles distance, and you will need all the help you can get. Given the right conditions you could be on maximum magnification at 60x, the only problem here of course, and lets face it there always has to be one, is that at top magnification you reduce the amount of light coming into the scope, so colour can become paler and the picture loses at lot of it's clarity, but without the higher magnification you would probably not even see the bird. Something is always better than nothing.

Then you can have the angle of view, which is very important. The three common types are straight on (you view straight through the telescope, or almost), or you have side angled view (here you view from the side of the telescope) and top angled view (down through the telescope). All of these have their good points and bad. My preference is for straight on, I find I can follow birds in flight far more easily than through the other two options. Top angled view is very good for seeing birds at height. On the tops of trees, up cliffs, soaring high in the sky, then it is much easier to look down a lens than straight on. Side angled I just cannot get on with at all, friends of mine swear by them. With both of the latter I find following birds in flight difficult, with straight on you just follow the birds direction. Try them all, before you settle on what suits you best.

As with binoculars, telescopes come in all shapes and sizes, plus weights, so when you buy do carry it about a bit to make sure you realise just what weight you are carting about. Buying your telescope does not end just there, you need something to put it on. So now you start to look at tripods and other accessories. If you can afford it straight off, buy a carbon fibre tripod, it cuts down the weight appreciably, otherwise buy the strongest you can, because in strong wind your 'scope will still move. Be careful of aluminium tripods, these may be light and strong, I have however found they flex in wind, and once again your 'scope moves. For viewing from inside a hide, a hide clamp works very well and is a lot more convenient than a tripod with legs all over the place. Finally a bean bag, these can work equally well, be it from a car or hide.

One final piece of advice, do not buy from off the net or by post unless you are fully aware of the type of equipment you are buying. You may only ever buy one 'scope or pair of binoculars in your life, take time to get it right, it is not just a case of price.

Back to the grind and I have returned from hospital, it is as I thought, an hip replacement operation is to be arranged. It is now just a question of when, as far as I am concerned it cannot come quick enough.

One interesting side effect of bad weather such as being experienced today, it can drive down birds which were just passing through, so you always have the chance of the unexpected, the only question being, where to go. In view of the heavy rain all my watching is likely to be done from either near to my car or even from it. Due to that I have decided to go across to Blithfield Reservoir, having a key and permit I can drive round the shore which could bring me close to any birds.

I decided to go to the dam, it was very quiet here, no boats out for obvious reasons, and neither were any anglers in evidence, this was just a day for crazy birders. I drove straight over the dam making my way along to Ten Acre Bay. As I approach the Bay I spotted a small wader walking along the water line, a plover of some sort, so I approached as slowly and quietly as I could. The bird stopped, so did I, and slowly winding down my window (I had not done this previously due to the rain which now, fortunately, had almost stopped), I raised my binoculars. The bird was very close, 10 metres or so away, and seemed completely oblivious to me, so I was able to get a very good view of the bird... dark bill, yellow ring round the eye, no more identification details were required, I had a little ringed plover.

Turning the car round I then slowly commenced my return journey I had only travelled a short distance when another movement on the shore line caught my attention, had the plover flown up here I wondered. I crawled along very slowly once again, this time with my windows open. This was no little ringed plover, a plover species though it may be, this was a lovely turnstone.

This was a nice turn up for the book, totally unexpected. The bird was in full summer plumage and really looked the part. They are a confiding bird and this one was not at all concerned about my close proximity to it. I enjoyed watching this bird for several minutes as it foraged away among the shore line debris, actually living up to it's name on occasion, turning over small stones.

Now what am I going to do with myself. There is little or nothing on the net close enough to home, so I have decided to have a day out round some of the Derbyshire lakes and reservoirs not visited so far this year. I am heading to Staunton Harold Reservoir, the Swarkestone gravel pit lakes and Melbourne Hall Lake, at these venues I can view either from the car or very close to it, so I am hoping not to put any strain on my legs so that I can manage a bit of a walk tonight after the nightjars.

Staunton Harold Reservoir lies just south of Melbourne and is a Severn Trent Reservoir. It has all the facilities, although the kiosk is closed at present, a Pay and Display car park, although Blue Badge Holders can park for free, several picnic areas, some of which have tables which cater for wheelchair users, and most of the footpaths are hard surface suitable for wheelchair users. Just be careful of one or two of these as they have short steep gradients so either a motorised chair or some willing muscle power may be required. The reservoir is used for sailing and angling as well as being maintained for nature.

I parked up on the main car park by the Visitor Centre which overlooks the dam. There are picnic tables only a few metres away from my parked car so I walk across to these to sit down and study the reservoir. Two tern were over the far side, once again too far away to be certain which, and a great crested grebe came sailing past with one youngster peeping out from among it's feathers, always a delightful scene – at the mention of which we should all go 'Ahh'.

I made my way back to my car for lunch, and opening all the car windows I sat down to enjoy this. I had hardly started when I picked up a large bird high in the sky over the far side of the reservoir, my initial thought being the buzzard, but there was something about the way this bird was holding it's wings which caused an adrenalin rush. Lunch quickly down and binoculars raised, just keep on coming you little beauty. As the bird came closer I could see the white on the bird, this just had to be an osprey, keep coming, keep coming. The bird then banked and I could see the full splendour if it, an osprey it most certainly was, it then flew directly across my vision, a truly wonderful sight, and slowly made it's way northward. I was able to follow the bird for several minutes before it vanished from sight. What a marvellous few minutes, a true birder's moment in time. We all dream of occasions like this when a bird as dramatic as an osprey puts on a show just for you.

Swarkestone is old gavel workings alongside the River Trent, and is a major flood plain which attracts large numbers of waterfowl during the winter, so I was not expecting a great deal today. Along the road, which incidentally is the A514, you cross over a series of old brick bridges which are ancient monuments and worth stopping to investigate in their own right, needless to say they are protected. I wanted the turning off to Ingleby, which I duly found. Going from memory, there is an area along this road where you can park up on the side of the sailing lake, something Dorothy and I had done several times before. My memory did not let me down, the only problem was the car park was now closed off with a good steel gate, locked and chained, but fortunately, the lane is wide enough to park a few cars, and at the side of the gate is an entrance for pedestrians, but I do not think it will take a wheelchair fully opened. Once inside the ground is flat from the many cars which had parked up over the years, and the lake is only metres away. It is now nicely overgrown, which illustrates just how many years ago it must have been when I last visited the area.

From the thick bramble and nettle patches whitethroats could be heard singing, from the taller vegetation both blackcap and garden warbler were in good voice and as I approached the waters edge I had a very pleasant surprise, I actually could hear a grasshopper warbler, I must have been standing right next door to the bird, but could I find it, could I heck. This must be the first time I have heard a 'gropper', as we call them, for over 10 years, I never thought I would have the pleasure of hearing one again due to the decline in my hearing capabilities. What a morning.

I moved to the waters edge, not wishing to disturb the little fellow any more, and looked down the lake. There was no sailing today so all was peaceful. The usual waterfowl to be expected were on the water, two terns, this time close enough to see, both were common. I was about to move off when something brightly white appeared on the far shore, a little egret had chosen that moment to walk into view, no complaints from me.

Melbourne is a delightful country town, boasting a superb piece of English architecture in Melbourne Hall, although today you could see little of it as it was all shrouded in plastic, obviously restoration work is being carried out, still the Hall was not my destination today, I was interested only in the lake.

I need not have bothered, it looked as though a fishing competition was taking place and anglers were strewn along it's shore line and the few birds about, which were not the 'tame' variety, were well out of sight. Never mind, back to Staunton Harold reservoir we will go, this time to view from the Calke Viewpoint Car Park. The car park, which is free, no facilities, over looks the two southern arms of the reservoir, and you can walk down from here to enter into the Calke Abbey parkland if you so chose, and this way you can get in for free.

Initially there was not a large amount to see. A few cormorants, Canada geese, several gulls, both lesser black-backed and black-headed, and a female pheasant was walking under one of the bird feeders. A calling nuthatch brightened up the proceedings and two tree sparrows put in an appearance. The odd buzzard was out enjoying the sun when I noticed a slightly smaller bird of prey coming in at speed towards a soaring buzzard, what had we here? My first thoughts were peregrine, but the shape was wrong, quickly putting my binoculars on the bird I had the shock of my life, the bird was a goshawk, and judging by the size difference with the buzzard, it was a male, and it was not here for fun.

The goshawk banked and dived at the nearest buzzard and feathers flew, two large feathers drifted down, the buzzard had been struck. I did not know buzzards could fly so quick the speed this one took off at. Buzzard may be larger than a male goshawk, but they are not the fighting machine a goshawk is, they are lethal. The goshawk turned his attention towards the remaining two buzzards, but they were having none of it, they sped away.

What a few hours birding, two 'Year Ticks', the goshawk and the osprey, and hearing my first grasshopper warbler for many a year was almost like a 'Lifer'. What can tonight bring?

Well we only had a small contingent of birders present, eight including me. We met on time and moved off promptly. Due to my leg I had taken with me a walking stool, I intended to sit out part of the walk once we got down into the Sherbrook Valley. We made the valley and as we did so a cuckoo called out his greeting, search as hard as we did we could not spot him. My friends went off and I sat down on my stool to survey the scene. The cuckoo was still calling and at last I did see him fly, my first actual sighting this year. He was not on his own as another cuckoo was calling from the plantation behind me. A tree pipit put in a brief appearance before dropping down into some thick vegetation where it no doubt had it's nest.

About an hour had past and I was just about to move off to another location when I caught sight of a bird flying across the horizon, a woodcock, this was one of my target birds for the night, I just hoped it had been seen by my friends. Woodcock do their flying late in the evening, when the male usually flies round the borders of his territory to protect his patch from any interlopers.

My friends returned, they had not seen the woodcock but had seen a pair of stonechats and witnessed a pair of meadow pipits chasing off a cuckoo, and also seen hobby, so they were happy enough with their birding. Time now to move on for the nightjars. I was becoming concerned with the prospect of seeing a nightjar, or hearing one for that matter. I had noticed as the weather had cooled down that the number of flying insects had dropped in proportion, and now none were to be seen at all.

Nightjars eat flying insects, moths and the like, which is why they are a nocturnal bird. I have long held the opinion that wild animals in general will not hunt if the conditions are such they are unlikely to find any prey, they do not wish to waste their energy, so will rest up until the conditions improve.

Last night was such a night. We held on until about 22.30 hours with not a sound of the nightjar, but as if to make up for the disappointment, as we moved off we were greeted by the hooting of a tawny owl. We made our way forward as quietly as possible, although walking on stones is difficult to do silently. An owl suddenly launched itself from a tree in front of us, completely silently needless to say and vanished in the gloom over the adjacent heath land. We thought that was that, but no, just ahead the owl commenced to hoot once again, we had obviously flushed the female, As both birds were out and about, this was a good sign they had large chicks in their nest and both birds needed to hunt to keep their youngsters appetites satisfied.

At Croxall the next day I initially have the hide to myself but a birder soon enters, a lad from Stoke. We have a chat and exchange information, it would appear he has come down to try to find the sanderling which were reported from here yesterday, with no success. We start to really study the far side of the lake, many oystercatchers to be seen, I count 11, all adults, which is probably the highest count I have ever made at Croxall. The odd redshank can be found along the waters edge, and near the outlet from the river I see a small bird scurrying along. A ringed plover, we are once again at concentration time due to the distance I am viewing. I bring the bird to my friends attention, so we are both studying it intently. The bird eventually turns, we can see the yellow bill, problem over, it is a ringed plover.

I was glad I had met this guy, during our conversation he mentioned he had been very successful with both nightjars and woodcock on the Chase a day or two back. I quizzed him deeply and found out he had seen them not far from my favoured area, and he had seen three nightjars in the air together. I now know where I shall be going when I next chase nightjar.

The Bank Holiday is upon us so today I am off to where the crowds do not collect, Blithfield Reservoir, Whitemoor Haye and Croxall, you should, by now, be getting to know these places as well as I do, but you could visit the same place for every single day in a year, and I would almost guarantee you would see something different every visit.

Blithfield was exceptionally quiet, I know I have had a few poor days of late, but today was particularly so. As I had not prepared any food I decided I would drive round via Lichfield where I could fill up my car with fuel, and buy myself a sandwich or something. In transit I called in at the Handsacre Flashes, only mute swan and mallard on the water, but I could at least hear both reed warbler and sedge warbler calling away, something at last to get interested in. I also stopped at the quail listening spot. The quail did not respond immediately, do they ever, but the skylarks were happy enough with life as they serenaded me. The usual yellow-hammer could be heard calling away, and a pair of lapwing were chasing off a carrion crow. I had been here for a good 20 minutes before I heard what I had come for.

Croxall was looking very quiet. The reed warbler were warbling away from the nearby reedbed, and a whitethroat was still doing it's best to attract a mate. Gate opened and I am on my way. I pass a dog walker, who I was amazed to see had her dog on a lead, so I gave her a cheery wave, and passed two bird watchers on their way towards the hide.

The hide was obviously empty, so I opened up the slats and proceeded to set up my tripod and 'scope, I had just about finished when the two birders came in, they turned out to be a father and daughter much like Sarah and myself. We passed the time of day, commented on how windy it was, and set ourselves up for a bit of birding. I quickly found a plover of sorts, and while focusing up on this bird I heard the father comment to his daughter that he had found an avocet. I asked where and by jingo he was smack on. The avocet was swishing away with it's long de-curved bill, what it was finding to eat in fresh water I do not know, but it must have been finding something.

Moving back to finding my plover, I was pleased to find a sanderling nearby, and a little further on two little ringed plover where chasing each other in what looked like a frenzy, is courtship this dramatic or am I too old to remember? Several oystercatchers and lapwings were scattered along the far shore and a small group of redshank flew in to join the birds on the scrape, that was seven waders already. We were chatting away about how lucky we had been when he said, 'A group of dunlin have just flown in'. Swinging round I quickly located his dunlin and after slowly working my way through them I noticed a small wader dashing about, what had we here? I drew my friends attention to this and wound up my zoom to get a larger image. I was delighted to find myself looking at a summer plumaged little stint, I just could not believe our luck at Croxall today, what a lovely collection of birds.

I called my two companions over to my 'scope so they could have a good look at the bird, my 'scope being more powerful than theirs, and they were thrilled to bits, it was their first ever little stint, and incidentally, a 'Year Tick' for me.

The Bank Holiday Monday is a field meeting for the Rosliston Bird Study Group, and eight of us have made the effort to visit Croxall. A quick drive down to the hide and into the hide we go. Fortunately, no other birders had ventured out, the hide only takes just about double figures, so we had almost filled it. Initially nothing of note was spotted, but Roy soon sorted that out, he located several ringed plovers on the far shore, eight in total, a very nice number, and into view quickly followed oystercatcher and redshank.

Moving our attention to the scrape, here we had further ringed plover, two little ringed plover and lapwing with a large youngster. Several of the black-headed gulls now had quite large young, with one or two having left the sanctuary of the rafts and were now moving about on the scrape. A coot got rather close to one of the young and this triggered off a very positive response from the chicks two parents who proceeded to dive bomb the coot. This action drew a response from the lapwings parents, they too joined in the attack on the coot, who decided discretion was better than valour, and swiftly moved away. Peace was quickly restored. Bird behaviour at times is simply fascinating.

As things quietened down a small flock of dunlin flew in, so I told my group to go through these carefully in view of my experience yesterday with the little stint, and this turned out to be a good instruction. I had not brought my telescope with me, but I was quickly called across to a friend who had, she had a small bird in her 'scope, what was it? It was jackpot time, right in the middle of her 'scope was my friend from yesterday, the little stint, it was marvellous it had stayed on for awhile longer. There was only Roy and myself who had ever seen little stint previously, and Roy's sighting was a few years back, so all the rest had a 'Lifer'.

Unlike yesterday when the dunlin and stint flew off they did not return, today, although very mobile, they kept returning back to the scrape, so we were able to enjoy the bird both in flight and on the ground, or should we say wading, the stint was rarely on dry ground, most of the time it was up to it's belly in water.

Barn Owl (Tyto alba)

Black–headed Gull (Larus ridibundus)

Blue Tit (Parus caeruleus)

Brambling (Fringilla montifringilla)

Bullfinch (Pyrrhula pyrrhula)

Buzzard (Buteo buteo)

Chaffinch (Fringilla coelebs)

Coot (Fulica atra)

Dunnock (Prunella modularis)

Little Egret (Egretta garzetta)

Fulmar (Fulmarus glacialis)

Gannet (Sula bassana)

Goldfinch (Carduelis carduelis)

Great Tit (Parus major)

Greenfinch (Carduelis chloris)

Greylag Goose (Anser anser)

Great Black-backed Gull (Larus marinus)

Great Crested Grebe (Podiceps cristatus)

Guillemot (Uria aalge)

Grey Heron (Ardea cinerea)

Kingfisher (Alcedo atthis)

Kittiwake (Rissa tridactyla)

Lesser Black-backed Gull (Larus fuscus)

Long-tailed Tit (Aegithalos caudatus)

Little Owl (Athena noctua)

Long-eared Owl (Asio otus)

Mallard (Anus platyrhynchos)

Mandarin (Aix galericulata)

Mediterranean Gull (Larus melanocephalus)

Moorhen (Gallinula chloropus)

Mute Swan (Cygnus olor)

Oystercatcher (Haematopus ostralegus)

Pintail (Anus acuta)

Pied Wagtail (Motacilla alba yarrellii)

Rock Pipit (Anthus petrosus)

Pochard (Aythya ferina)

Puffin (Fratercula arctica)

Red Kite (Milvus milvus)

Robin (Erithacus rubecula)

Reed Bunting (Emberiza schoeniclus)

Sanderling (Calidris alba)

Common Sandpiper (Actitis hypoleucos)

Sandwich Tern (Sterna sandvicensis)

Shelduck (Tadorna tadorna)

Swallow (Hirundo rustica)

Snow Bunting (Plectrohenax nivalis)

Tawny Owl (Strix aluco)

Teal (Anus crecca)

Turnstone (Arenaria interpres)

Waxwing (Bombycilla garrulus)

Whooper Swan (Cygnus cygnus)

Wigeon (Anus penelope)

Tuesday, and the latest reports of osprey were from Tad Bay, so I decided to park up in the causeway car park which provided me with a full view of Tad Bay, anything the size of an osprey would be easily seen from here. After nearly half an hour of watching, it could not, but I at least had something of interest to keep away any boredom. Along the shoreline of Admaston Reach, and well in view with my binoculars, two sanderling were busily feeding away as they continually moved backwards and forwards over the same piece of shoreline, there was obviously something of interest to be found. I decided to move on across the dam and on to Ten Acre Bay, I do not think I have visited this spot so frequently previously, but it has been quite good to us, and I can at least drive all the way down to it, a major consideration these days. At first glance there seemed little of interest, a few greylags, mallard, the inevitable coot, and as I was going through these, three small waders came hurtling past, fortunately, although I only had them for seconds, their black bellies really stood out in today's light, dunlin. As with the sanderling, these birds seem to be hanging on a bit this year, normally I expect the majority to have left our neck of the woods by mid May, it is 1 June tomorrow. Crossing the dam I noticed something white in the River Blithe, as I was the only vehicle on the dam I could stop to look at it more closely. It was a little egret, not a bad bird really to end the month on.

So how are we with yearly totals, I close for May on 192, not bad at all. This time last year I was on 184, and by that point I had visited Scotland, so I would consider this year I am doing far better than 2010. Last year, or at least for a part of it, I could walk a mile or two whenever I went out. This year many a time, such as today, I have not even got out of the car from start to finish. But it at least shows what can be done. See you in June.

Map references:
Foremark Reservoir – Carver's Rocks entrance: SK 335224.
Foremark Reservoir – Main entrance: SK 336248.
Bempton Cliffs – RSPB: TA 198742.
North Landing – Flamborough Head: TA 239720.
Blacktoft Sands – RSPB: SE 843232.
Shustoke Reservoir: SP 224910.
Handsacre Flash: SK 091167.
Whisby Nature Park – Car Park: SK 914661.
Catton Hall: SK 210155.
Tittesworth Reservoir – River Churnet Woods: SJ 997605.
Staunton Harold Reservoir – Car Park: SK 376245.
Swarkestone Sailing Club Lake – Old Car Park: SK 361276.
Melbourne Lake: SK 387249.
Staunton Harold Reservoir – Calke Viewpoint Car Park: SK 375227.

Chapter VI

June

June has come in but unfortunately birding is off the menu for today, unless it appears in or above my own garden as I must really do some work out there. While sitting working away, I had a lovely encounter with a young blackbird. Knowing how dry the earth would be with a lack of worms near the surface, I had taken a supply of suet pieces and a bag of dried fruit out with me so I could put this out for the birds, and the birds came in regularly for it. One young blackbird was extremely confident and it came right up close to me and on more than one occasion actually stole a sultana from the bag, the cheeky blighter!

I positioned the bag right between my feet and waited to see what it would do, nothing was going to stop this bird, straight to the bag it went and ran off with it's pickings. I began to wonder just how confident this bird really was so the next time it was around I closed up the bag and held out a sultana between my fingers. Initially the bird seemed bemused by the change of event and just stood looking at me and then at the bag which it could clearly see, although it could not see the fruit. Then, with a sudden dash it flew at my fingers, snatched the sultana, and was away. Remarkable behaviour, and I was able to repeat this several times and it was quite noticeable how more calmer the bird became, not so hasty in it's approach.

As I have some time before having a light lunch and going out, I thought I would investigate just how far I had actually walked this year for my birds. Over five months I have walked a total of 24 miles, with the longest in a single day of 1.5 miles. I suppose I average 4 -6 trips out each week, let us call it 5. By the end of May we had completed 21 weeks, so that gives us a minimum of 105 birding excursions. A quick division exercise, 105 trips into 24 miles comes out at a little under a quarter of a mile per round trip. We have seen a lot of birds per quarter of a mile, and of those 105 excursions, well over a half could have been experienced from a wheelchair. As with many things in life, a bit of careful planning can save a lot of wasted effort.

The day was very calm and I had high hopes of hearing the quail well today. I parked up to the accompaniment of two singing skylarks, they certainly sounded as though they were enjoying the weather. I did not have to wait long, out of the field came the familiar song of the male quail, but this time he was being answered by a female, wonderful, we now have at least one pair in situ.

I have decided to visit Derbyshire once again to see if I can repeat the success of last week. This time I will visit the north of the county. I pulled in on the North Bank Car Park at Ogston, parking free, although there are no facilities, apart from a bench or two. The car Park directly over looks the reservoir with no apparent access to the shore. A telescope here would be advantageous. The West Bank Car Park is also free although this one does boast a toilet along with a disabled toilet if the sign is to believed. This car park is right by the side of the sailing club and from here a wide sweep of the reservoir can be viewed. Telescopes advised for both. There is a bird hide close by but I did not investigate as it clearly stated for use by Bird Club members only.

The reservoir is most attractive, if it was not for the dam you would think it was a natural lake. I parked up within 10 metres of the fence over looking the reservoir, and made my way across. I was accompanied by both a calling chiffchaff and a singing garden warbler, all very delightful. I could see a couple of anglers on the shore and across the bay was a sailing club, although no boats were out on the water today. It was a picture of complete tranquillity, and my car was the only vehicle on the car park as well.

I was pleased I had brought my telescope with me because I was most certainly going to need it. On the foreshore were just two mallards and a family part of coot, so it was a question of concentrating further afield on the far shore. A pair of great crested grebe were displaying, always a delightful sight, and a cormorant was busily diving in search of a fish for it's dinner. Working my way further along the shore I caught sight of two small waders running about in a small shallow pond of water, left behind by the retreating tide, the reservoir was quite low.

After a bit of careful focusing up, the heat had created quite an haze, two dunlin, both in their full summer regalia, at last something a bit special. Little else was to be seen from this viewing point, although one of the benches was at a nice vantage point so I was able to sit down to do it. I had a moments excitement as a bird of prey flew out of the wood a kestrel.

I am of the opinion Ogston is a location for seasonal and passage birds, and as such is probably better visited between August and April, but forgetting all of that, it is a delightful spot, and on today's evidence, not over visited.

After the peace of Ogston, Cromford was full of people out enjoying the last day of the school holidays and with such beautiful sunshine to boot. I had a stroll down to the river, only about 40 metres or so away, you cannot visit Cromford without looking for the dipper in the Derwent. Two birds were quickly located, an adult and youngster, that was nice, and they did not seem the slightest bit concerned by the many people walking the Derwent. Now for Carsington.

After the crowds at Cromford, I should have known better but as I was about to swing into the driveway down to the car park a large notice was seen 'Car Park Full – Overflow Car Park' with an arrow pointing. Now what to do? I initially thought of JCB at Rocester, but logic told me as it would be crowded there. It is too early to go home so I decided to have a ride round Blithfield and at Dapple Heath, a small hamlet, I had a pleasant surprise, a male hobby flew directly in front of me as it flew over the lane. A bird I always love to see.

From the causeway car park there was also little to be seen apart from a large congregation of mute swans. I counted these and I made it 74, all of which were adults, these birds were collecting for their annual moult, although the 3 June did seem a little earlier than usual.

Today has tuned out to be a typical June day in our neck of the woods. Most of the returning migrants are in the middle of their first breeding cycle, so the males have little reason to sing all day, they are too busy collecting food for their broods. You can still hear the 'Dawn Chorus' but it does not go on for as long as a couple of weeks or so ago. The majority of the passage birds have moved through, especially the waders and terns.

For the avid 'Ticker', they have to travel to pastures new to seek further names for their lists, so many head off to the coast for their days birding. The only alternative for them is to seek out the odd local breeding bird they have not seen and this can take time, otherwise they would have already seen it, (the nightjar would be an example for me). Secondly await the report of some rarity or other, believe me something will crop up. We have a red-necked phalarope at Upton Warren at present, and then chase after that bird in a very single minded manner.

So today has been rather quiet, although to be fair if I had listed every bird seen it could have been a nice little list, I have tended to concentrate more on the unusual than the common place, although the common place in many instances are more colourful than the unusual.

Back again in Blithfield which was very quiet once again on the bird front. I parked by a large dead tree trunk lying on it's side, and I quickly realised this was home to a pied wagtail. A male bird came in with a beak full of food, and sat glaring at me,. I could see the bird was very agitated so I moved back a short distance, and the bird quickly vanished into a large crack on the side of the trunk. Leaving the pied in peace I studied the reservoir, a few gulls, mallards, coots and a pair of great crested grebe was all I could find.

Sunday I travelled to JCB at Rochester and managed to park up easily. The usual collection birds were strutting about, although there was no one feeding them at present. While looking through the birds on the water three Egyptian geese came flying in, quickly followed by two drake red-crested pochard. Seeing free-flying birds among collection birds always raises the question of their 'Pedigree'. Purists would not include these sightings on their lists, claiming them to be escapees, I personally believe if it is flying free and it is on the British List, then I will count it. Many a bird, and especially waterfowl have originated from escapees, the Canada goose being a prime example.

I still had time to spare so I went to Blithfield Reservoir. The view from the lane overlooking Tad Bay was quite good, light conditions being well nigh perfect with no hint of any haze, which you usually get over water in warm conditions. Initially there did not seem a great deal of interest, the birds were the ones you would expect, a few duck, geese, cormorants and on the exposed muddy areas many lapwing. While studying these closely I heard redshank calling and two birds landed in among the lapwings, this caused a little disturbance and two small waders appeared from among the lapwings, these were different sizes so we had two different species. The one was obviously a plover species, the other was a slim sandpiper, and here my pulse commenced to race, had I at long last got my wood sandpiper? Zooming up to 50x I had what I wanted, a marvellous summer plumaged wood sandpiper, my bogy bird was now put to bed. Believe me, if you wish to prosper in this game, patience is as important as luck. Sandpipers are very active feeders and I spent several minutes enjoying this bird, I may not see one for another 12 months. The bird eventually worked it's way round the corner of the mudflat which was obscured from view by trees.

I was thrilled to bits to also see a small number of Beautiful Demoiselle damsel flies flitting nearby. I have not seen one of these lovely insects for many years, no name could be more apt, they are a gem, a piece of pure exotica. I almost forgot what I had come here for, but not quite.

Driving home through Hoar Cross I stopped to see a couple of buzzard sporting about, they seemed to be thoroughly enjoying the weather, and shortly afterwards came the moment of the day. Something to beat my wood sandpiper – impossible I can hear you saying, but to be perfectly honest, yes.

Midway between Hoar Cross and Woodmill there is a plantation which we locals refer to as Cross Hayes Plantation as Cross Hayes House lies close by, and flying across the field in front of this wood is a large bird of prey, my initial feelings being buzzard, but something about it's flight was not quite right – had I a red kite? No I had not, as the bird banked I had the surprise of my life, I was looking at a superb honey buzzard, I could not believe my luck. Honey buzzard are rare, and I mean rare, they are one of the most rare birds we have breeding in the UK, probably less than 60 pairs. They are a returning summer migrant and it would be absolutely marvellous if a pair were to breed locally, as long as egg collectors do not catch on to it.

Monday morning is upon us, the Rosliston Bird Study Group are visiting Branston Water Park, and we have a very good turnout, 26 in all. The morning has started out quite dull and overcast, no rain is promised, but it is a morning for a light pullover to be worn. We will make our way round the lake anti-clockwise, walking the canal tow path initially as here we normally hear many warblers.

Before we leave the car park our first chiffchaff of the day can be heard, and by the time we reach the canal both whitethroat and blackcap can be added to our day's list. In the canal two family parties of mallard can be seen, the first with four quite large ducklings, the other with seven very small ducklings, only a day or two old I would estimate. We had not proceeded much further when we had our first bullfinch of the day, they are almost guaranteed here. It was not long before the first sedge warbler could be heard, our fourth warbler in about 20 minutes, and all heard, none seen.

A chiffchaff sat out on an overhead wire, calling his little heart out, and close by a blackcap was doing similar. As we were enjoying these two birds a garden warbler started up from dense undergrowth close by, this provided us with a wonderful opportunity to compare their song with that of the blackcap, and a useful few minutes this turned out to be.

A singing sedge also popped out to join in the fun and for one or two of my friends this was the first time they had seen a sedge warbler, so his presence was very welcome. A willow warbler then joined in, he obviously was not going to put in the shade.

Leaving the canal towpath we rejoined up with the lakeside walk, and it was not long before we had our first singing reed warbler. We could not find the bird as he was singing from the centre of a dense reed patch, but this also gave us the opportunity to compare the bird's song with that of the sedge heard but a short time ago. The reed was our seventh warbler of the day, not bad going.

The woods were quiet by comparison, just the odd chiffchaff calling away, and we had the briefest of views of a male reed bunting, so out of the woods and onto the shoreline once more. While in the woods the sun had broken through, and with it had come large numbers of swift which were hurtling round over the lake surface. While watching these we had a pleasant surprise, just off shore sat a superb drake ruddy duck.

Friday is here, and Croxall today was very quiet, both for people and birds, apart from a noisy bunch of oystercatchers the only interesting birds seen were two ringed plover, and these were right on the far side of the lake. The water levels are still disappointingly high with little or no scrape visible, so passage waders will long have departed I would think. Some of the black-headed gull chicks were now quite large and out of their nests, and one black-headed was valiantly defending her young against the attentions of a lesser black-backed gull, and I am pleased to report, she won, driving the larger gull off.

After about an hour I decided I would move on to Whitemoor Haye. The main lake was very quiet, so straight down to the rough lane for the quail. They were reported singing a couple of days ago, let us hope they are today. It only took a few minutes today to catch their call, just one bird by the sound of things, but one bird is better than none.

Slowly driving along the rough lane I caught a flash of yellow on the edge of the neighbouring potato field, I know we have yellowhammer here, but this bird was not performing like a bunting, so I slowly eased my car forward to obtain a clearer view. I was pleased I did, the bird was a magnificent male yellow wagtail, and it was collecting food, it had a beak full of small insects. He was either taking this back to the nest to feed his mate, or to feed possible young.

Tomorrow, weather permitting, we will go osprey hunting, Sarah would also like to do some wild flower photography, and Blithfield has much more on show than Croxall. At Blithfield we have masses of foxgloves and two nice patches of corn cockle and viper's buglass for her.

Later on in the evening I happened to be looking out into my garden when I had a pleasant surprise. On my seed, a solitary stock dove was feeding away, and it was consuming the seed as though it had not eaten for days. Stock doves, locally, are not rare, but this is the first time I have ever seen one in my own garden, and I have certainly never been so close to one. I had to call Sarah through so she too could enjoy the moment. It will be very interesting to see if the dove calls back, or if this was a one off venture on it's part.

Driving down the lane at Blithfield on Saturday we notice three birders looking into Tad Bay through telescopes, this looks a bit serious, so I ask Sarah to pull in. We were only metres away from the birders and as I walk back to ask them if anything is about, one of them shouts 'Spoonbill', I must admit I thought they may have had the osprey. A spoonbill is in a different league, especially for Sarah who has never seen one before. What a start to our morning.

My 'scope was already fitted to the tripod so we were quickly focused up on the bird. It was standing among a few cormorants, so finding a large white bird among a dozen or so black was simple indeed. The bird, unfortunately, was standing as though asleep with it's bill tucked in it's back so we were unable to see the spoon shaped bill from which the bird obviously gets it's name. The bird was standing on one leg, and then it started to preen, and for no more than five seconds the bill was visible, no doubts now about what we were looking at. Sarah was over the moon, and I was very pleased these three birders were here, we could easily have driven straight past and not seen the bird.

We drove on round to the Permissive Walks car park, I thought from here we may obtain a better view of the spoonbill, plus it was here Sarah hoped to do some floral photography. I showed Sarah were the corn cockle and viper's buglass were growing, and we then walked on to the first view point. I was right, we had a very nice view of the spoonbill from this angle, although it was still asleep, or at the very least gave that impression. After a short while Sarah decided to go off to do her photography, I was quite happy to sit down and study the spoonbill.

A new day and I take a trip to Blithfield, especially as I may see the spoonbill again. Just to make it a little more interesting I will list every bird as we see them, be very interesting to see just how many we find. In transit to Blithfield I see, rook, jackdaw, magpie, carrion crow, flush a nice buzzard from off a kill on the verge, I am pleased to say it quickly returned to it, and at Hoar Cross church a wood pigeon. At Blithfield, from the Sailing Club car park, I can add lesser black-backed gull, black-headed gull, mallard and coot to my list. Now over the dam to the Angling Club. Crossing the dam grey heron and pied wagtail, and at the Angling Club car park a moorhen.

The drive down to Ten Acre Bay I collected swift, house martin, sand martin and swallow, all feeding low over the water. In Ten Acre Bay I see shelduck and lapwing. From the Abbots Bromley side I see common tern, three of them feeding close in and a great crested grebe. Crossing over the causeway we flush an oystercatcher from off the parapet and on reaching the far side two cormorant provide us with a flypast. From Tad Bay the first thing I look for is the spoonbill, I am pleased to say I quickly find it and it is mobile, the bird is walking in the water slashing it's enormous bill from side to side as it searches for food, a most impressive sight. Now what else have we on the water, gadwall, shoveler, greylag geese, tufted duck and a small flock of Canada geese fly in. Several mute swan are on the water and a pheasant calls noisily from a nearby patch of woodland. What are we up to now – 31.

Driving back through Abbots Bromley we knock off collared dove and starling and at Woodmill we see goldfinch and blue tit, 33 now in total, but we are not finished there. In Yoxall blackbird and house sparrow can be added to our list.

There you are, 35 birds without once getting out of the car.

Monday is upon us, and after the rain of yesterday it is rather nice to welcome in a nice dry morning. Today the Rosliston Bird Study Group is visiting Cannock Chase, Seven Springs to be precise, for our last stab at our returning migrants. We have a good turnout, 23 hardy souls plus yours truly.

Considering we are nearly halfway through June, birds are very vocal today, probably celebrating the sun after the rain of yesterday. We had hardly got out of our cars before the first blackcap started up, a very nice and bright greeting, and he was quickly joined by a song thrush who gave us his full repertoire. Walking a little way from the car park is an area I always associate with redstarts because nine years out of 10 a pair breed here. Today we were not to be disappointed, a bird is spotted with a beak full of food, a male redstart who is busily collecting food. We stop our advance and just let him get on with it, the last thing he needs is interference from us. Further on activity in a small oak tree draws our attention. Here we have a family party of nuthatch, six in total, feeding away on the insects found on the oak. An oak tree carries a far greater range of insects than any other native tree and is a vital food provider to many insect eating birds, and today the nuthatch were proving this point.

While enjoying the nuthatch, and who does not, I asked for a bit of hush – singing, and not too far away, was a wood warbler. Over recent years this bird has declined in numbers, worryingly so, and Cannock Chase is one of the last places, locally, where we can experience this bird, and I doubt if above half a dozen pairs inhabit all the Chase. The UK breeding population is probably less than 1500 or so pairs, when you look at a figure like that, six pairs on the Chase is quite a lot! While I am typing this narrative I am listening to a CD, Frank Sinatra's *ol' blue eyes is back*, and the final track on this disc is *Noah*, I am always moved by this record, for two reasons, it was one of Dorothy's favourite songs, and secondly for the sentiments it expresses. This song should be the anthem for the Green Party.

From the Chase we arranged to meet up at the lay-by in the lane off Tad Bay to see the Spoonbill, here we can at least park up a few cars as long as we are bumper to bumper so to speak. Our luck was also in, on the near shore stood our quarry, once again with it's head tucked in, does this bird do anything else but sleep I wondered. We quickly got all of our telescopes set up and waited for the bird to show some activity. Several times the bird had a scratch when it used both it's feet and it's bill, not all at the same time needless to say!

As well as the spoonbill, three dunlin were running about on the exposed mud, and a couple of ringed plover species could be seen, these once again were too far away for positive identification. For most of the time we were here at Blithfield, a cuckoo had been calling almost continuously, I have only heard a few this year, where are they all?

On Tuesday I decided to give Chasewater a visit, it must be about a couple of months since I was last here. Looking at the dam repair work, little seems to have happened, the reservoir is still just a series of small lakes/ponds, which are some distance from the nearest vantage point, it is a good job I have brought my telescope.

A fairly large number of lesser black-backed and black-headed gulls are in attendance, the odd mallard and tufted duck have stayed, a decent sized flock of Canada geese are evident, two or three great crested grebe are on the water, with no sign of breeding obvious, and a dozen or so mute swans are loafing about. Not a lot to get excited about.

As I was driving along the Lichfield bypass I noticed a very dark bird perched on a street light, it was too large for a buzzard and fortunately for me the traffic lights decided to change to red. I managed to get a nice view of the bird and could clearly see the white tail from my angle, it was an escaped Harris hawk, some one was not going to be a happy man. I understand Harris hawks are a very popular captive bird of prey. From what I understand, they are a lethal bird of prey, in the States from whence they come, I believe they even hunt in family groups. Although they are not on the British list, I will report this sighting just in case the owner picks up on it, he may then be able to recapture the bird.

On Thursday afternoon I revisited Croxall once again finding it very quiet both on the bird front and visitor numbers, only one car on the car park, and they were dog walkers, so I had the hide to myself. Water levels were again high which was not good news for the smaller waders. The usual oystercatchers were evident, I counted seven on this occasion, and three redshank were feeding on the far shore, but no sign anywhere of any plovers. From the hide the nesting little ringed plover was not visible, and as several carrion crow were about I did not intend to go and see if things were OK, the last thing I wished to do was make them aware of the nesting bird. If it was located by them the plover would have a torrid time defending her eggs against these villains!

Quite a few young black-headed gulls were on the water, and the odd one was capable of flight, it is amazing just how quickly some birds grow, they may not look like their parents, but they soon learn what it is all about.

A family party of shelduck swim past, nine youngsters, she will do very well if she manages to raise all of those, there are three or four lesser black-backed gulls about and they will not turn their noses up at a fluffy young shelduck, life can be very hard when you are young.

On getting home I put out further supplies for my birds and I had hardly got back indoors before the stock dove came in. This bird is now in the garden several times a day, added to my two ducks who are also regular visitors my seeds stocks are going to diminish rapidly, but the pleasure they bring is well worth the cost.

Friday looks very bleak to say the least, heavy rain is forecast for later in the day, and this evening I have a field meeting with my Rosliston Bird Study Group, we are after nightjars once again.

Prior to that event I will have my usual reconnaissance run for Sarah in preparation for tomorrow, and at present I have no real idea of where we will go, there is so little on the net, so it may well be Blithfield once again, here at least Sarah can do some more photography.

The day so far has been one of scattered showers so it is likely to be a day for bird watching from the car. I stop in the lane to view Tad Bay, a decent number of birds but mainly of little interest. As I drive back along the Dairy House Reach I spot a plover legging it along the shore line, eventually it stops, and so do I, it is a ringed plover, so at least I have a bird to report for my efforts.

Come the evening the turnout is very poor really, only five of us, and the tragedy is the fact the forecasters have changed their minds and we may have a dry evening. As with our last visit I send my friends off down into the Sherbrook Valley for an hour or so having shown them where we will meet up at 21.00 hours. I find a suitable spot to sit, under a large beech tree as it so happens, just in case it should rain, I must admit I find my walking stool a perfect tool on occasions such as this. Dorothy bought it for me many years ago when she used to do voluntary work for the NT, little did she know how I would come to use it so frequently.

I had been very pleased to note that several moths were on the wing, the night was pleasantly mild and there was little or no wind. I thought it was building up as the perfect night for nightjars. By now others were arriving on the scene, this location was obviously well known. One large group arrived, 'Friends of Cannock Chase' I believe them to be, but they did not stay by us they moved on further afield. It was now just a question of time and patience.

At about 21.30 hours our first woodcock of the evening came over, and right above our heads, we could not have chosen a better spot. The bird was on it's 'roding' flight, the male patrols it's territory boundaries to protect them from intruders, in much the same way as a blackbird will sing to announce his presence, and woe betide anyone who tries to move in. For three of my friends this was their first ever woodcock, so they were delighted. Over the next 20 minutes or so the bird flew past us on about five occasions, so we had splendid views. Then came the sound we had been waiting for. From a line of beech trees, the very trees I had been sheltering under earlier in the evening, came the call of the nightjar, a mysterious 'churring' sound is the only way to describe it. This only lasted for 20 seconds or so, then all was quiet. Almost from in front of us came the 'kru-ik, kru-ik' flight call of the bird, I quickly brought this to the attention of my friends, out there, just in front of us somewhere, the bird was flying, hunting for night flying insects.

Then the silhouetted shape of the bird came into view, the wings held in the characteristic 'V' that so identifies the bird. While enjoying the bird's skill another bird appeared, we had both the male and female out hunting together, they obviously had large nestlings to feed. At times you could also hear their wing clapping, which in the stillness of night sounds most mystical.

The birds kept vanishing for a short period, obviously they were feeding their young, before back they came, and this was repeated for many minutes before stillness returned, and the birds did not return. They had no doubt satisfied their nestlings appetites as well as their own. What a wonderful climax to the evening, the woodcock had been wonderful, but this had been sheer magic, and I had my 'Year Tick' at last.

These birds have flown up from Africa to breed on Cannock Chase, they are only with us for a short time, and tonight just five of us are standing here absolutely enthralled by two birds, only weighing in at grams, putting on a spectacle such as this. All I know is the fact tomorrow is going to have to produce something special to even compare with this, let alone beat it. At times such as this I realise bird watching is keeping me alive and allowing me to think only of the present, and not to dwell on the past, not that I will ever forget the past, Dorothy and I were too close for that to ever happen.

Saturday again looks dull with rain promised. Blithfield it is to be, and we drove across in dry weather at least. On our arrival a large black cloud slowly moved across and right in our direction. We pulled in at the Tad Bay view point, no spoonbill today needless to say, but a large flock of lapwing had two or three smaller wades among them.

I had just set up my 'scope when down came the rain, fortunately there are many thick trees about so we were able to shelter, mind you the bench was now dripping so I could not sit down. The shower passed over, so up with the telescope once more, focus up on the lapwing, the smaller waders were dunlin, nice summer plumage birds, so although not rare we always like to see them so attired.

As photography was now out of the question for Sarah, we moved on to the causeway, from where we can look down both the bays, Blithe and Tad. Initially nothing of interest was to be seen, until a tern drifted into view. This bird was very accommodating, it landed very close in, we could see the bill colour and also the length of leg, no problem identifying this bird, a common tern.

As we were about to leave I picked up a gull flying towards us, my first thoughts were black-headed, but something was not quite right, so I told Sarah to stop and switch off the engine. The bird got closer and I was very pleased to see it was a first summer plumaged Mediterranean gull. Gulls are notoriously difficult to identify due to their various plumage stages, plus their variance between summer and winter, but I have made a big effort with the Med' gull, as we term it, and today my efforts proved their worth.

Later in the afternoon I decided to have a run over to Whitemoor Haye, popping in at the Alrewas National Memorial Arboretum on the way. I parked up and studied the area through my binoculars initially. Not a lot going on until my gaze moved upwards.

High up above a large bird of prey was circling round as it tried to avoid the attention of a group of corvids, my initial thoughts were buzzard, but no buzzard had wings like this bird, nor such a long tail, what had we here?

Fortunately the bird was circling in a very tight circle, a chance here for the telescope. After a bit of trouble I managed to locate the bird through my 'scope and thought I could see a forked tail, a red kite? Focusing up more critically, this bird was no kite, we had a harrier here, but which species? Time to put brain in gear. I was very pleased the bird was not flying away from me, although it was climbing higher and higher due to the attention of the corvids, they did not like this bird on their patch. I eventually got the view I wanted of the under side of the wings, we had a female hen harrier, and I was delighted. .

Time now to move on, and the Haye here I come. I called in at the quail listening spot, nothing doing today, although I did have a nice dark phase buzzard fly overhead, who for once was not being pursued by the corvids, unlike the unfortunate hen harrier earlier on.

The last couple of days have been very productive, far better than I had anticipated, two 'Year Ticks' for me and one for Sarah, so no one is complaining. The only problem now is what do I do tomorrow, as it is 'Father's Day' which will make some places quite busy, so I am going to have to be a bit selective. I decided I would visit the RSPB reserve at Middleton Lakes. This was not so much of a birding trip, I was more interested in what the reserve had to offer. A new reserve in the Midlands has been long awaited, especially one so near to Birmingham, and when you include this new reserve with Kingsbury Water Park and Dost Hill, it opens up a very large area of the Tame basin. An area well known to us Midland bird watchers, but to have it finally linked up is wonderful.

The entrance to the reserve is off a minor road from the A 4091, the map reference for this will be found at the end of this chapter, and you have to drive for about 1.5 kilometres to the reserve car park. In the past you have been able to entrance from Middleton Hall, but you are requested to no longer use this entrance.

The reserve currently has no information centre or other permanent facilities, but these are due in Phase II I understand, staff were around to assist as required and to pass on information with regard to the birds likely to be seen. There are a few Blue Badge car parking areas, but as parking is free this is not important, the car park being quite large.

I wanted to see just how well us Blue Badge holders would find the reserve, and in this aspect I am a little disappointed. The pathways are wheelchair friendly initially, but within the first 200 metres or so you come to a series of steps, and there is no way you will get a wheelchair down these without assistance, I found them difficult with my sticks being on my own. This being said I found the short distance walked to be very interesting. There is a view point area which overlooks the heronry, this is from a board walk, and although the nests could not be seen at present due to thick foliage, you could certainly hear the herons going about their business. I would think you would get wonderful views of these birds earlier in the year prior to the trees leafing.

Between the board walk and the heronry is a nice open area full of reeds, and reed warbler could be heard singing away. A feeding station at the side had various titmice and finches feeding, a green woodpecker flew across to land on an old tree, and a hobby flew over head. Heron were drifting in an out of the heronry as they flew off seeking food, and the odd one or two of these were this years young, and quite ungainly they looked. Willow warbler and chiffchaff could be heard singing and a whitethroat was kicking up a commotion from a nearby bramble patch.

In this short distance enough could be seen and heard to keep you happy for some time, and earlier in the year it would have been far better. To be fair to the RSPB I do not believe they could have done much more to accommodate disabled people than they have, due to the terrain of the site, and if they had chosen to do more they would have destroyed a lot of what they are trying to preserve. Nature reserves are unique areas and we have to ask ourselves a couple of questions, those being are the reserves set up to protect and encourage wild life or are they there for us to see wild life and hang the consequences of our so doing? It has to be the former statement, not the latter, surely! I will try Middleton Lakes again, probably during the winter if I am fit and able, I feel sure it has much to offer.

I popped over to Blithfield to see if I can find the 7 Sandwich terns that had been reported, I have yet to see one this year. A bit of a 'Twitch' you may say. Twenty minutes at least went by and I was beginning to think my luck was out, when two birds flew out of Tad Bay into the open water in front of Beech Tree Point, and due to their deep wing beat I at first took them to be black-headed gulls. One, however, hovered slightly, and dived, beak first into the water, black-headed gulls just do not do that, I had my quarry.

Sandwich terns are a large tern, being the largest of all our breeding terns, and just in case you are wondering where the name Sandwich came from, they were first identified as a separate species in Sandwich Bay in Kent, they are not particularly tasty on whole meal bread! They are very much a marine tern, breeding round the coast, and few travel across country on migration, they tend to follow the coast. This is why birders are excited to see them so far inland and the original seven, which were first reported, would have been the largest number I had ever seen locally.

The last three days have been exceptional for the time of the year. The nightjars I know were there to be seen, but you had to find them first. The hen harrier and now the Sandwich tern were never on my radar, so thanks to luck in the first case, and the net in the second, I have picked up two unlikely birds to add to my list, which now totals 198.

The Rosliston Bird Study Group and I are at Belvide Reservoir, another reservoir managed by the West Midland Bird Club, and you have to be a member to be allowed to visit. It is a lovely morning for a day out, so I am hoping that Belvide will provide us with some interesting birds. We have a good turnout, 23 in all, so we promptly separate into two groups as no single hide will take that many, so Roy marches off with his party and Len and I take the remainder. We go to the hide closest as I doubt if I will move on from here, the next hide being some distance away, so Len will take them on.

In the reed bed in front of the hide there is much activity from reed warblers, both vocally and physically as they dash about among the reeds, no doubt chasing after insects. Common tern appear to nesting on a raft in front of the hide and they are providing us with superb views, their black-tipped red bills and long legs are really visible, leading us into a perfect identification exercise. A grey heron came gliding over and was obviously going to settle on a tern raft, the one I thought they may be nesting on. Off the raft came two terns who proceeded to attack the heron with such force they drove it off.

Should you visit Belvide it has good footpaths and the first hide is wheelchair accessible, and as you approach the hide there is a well stocked feeding station to view, here we have seen lesser spotted woodpecker in the past, but not today.

It is now Wednesday and the weather today has been very poor, sign Wimbledon is upon us, but I hope to be able to get out for a short while later, with Blithfield being in my sights. My journey across was uneventful, a couple of buzzard and a kestrel was all I could muster, and as I approached Abbots Bromley the sky darkened appreciably. As I pulled into the causeway car park the first spots fell, and within a couple of minutes the heavens had opened. The rain was pounding off my car roof like machine gun fire, and the roadway in front was soon a running torrent of water. Visibility over the reservoir was down to almost nil, all I could do was stay put and await the passing. It did not pass over but my birding for the day was.

Thursday is a far better day so I visit Croxall and I park up at the hide at Croxall and make my way inside, smiling to myself as three oystercatchers fly directly overhead, very vociferously, almost as though they were hurling abuse directly at me. Soon as I opened up the viewing slits I knew I was in for a disappointing visit, the water levels were very high with none of the scrape area visible. A very large flock of Canada geese were on the water, I would estimate at least 300 of them. Today's flock was well spread, probably 200 metres or so, with several being on dry land, so I had a few minutes work ahead of me. I was almost halfway down the flock before I came across something different, a solitary barnacle goose. Continuing on my way two greylags appear and towards the end of the flock a further barnacle, it had been worth the effort put in.

Time now for home, and still none the wiser of where I would be taking Sarah on Saturday. On the way home I stopped off at the Kings Bromley lay-by for a quick look, and who should be strutting off down the river, none other than out old friend the little egret, a nice end to the day. One thing I had noticed today was the number of wild flowers in bloom, so if the birds are not very co-operative, we could well try another photography day, the corn marigolds and poppies looked particularly lovely.

Tomorrow has arrived, and little new with it. So I have a quick look round the Blithfield area, both for flowers and birds and finish off back down Whitemoor Haye. We are at that quiet period of the year, by which time we should have accounted for all the birds locally and just hope for something of interest to pass through. I reached the Newton Shallows picking up nine little ringed plover on the way, got a bit excited over a gull I thought was a yellow-legged, it was not, it was just a pale lesser black-backed, and as I was about to drive back a plover landed on the shore near to me. Was this to be number 10 for the L.R.P's, no, this one turned out to be a ringed plover, which I was more than happy with.

On the return journey I stopped to admire a graceful raven which was flying as though for the sheer enjoyment of it, and why not. Magnificent birds at any time, but this one really put on a show. Time now for a quick tour round the Haye, see if I can locate any birds of interest, if not to make sure Sarah can get at the poppies and corn marigolds for a bit of photography. Just as I started to drive off a partridge dropped into the lane and proceeded to eat pieces of gravel, I was very pleased he had, I can say he, for I was looking at a male grey partridge. I stopped by a nice patch of corn marigold to make sure Sarah could get close to them and I was delighted to find growing in the ditch nearby, a lovely clump of yellow archangel. A cracking bonus for Sarah I would think.

Saturday morning has come in damp and miserable, not a morning for either birding or photography, but we decided to venture forth just in case, we need not have bothered. There were plenty of swifts and hirundines feeding over the lake at Whitemoor, we also managed to see a smartly plumed male yellowhammer, and that was about it The overnight rain had battered down the poppies and even the corn marigolds looked sick, and due to the damp ground we could not get close enough to the yellow archangel to make photography worth while. It is not often we experience a morning such as this, not that we could have done anything about it.

Typically after yesterday, today is going to be a scorcher, or so the forecasters claim, and even at 08.00 hours it feels as though they may well be right. On the net this morning I saw reports of spotted redshank and black-tailed godwit from Blithfield. The journey over was very peaceful and the reservoir car parks were no where as near busy as I had expected. Dairy House Reach was also quiet, just three anglers fishing from here, which no doubt accounted for the absence of birds. On to the Newton Shallows, and as with my recent visit, many birds were to be seen in this quiet bay, far too shallow for the anglers wishes, but perfect for us birders.

I scanned the bay with my binoculars, many duck, a lot of whom are going into eclipse, almost triple numbers of mute swans who, judging by the amount of white feathers along the shore line, have commenced their moult, and a large mixed flock of Canada/greylag geese. Lapwings we have a plenty, many young, and oystercatchers are well up into double figures, but where are the waders we have come for. As I was thinking this to myself a sudden eruption took place, all the smaller birds up to black-headed gull size took off in a frenzy, looking up I could see their problem, a large female peregrine falcon was slowly drifting across. Fortunately for the birds she did not look in hunting mode.

Four large waders, each with a pronounced white wing bar, came flashing in and landed only 30 metres or so from where I was parked, my black-tailed godwits were here. Three of the birds looked quite spectacular, they were in full summer plumage, the fourth, who was not, looked quite dowdy by comparison. They started to feed, now looking completely relaxed. I started to go through all the birds once again, quickly picking out two ringed plover and several little ringed plover, I had not noticed these before the peregrine came through, she had done me a favour that is for sure. A group of Canada opened up and at the back of these had been my spotted redshank, hidden from my view by the bulk of the geese. In today's light the bird looked completely black, it was only when I put the telescope up on it that I could clearly see the silvery speckles on the plumage, they are a gorgeous bird, and we are very lucky to have one in this plumage to enjoy, it really should not be here.

The the Rosliston Bird Study Group are off the Carsington Water for the last session of our term but the turnout is a bit disappointing, only 14. Our first call will be the Sheepwash Hide, a walk of about 200 metres or so, and the track is wheelchair friendly, as is the hide. The only thing to note is the fact a large oak grows alongside the path and a root from the oak has raised a sharp ridge in the path itself, this is about halfway down the track, so do not go racing over this like a Jenson Button, take care.

We have the hide to ourselves, so we settle in and start the business of the day. The shoreline looks very quiet and there are only a few duck out on the water, mainly mallard and tufted. A couple of teal are feeding in shallow water just in front of the hide, and a great crested grebe suddenly pops up with a large fish in it's bill. After a bit of careful a manoeuvring the fish is soon dispatched, I should not think the grebe will want anything else for some time. Len brings me back to earth, he has a plover on the far shoreline, a distance of about 75 metres, so we are going to have our work cut out identifying this one.

We began to piece this bird together, it had pale legs which looked quite orange at this distance, the bill was dark, two conflicting features: the ringed has a black tipped yellow bill and orange legs, the little ringed has a dark bill and muddy looking legs, neither has the description we thought we were looking at. Unfortunately the bird had no intentions of coming nearer, then a bit of luck came our way. A lesser black-backed gull decided to land just where the plover was, the plover took to flight, no distinctive wing bar, we had ourselves a little ringed plover. But this little exercise does illustrate how the light can play tricks with colours, without the lack of wing bar we would probably never have sorted it out. This shows just how easily mistakes can occur, and they are not deliberate.

During the next half an hour or so we saw several little ringed plover, all providing us with the views we required, including the yellow eye ring which is so diagnostic. A couple of local birders came in, whom I knew vaguely, and I was telling them about of experience, when one of them laughed. He said to us, 'Don't worry we have all done it, the best way to identify them at this time of the year is the simple fact we never get ringed plover here, we only have little ringed'. The heat by now was becoming most unpleasant and sticky, so we called it a day and made our respective ways home, most of us thanking our lucky stars for modern cars having such efficient air conditioning.

The next day has started very badly. My old friend Mike Dix, whom I have mentioned previously in this journal, finally succumbed to cancer, and died yesterday morning. Although this was obviously anticipated news, it does not make the coming any easier as I know only too well, so I must get in touch with his wife Sally to offer assistance if required and to also pass on both mine and Sarah's condolences. My times of birding with Mike are now over, but I have my memories of a man whose hearing and eyesight were second to none.

June has now almost come to a close, half of the year is now completed. It looks as though I will close this month on 198 species, I am down by about 10 when compared with the same position last year, and I will be very fortunate to add many more over the next couple of months.

Map references:
Ogston Reservoir – North Bank Car Park: SK 376610.
Ogston Reservoir – West Bank Car Park: SK 375604.
Blithfield Reservoir – Tad Bay View Point: SK 059259.
Middleton Lakes RSPB Reserve Entrance: SP 192966.
Belvide Reservoir: SJ 869097.

Chapter VII

July

My visit to hospital yesterday was not as successful as I had hoped. My various tests were completed and where the results were instantaneous there were no problems, the results of the others I will know within a few days. They obviously were unable to give me a definite date for the replacement, all they could say was I would be in within 12 weeks, which was not the news I had hoped for. This throws all my plans into complete disarray, and could almost write this year off. It could now be the end of September before I have the op', a further six weeks before I am able to drive again so any plans for a few days holiday are now completely on the back burner. I just hope a cancellation comes my way. Unfortunately the medication my doctor gave me has not kicked in as yet, and last night I tried my first sleeping pill, that too had little or no affect, so come tonight I will try a double dose to see if that works.

I am very pleased to see so many house sparrows and greenfinches in the garden, with well over half being young birds, it looks as though they have both had a good breeding season. At times the jackdaws are in double figures and a goodly proportion of these are young, as is the case with the rooks, and the noise they both make is unbelievable.

Today I am off to Blithfield and Croxall and my first port of call was the dam. Driving across it I flushed a few pied wagtails, a couple of lesser black-backed gulls and three meadow pipits. Nothing to set the world on fire there so I drove on down to Ten Acre Bay, here it was also quiet although I did see one little ringed plover while in transit and a family party of lapwing were bathing away at the waters edge, this pair had done very well as they had three large young, all capable of flight. I turned round to drive back and after a short distance my single little ringed plover had become two and a small flock of greylags came crash-landing onto the water, nearly decapitating a cormorant as they came in.

As I was driving onto the dam once again I was considering calling it a day at Blithfield to concentrate my efforts at Croxall, when a large bird disturbed my thoughts. This bird must have been big I remember thinking, as it was right at the far end of the dam and it still looked big. No other traffic was on the dam so I stopped and reached for my binoculars, I was having an adrenaline rush as my heart kept shouting osprey at me. I focused up on the bird just as it vanished from sight, but I had seen enough, it was definitely an osprey, so I raced across the dam, pleased there was no one about to see me speeding.

I pulled in on the Sailing Club car park as the bird circled round, it certainly was a beautiful sight, an osprey no more than 50 metres away, binoculars were not required for this one. A car came from the direction of the club, and I realised it was my friend Eric Clare. We only had the osprey for company for about three minutes but it did put quite a show on for us, including hovering, so we were not complaining. Eric had been down Blithe Bay during the morning and he had seen a wood sandpiper and several common sandpiper, so I decided to go there rather than visit Croxall.

My 4x4 has earned it's keep lately as I bounced, merrily, down the shores of the reservoir. A pair of little ringed plover were going about their business in Admaston Reach, three common sandpiper were rushing along the shore line in Dairy House Reach with four oystercatchers standing quite still watching all this frenzied scurrying about, they obviously did not approve of all this wasted energy! So I finally made my way into Newton Shallows, where I parked up near to the hide.

A large number of lapwings were out on the mud in front of the hide and it was here I intended to concentrate my efforts. Initially, all I could find was a solitary redshank, but there were so many lapwing standing on the mud a small bird such as a sandpiper could easily remain hidden, so I put up my tripod and telescope ready for some serious work.

Behind the bulk of the lapwings a small dark wader was walking quickly by, tail flicking as it went, a sure sign we had a sandpiper of some sort, and only one is as dark as this, it was the wood. Moving on I paused at another wader, thinking it to be the redshank seen earlier, put your brain in gear Brian, look at the markings on the birds back. The bird was a ruff, well the reeve actually as it was the female of the species, and I nearly ignored it. She turned out to be the last quality bird of the afternoon, but it was a lovely start to a new month, eight different waders today: little ringed plover, oystercatcher, lapwing, common sandpiper, wood sandpiper, redshank, ruff and dunlin plus the osprey, and a dozen or so common terns.

On saturday on our way to Blithfield we had one of those wonderful moments, and this was nothing to do with birds, the feathered kind anyway! As we drove down towards the reservoir a large, dark aircraft could be seen coming in our direction, and very low, we managed to pull up to watch it's passing, it was a Lancaster. I believe it to be the only Lancaster still in flight, and what a magnificent sight just a hundred or so feet above our heads, here was our 'bird' of the day. It is going to take something a bit special to compete with this.

We drove off down the side of the reservoir taking the same route as I did yesterday. As we drove through Dairy House Reach a small group of oystercatcher were sitting it out on the shore, a family party of shelduck were out on the water, the ducklings beginning to actually look like shelduck now. We parked up, set up the 'scope, and started our serious birding. The lapwing flock was still in attendance, when Sarah drew my attention to a largish wader. Swinging round to see what it was she beat me to it, a godwit.

Eventually we hit lucky, the wood sandpiper came round a bend in the River Blithe where it had been feeding and proceeded to feed right in front of us, we could not have been in a better position to really study the bird, Sarah was delighted, her 'Year Tick' was in the bag. A very pleasant morning, one Lancaster and one 'Year Tick' for Sarah. We will now have to wait to see what tomorrow may bring.

According to the bird line there is a garganey at Blithfield Reservoir, unfortunately the report does not sex the bird and with the rarer duck I feel they should. You can save a lot of time and trouble with duck watching if you know the sex of the bird you are looking for, so many female ducks are just brown jobbies, and here you really do have to concentrate the mind. Drakes on the other hand are usually bold and colourful, as long as they are not in eclipse.

As I approached Newton Shallows I could see bird numbers were certainly down on yesterday, which I did not mind really, it gave me less to have to look at, and today it was waterfowl not waders which held my attention. The most common duck were tufted, the family party of shelduck were also in the bay, a couple of mallards were escorted by flotillas of ducklings and a flock of about 20 teal were very active, bathing and flying round as though they were enjoying themselves, and why not? Teal were showing well, and teal, especially the female of the species, are very, very similar, to a female garganey, and of course I still did not know which sex I was searching for. A small brown duck sitting fast asleep caught my attention, I could only see the bird's rear end on but it was not exhibiting the pale feathers usually seen at the rear end of a teal, time now for some serious work.

Should the bird I am looking for be the female there were only one or two distinct differences to concentrate on, bill colour being one, this also being stouter and longer, a more pronounced forehead and the lack of pale colour at side of tail base as in the teal. It was now a time for patience and when I am hunting a speciality, I usually have that in an abundance. Nearly 40 minutes passed before the bird raised it's head and started to preen, but the wait had been worth it, a female garganey, I had a 'Year Tick', my first for about three weeks, but it had been worth the wait. As if to say you have seen enough, the bird promptly went back to sleep again, I was a very fortunate man, and this was 199 for the year so far.

Monday has dawned very pleasantly, and having picked Audrey up we arrive at Blithfield by 10.10 hours to find several of our friends from the Rosliston bird group are already there and in birding mode. I sensed excitement in the air, what had they seen?

Apparently, a largish bird of prey had just flown through, only seconds before our arrival, (how many times do you hear that), a bird just slightly smaller than a buzzard. I asked a few questions about just what they had seen between them, and from Alison I got the answer I was searching for, the bird had moustachial streaks, and a pale brownish back, they had obviously just seen a peregrine, and from what I could gather, it was a juvenile female. A cracking bird to start the day with, and we had missed it by seconds. 24 of us turned out this morning, and half of us had missed the peregrine, so let us hope we see something of merit to make up for that disappointment.

We make our way down to the viewing area over Tad Bay, where I can sit on the bench, this is as far as I shall be able to walk today, Len will be taking them round the permissive walk. Just before they move off a little egret flies into Tad Bay. Waving our friends off, the remaining few start to work the mud for waders, there are a large number of lapwing which is to be expected. One small bird quickly becomes five small birds, we have a family party of little ringed plover who are actively chasing flies on the muddy surface, and they are having a bean feast by the look of things. Through the telescopes we can see the muddy surface is crawling with small insects, I can only presume an emergence of some flying insects has taken place, and the plovers are making the most of it. The lapwings suddenly seem to have woken up to the event and they proceed to feed as energetically as their smaller cousins. It is not a morning to be a small fly, that is for sure.

A loud mewing breaks our concentration, a buzzard drifts, very lazily, over our heads, no more than 20 metres or so above us, providing us with a splendid view. You could see it's bright eye as it twisted it's head side to side studying the ground beneath, unfortunately it located nothing so we did not have the pleasure of seeing it stoop, instead it just lifted itself over the trees and was gone.

Not a lot else occurred, the little egret kept on flitting about, and our friends arrived back on the scene. They had not seen a lot, we were able to show them the little ringed plovers which they enjoyed, and it was then time to go home. As we made our way back to the cars, I was bringing up the rear needless to say, I spotted a large bird flying over the trees towards us, quickly drawing it to the attention of the few who were with me, I realised we had the osprey. For only about 10 seconds the bird glided over our heads and was gone from sight.

It is now Thursday and I have done little or no birding since Blithfield on Monday, my mobility has been very poor, so all I have done is watch the birds in my own garden. I have been very pleased with the numbers of young birds seen, especially of chaffinch, greenfinch and goldfinch, if numbers locally can be taken as a yard-stick, they have done very well indeed.

Today I'm off to blithfield, no walking required here. The drive down to the Newton Shallows is not very rewarding, apart from the odd common tern, a solitary little ringed plover and a flotilla of greylags, little is seen. As I approach the Shallows I was delighted to see that a group of birds I first thought to be lapwings were in fact, black-tailed godwits, and there were 23 of them, the majority of which were in summer plumage. A flock this size is quite memorable for our neck of the woods. While enjoying these a small black and whitish wader flew through and landed nearby, it was a green sandpiper, another nice bird to notch up for the day.

The lapwings and black-backed gulls all suddenly took off, only one thing could trigger this type of panic, a bird of prey must be about, a peregrine probably, thinking back to Monday, but I was wrong. Gliding across came our osprey, this had frightened them all off and they need not have worried, osprey are unlikely to take a bird for dinner when the lake is full of trout.

I was driving slowly along the Dairy House Reach when I became aware of a group of sand martins flying very erratically, and glancing in their direction I quickly realised why, a merlin was in their midst, and merlin do not hang about. The bird quickly sorted out it's target and flew rapidly after just one bird, the martin had no chance. The merlin hit it at speed, catching the by now probably dead bird as it plunged to earth, and flew off with it's meal safely held in it's claws. The whole incident took only a few seconds, probably 30 at the most, but what an amazing few seconds. These type of incidents are what makes bird watching so interesting, rarities are fine but when you have the opportunity of this type of experience, you quickly realise the real meaning of bird study.

Friday has come in as a damp and miserable but I have decided to cross the borders into Derbyshire, pay a quick visit to Carsington Water, here, as you may remember, Blue Badge holders park for free, and spend some time in the information hide. If I see nothing else I should see a few tree sparrows, and a yellow-legged gull has been reported. It turns out to be remarkably quiet. I was able to park my car right on the nearest corner to the Visitor Centre/Hide, leaving myself with a walk of about 100 metres. I had the hide completely to myself so I settled myself in for a comfortable spot of birding. The usual duck were in evidence, only one Canada goose funnily enough, they are usually found in droves here, and a nice flock of lapwings. Most of the mallard seemed well into their eclipse state and they were sitting out on the island, and as I was looking through these I came across a large wader, standing erect upon one leg, a black-tailed godwit, a solitary bird, he should have popped down to Blithfield where he could have joined his mates. This bird was in it's full summer plumage like so many of the birds I have seen lately, I can only presume many of the birds have not attempted to breed this year as they should be much farther north than the Midlands.

After several more minutes of reservoir watching I turn my attention to the bird feeders to see how many tree sparrows I can find today. According to a notice up in the hide, 28 is the largest reported total so far. The most I see at any one time is 17, and I was pleased to note that at least half of these were juvenile birds, so it looks as though they have had a good breeding season.

Time to move on, Beeley Moor here I come. The village of Beeley lies just before you reach Chatsworth House, coming from Ashbourne, turn right and drive straight through the village for a couple of miles or so and you arrive on the moors, about 300 metres above sea level, and the whole area is collectively known as the East Moors. Summer is not the best time to visit for the birds, but it certainly is for the wild flowers, and the area I am in today is a blaze of colour, especially from masses of meadow cranesbill and yellow rattle.

The principal areas for birding are the spots west and north of Slagmill Plantation, between the small gas plant and Wragg's Quarry on Beeley Moor, and the Beeley Triangle, where I am today, (Map references for all three sites will be found at the end of this chapter). The minor roads which cross the moors make good vantage points and you are unfortunate if you find yourself disturbed by a lot of traffic. Just be careful where you park obviously. As I start to get my tripod and telescope fitted up the sky goes dark, thunder once again roars about and down comes the rain. The moor just vanished in torrents of falling water, and lightening again flashed round. The rain persisted and after nearly an hour I realised my days birding was a complete wash out.

Saturday has come in a little improved on yesterday we are pleased to say. However, in transit to Newton Shallows the rain did come, but fortunately it did not last long. Oystercatcher, little ringed plover, greylag geese and common tern were all very much in evidence as we approached the shallows, and looking ahead the black-tailed godwit also appeared to be in situ, although the flock did not look so big. It was not, today's numbers were down to 14, so a few have moved on.

Concentrating back on the godwits, I picked up a few smaller waders, two of which were definitely common sandpiper, but three others were partly hidden from view. After a short while they moved into vision, three dunlin, and while watching these a little egret flew directly above them.

For a few days now a Slavonian grebe has been reported from Pitsford Reservoir, in Northamptonshire, so I will go across to have a look for it. I have never visited Pitsford so this will be a chance to see a nice bird and get to grips with a new location. It is only about 70 miles distance, good roads, so it should only take about 90 minutes to do the journey, so unless something mega pops up locally, Northants' here I come. After a bit of late night mugging up I have learned that Pitsford is Northamptonshire's premier bird watching reservoir, and Slavonian grebe are an annual visitor, plus other interesting species, and I have never visited the location! The reservoir appears to have three car parking areas, two at either end of the dam, both having facilities, and one car park at the causeway, this is the one I intend to use as the grebe is being reported from this end of the reservoir.

First impressions of Pitsford are very good. There are large numbers of water fowl to be seen, waders are feeding along the shoreline, several species of gull can be seen and common tern are plentiful The first wader I clearly pick up is a greenshank, that is a very good start to the day's proceedings. This is quickly followed by common sandpiper, little ringed plover and a nice black-tailed godwit, along with many lapwings and just one oystercatcher. No complaints so far.

Time now to move on down to the Scaldwell Arm area, it is from here the latest reports of the grebe have been made. From my vantage point I could see probably 80% of the bay. I must have spent a good quarter of an hour working the area, all to no avail, so I moved further across towards the Walgrave Arm, as large numbers of birds could be seen here. Although I saw many great crested grebe my quarry was escaping me. Second time round I was lucky. I picked up a small grebe diving persistently, but this one had a slender neck so it was not a little grebe, and great crested were far too large to enter the equation. Eventually I got the view I wanted, my Slavonian grebe was in the bag, and I had reached my 200! .

Studying the Walgrave Arm shoreline I came across a large gull eating a dead fish, initially thinking it to be an herring gull I moved off, then something hit me, go back this bird had yellow legs, so it could not be an herring gull. Closer inspection showed this to be correct, I had in fact found an adult yellow-legged gull, another nice bird for the day, Pitsford was living up to it's reputation.

Yellow was soon to become the colour for the day; two yellow wagtails flitted along the causeway, dad with a junior in tow. There were lots of small insects on the warm concrete of the causeway and the adult was picking these up and feeding the young, if I had brought my camera with me I could have got some very nice shots, but you never do, do you? I had not realised how time had flown, so I decided to have one last scan over the reservoir, see if I can find the grebe once more, then we must be on our way home. I did not relocate the grebe, I saw something else which gave me the surprise of my life. A bird I at first thought to be a moulting wigeon started to bathe and raised it's wings but when I caught sight of a white area in the arm-pit, or axillaries to be more scientific, I realised that it was the American wigeon that has this. I went to my car and got out my field guide, I cannot remember the last time I had to do this for myself, but I just had to check to see if my memory was right, it was. The American wigeon does have the white axillaries, what a bird to end the day with. I have not seen an American wigeon for probably 10 years or more.

Monday has dawned, another Rosliston Bird Study Group day, and we are due to visit the Sence Valley Forest Park at Ibstock in Leicestershire, a delightful spot. It is hard to imagine the area was once opencast mining, over 98,000 trees have been planted on the site and it was only opened up to the public in 1998 as part of the National Forest. It is now a very popular area for many people, car parking is free and it has toilets. A very good feature here is the condition of the pathways, without exception they are all wheelchair friendly, there are a few gradients so it may pay to plan your route well, unless of course, your chair is mechanised, then you can whiz along with gay abandon. During holidays and at weekends in the summer months, you regularly get ice cream vendors and soft drink sellers.

The morning is superb, bright sunlight with only a slight, but cooling breeze, and we have 28 members out to enjoy themselves. Due to my current situation with my leg, I am unable to walk with them, so I will drive down to the lower car park where there are picnic tables and await their arrival. I was able to inform them of reports of grasshopper warblers singing and show them the location, so I did not feel completely useless. Roy and Len, needless to say, lead them off.

I sorted myself out a picnic table and sat down to watch and listen. I was being serenaded from a nearby reed patch by at least three reed warblers, a jay was hurling abuse at me from a patch of trees and as I was idling things away a large bird caught my attention as it circled, high in the sky. I had not brought my telescope with me today, so it was down to my binoculars. The bird was gliding on stiff, straight wings, with the primaries down turned slightly, not usual buzzard pose. As I tried to improve my focus the bird hovered. My heart skipped a beat, had I an honey buzzard? Unfortunately, as the thought crossed my mind the bird took off and vanished from sight very quickly. My gut feeling is honey buzzard, but I will never know the answer to the question. I quickly 'phoned up Len on the mobile to tell him what I had seen so they could keep their eyes open.

Time passed by very pleasantly, I saw some common buzzards, heard raven calling, enjoyed the many butterflies which were on the wing in the warm sunshine, and had one or two pleasant conversations with passers by. My friends returned, they had not seen my buzzard but they had notched up the grasshopper warbler, only vocally, but everyone had heard it which is nice. They had also heard chiffchaff seen green woodpecker, common tern, blackcap, kestrel and buzzard, so they were more than happy. We made our respective ways back to the top car park, I was able to give lifts to three, and just before we left we had a nice couple of minutes watching a sparrow hawk attacking a buzzard, and the buzzard did not like it.

Today is my old friend Mike's funeral and it is not often I wear a suit these days. Funeral type services bring back too many memories I am afraid but I am very pleased to say Mike's Memorial Service went very well, the Minister knew both Sally and Mike which showed through in the manner he conducted the service. The church was full of mourners, and I would estimate there were at least 250 people in attendance. Mike certainly had a good send off.

Wednesday and I am off to Blacktoft the journey was uneventful and I arrived at a little after 11.00 hours to find the car park quite full so I was pleased to have the advantage of Blue Badge parking. A report of a marsh sandpiper had certainly brought the birders in, let us just hope it has not flown out overnight! I walked towards my destination I met up with a birder who was able to inform me the bird was to be seen from Townend Hide, and this was 100 metres away from where I now stood. The hide was quite full, but a couple of birders' made way for me to sit, which was very kind of them, so I had a grandstand view of the lagoon. The bird, I had been reliably informed, was to be seen on a small island towards the back of the lagoon, and my informant was smack on. A pale wader stood asleep, standing on one leg, with it's head and bill tucked well into it's back. Not the best of views, but I could see enough to know it was my quarry.

As I slowly panned the lagoon I had a very pleasant surprise, two spoonbill came into view, these were also asleep, bill tucked in and standing on one leg. I had completely forgotten about these birds as I was far more interested in the sandpiper. After a couple of minutes or so the spoonbills started preening and their ponderous bills could be clearly seen both of which had yellow tips to the bill, so these birds were in fact adults, but as they lacked the yellow neck-ring, these birds were both none breeding. As I was enjoying the spoonbills, a whispered, 'The sandpiper is on the move' was uttered, so swinging back to the sandpiper it was now a fully alert bird. It appeared a lapwing had flown in and decided it wanted to land on the spot occupied by the marsh sandpiper, so the sandpiper was left with no alternative but to move a short distance, which enabled us all to get the view we wanted.

As I mentioned earlier, it is a pale looking wader, not unlike a smaller edition of a greenshank, with which it is frequently mistaken if no size comparison is available. Obtaining a far better view of the bird than when it was asleep, I am of the opinion it is a juvenile, and if I am correct the bird may well be only a matter of a few week old, and it has already migrated down to the UK. These birds are not a British breeding species, they are what we term, birds of passage. Nature is marvellous, this little bundle of bone and feather may well have already flown over 1000 miles in it's short life, and I trust the many birders enjoying it today fully appreciate this.

On one of the small islands an avocet is sitting a clutch of eggs, I think she has three. This is late so she may well have lost her first clutch to predation, for ground nesting birds predation is always a problem. A roaming badger, fox or even a rat will not turn it's nose up at the chance of egg eating, plus the fact there are enough marsh harriers about to take the young when first born.

News of the marsh sandpiper's appearance from this hide has obviously spread and people are waiting outside to get into the hide, so I at least will move on and give someone else a chance. So I call in at Townend Hide, and I had only been there for about 15 minutes when I heard the 'ping-ping' call of bearded tits, this call is almost like the twanging sound heard from a guitar cord, and there moving about in the reeds nearby were three bearded tits.

It was now getting close to lunch time, so I called in at the Reception Hide to report my sightings and there I met up with Pete Short, the Head Warden, or to give him his correct title 'RSPB Humber Reserves Warden & Wetland Management Advisor', how would you like that as a mouthful to write down every time you sent out a letter? Pete is one of the old school, a very knowledgeable and respected member of the RSPB team on Humberside. He learned his work from experience in the field not studying at college and this experience shows through in conversation with him. This job is no 9 to 5 effort, it is their life, the clock does not exist for people of this type, and the RSPB are very fortunate in having many like him. To visitors such as me they are a wealth of information and advice. Time now to make my way home, Not a large number of birds to report upon, but they have all been quality, and two of them, the marsh sandpiper and bearded tit were both 'Year Ticks'.

Sunday has come in with mixed weather conditions, but three garganey and a whinchat have been reported from Blithe Bay, so a slow drive down there later today will be my aim. I drive down Admaston Reach, picking up a common sandpiper and two oystercatcher in transit. I notice a bird's head sticking up behind the ridge of the shoreline, obviously a duck of some sort, so I stop to investigate. I was pleased I did, it was a duck goosander, always a pleasing bird to see.

I pull over near the hide in Dairy House Reach, not a spot I usually stop at I must admit but the water levels at Blithfield are still reducing and the mud line is now opposite this hide, and a large number of waders are standing on the mud, the majority of which turn out to be lapwing. The odd smaller wader is busily foraging away among the lapwings so this now becomes a telescope job.

A small group of dunlin first catch my attention, five in total, and two further common sandpiper soon come into view. I am rather surprised to see no black-tailed godwits in attendance as these have been rather regular this year, as you will have gathered yourselves. I give the duck a good going over, although I see a few teal, the duck I would really like to find, the garganey, are no where to be seen.

Tomorrow the Rosliston Bird Study Group are off to Kingsbury Water Park, as both Roy and Len are available for this one I will give it a miss, walking is not my forte at present. Should you wish to visit Kingsbury Water Park be very careful which entrance you go in at, so check the map reference at end of this chapter. This part of the country park is the bird watching area and there are both hides and good pathways all accessible to the wheelchair user, apart from the final hide, this has steps not a ramp, so avoid this. The car park has toilets and is pay on entrance, currently £2.50 per vehicle with no concessions for Blue Badge holders.

Roy called in on his way back from Kingsbury, apparently 14 members of the course turned out this morning, and they had a very enjoyable session, the weather, fortunately, remained dry until they were almost ready to leave. Not being out with my friends for the session seemed a bit strange, but it provided the time to complete my bird breeding survey carried out for Croxall, so the time has not been wasted.

Roy has been doing some work on our behalf with regard to a group bird watching holiday next year, and this afternoon we were hoping to finalise the details. We are looking at the prospects of a week in Scotland, sometime during May, staying at Grantown on Spey, a spot we have visited previously. Roy is awaiting confirmation of the prices they have quoted. Today, we are looking at the locations and the birds we would expect to see, working out the distances of travel and coming up with an anticipated cost. After a couple of hours we had the first draft ready, so once we receive confirmation of the hotel costs we can go to print.

It is Wednesday morning and I have decided to have an afternoon at Blithfield once again, a few waders have been popping through and you never know what may be hidden among them. It is once again very quiet on the birding front, I look as though I have it completely to myself, not that I am concerned with that, I am more than used to being out on my own these days. After a quick glance along the causeway where all I see are a few pied wagtails I start to open up the gate to drive in. As I am doing this a movement on the shore line close by reveals two small sandpiper type species.

One of the birds is certainly a sandpiper, a common sandpiper in fact, but the other bird is slightly larger and more uniformly darker, for a second or two I wonder if I have a pectoral sandpiper and a bit of an adrenaline rush starts on this thought.

Calm down, it is not, the bird I am studying is a wood sandpiper, not that these birds are to be sniffed at, this is probably only my third sighting of the year.

Time now to drive down to the Newton Shallows. Once again there are many wagtails about chasing small flying insects of which there is a still an abundance, fortunately they are not the biting type, they are just an irritation. The shelduck family group are now well broken up, common terns are plentiful with a goodly smattering of youngsters among them, and a small family party of tufted duck swim by, mom with four ducklings. Cloud is now starting to build up, the rain may well arrive after all, even if later than forecast, so I drive on a little further along the shore, this time pulling in a hundred metres or so from my usual parking spot in the Shallows, here I have a sweeping view of the bay. It is a case of up telescopes from here, this quickly done I start to pan the bay. I quickly locate the lapwing flock and slowly make my way through these, and tucked in among them are three greenshank, a juvenile and two adults, no doubt a family moving through on migration. I could find nothing else and the first spots of rain started to fall, so home it will be.

Thursday has dawned, grey and miserable looking, but no rain is actually falling at present, although the ground is damp from overnight rain. I am hoping the rain does pass over, as looking in on the net I see a group of 30 or so crossbills were reported from Coppice Hill, on the Chase, yesterday afternoon. I have seen crossbill previously this year, but that was just a small number early in January, a nice flock is something different, a very good reason to get my morning duties completed as quickly as possible.

Coppice Hill is located in the middle of the Chase, there is a parking area provided, this is rough, but as no charges are levied we cannot really complain. This area can be very quiet, so when parking leave no valuables in view as the odd break in has occurred, it actually happened to me one night many years ago. Because of this I only visit this spot during daylight hours, and I am pleased to say I have had no problem since that occasion. The birds were last seen in a nearby larch plantation which lies about 50 metres due east of the car park. The pathways and tracks in this part of the Chase are just about wheelchair passable, but do take care. And I suggest you go with company, just in case of a mishap. To give you some idea of the terrain, I was quite happy to do it with the aid of sticks, so conditions underfoot are not that bad, just be cautious.

I must have stood around for nearly half an hour when I heard a sudden burst of sound, the birds flew in directly above my head 'Chip, chip, chipping' away, as though their very lives depended upon it, to land in a flurry on a larch close by. The noise of their eating was quite audible to say the least, and pieces of cone were drifting down onto the ground beneath.

Crossbill love larch, unlike many of the other conifers, the cones of the larch are quite flaky and soft, so they can get at the seeds contained therein, with the minimum of effort. Their calls at this stage sounded very conversational and had quite a musical tone to it, something I had never been aware of previously. After a good 10 minutes they erupted into noise and off they flew, crossbill time was now over. I waited several minutes for their return, they did not, so I made my way back to the car, while doing so a green woodpecker flew across my path 'yaffling' away as he went. I did not mind him laughing at me, I had seen what I came for. And he was not a bad looker either!

Should nothing new come along, Sarah and I will probably come across here on Saturday, for, hopefully, a repeat performance. When entering my report of the crossbills on the net I noticed a Brent goose had been reported from Blithfield, if that hangs around then this will be our target bird for Saturday, Sarah has yet to see one this year so far. The only problem, once again, with this report, the location at Blithfield for the goose was not logged, and with a 10 mile shoreline it could be anywhere.

The weather today is absolutely glorious, light cloud shielding the real strength of the sun, a very slight breeze, and a nice temperature of about 20 degrees, what more could you ask for? The Brent goose hopefully!

The water at Blithfield looks like a mill-pond, hardly a ripple, just the odd fisherman about, and surprisingly in view of the weather, very few visitors, the ice cream vendor was not doing a brisk trade today for some reason. I let myself in, no excitement today with sandpipers, only a solitary oystercatcher to greet me today. I completed my first sweep of the lapwing flock without too much to get excited over and started to work my way back through them, while doing so, something small and yellowish flew through my 'scope. Quickly, trying to relocate the bird, I came across it again, it was a delightful female yellow wagtail, a bird always worthy of a second look. I was about at the end of my sweep when a wader ran, quite briskly, into view, a greenshank, another bird it is always nice to see, you certainly can never see too many.

My experience of Brent geese has always lead me to the conclusion they do not like to be a solitary bird, they are far more contented when they are in and among other geese, not necessarily Brent's, any species will do. As I knew the largest number of geese at Blithfield were regularly to be found down Blithe Bay, I had assumed this was the spot for the Brent, it was now time to put the thought to the test. Through my telescope I could see a large number of geese tucked in at the top end of the bay, so I drove myself round to the last hide in the Newton Shallows, and here I set myself up.

The geese were across the other side of the bay, about 100 metres or so, but through a 'scope this was of little consequence, geese are, after all, large birds. I started my sweep at the extreme right hand end of the geese and slowly worked my way along, they were spread out in a long, thin line, which helped me as not many of the birds were obstructed from view by one of their fellows. It did not take me long to finds the bird I was after, it was right in front of others, almost as though it wanted to be seen and admired, and why not?

We usually associate Brent geese with winter when we experience very large numbers wintering along the coast, especially the east coast, and you will recollect my writing about them when I was in Norfolk in March. They are a beautiful small goose, and to see one locally is always a moment to saver. I just hope this one hangs around for another 24 hours so that Sarah will have a chance of seeing it.

Saturday has come in very pleasantly. Driving down the track at Blithfield we saw very little, just the odd oystercatcher, lapwing and mallard, with many moulting mute swans needless to say. The most exciting sighting was a family party of three little ringed plovers. Time now to up telescope and start to do some serious work. I worked my way through the flock twice, no Brent, Sarah took over with the same lack of success, the goose was no where to be seen. We decided to pop round to have a quick look in Tad Bay just in case the bird had moved round the corner but as we got into the car we heard that most magical of bird calls, a curlew was letting rip and swinging round we could see the bird flying low over the water, calling as it went. I do not suppose we heard the bird for more than 30 seconds before it had vanished, but what a 30 seconds, we did not care about the Brent right now. This was a good job, as we could not find the goose in Tad Bay either!

Sunday, and as a little tern has been reported from Blithfield, I made my way to the dam. I had hardly stopped before I noticed several terns flying close to the dam, and what was of particular interest was the fact two of the terns looked decidedly smaller than their companions, surely I cannot have hit straight onto my target bird this easily. I got the view I was after, both the birds had yellow bills with a dark tip, and when combined with their smallness in size, these were obviously little terns, and both adults. Driving over the dam I got a much closer view as one of the birds rose above the parapet at I drove past, no need for binoculars here. I drove on down towards Ten Acre Bay which did not look too good, a couple of anglers were fishing from the shore, this type of angling and birding are not compatible I am afraid. My first pass found nothing so I repeated the process and as I did so a small bird rose up and ran along the island, a common sandpiper, had it not moved I doubt if I would have seen it, the birds camouflage was perfect for the terrain.

Two nice birds so far, now off down to the shoreline from Admaston Reach, would we be lucky here? Initially no, there was hardly a bird to be seen along the shore and only the odd grebe and cormorant on the water, it is a long time since I have seen it this quiet. As I reached the Dairy House Reach, where there were a few more birds to be seen, terns and gulls mainly, these suddenly erupted. Flashing across the reservoir came a female hobby, and this bird was motoring. She just veered off and within seconds was gone, this bird was just out for a bit of fun. I motored on to the last hide, and here I pulled up to survey the goose flock and study the waders still to be seen in the bay. The geese were just greylags and Canada geese, no Brent once again, and the waders looked to be all lapwing, until a smaller bird ran into view, a dunlin, and eventually one became four. Here I ate my lunch, and while I was enjoying this I heard a deep croak, and gliding in came two raven. They settled onto the ground where they had obviously seen something edible, and proceeded to hack a dead fish to pieces, much to the annoyance of a nearby heron who looked as though it also had designs on the carcass. Large as a heron may be, I doubt it would have tackled a raven, specially when it is two!

Driving back, I just called in at the Kings Bromley lay-by and I was pleased I did, two little egrets were strutting about in the river, and they seemed to be finding much to savour.

Monday looks to have the promise of being a beautiful day, not overly warm early on, a nice cooling breeze and rain not on the agenda, we can but hope. The Rosliston Birders and I are off to Belvide but I think this may well be my last venture forth with them prior to having my op, whenever that may be, I do not think it is fair for them to be lumbered with me. They are all very kind, but these are their trip out, and I have no wish for any of them to think they are obligated to stay with me, so it is time to withdraw I think.

While we were getting ourselves ready for the off Len called me across to his telescope, he had found a small, bright yellow bird, in a small tree nearby. I moved across to have a look, we had a juvenile willow warbler or chiffchaff, but which? We needed leg colour, but seeing legs on a very small bird at this distance is not easy. Eventually Roy came to our aid, black legs, we had a chiffchaff, and a very bright coloured bird it was. A nice start to Belvide, and a very good example of how important small detail can be. Since our last visit to Belvide the Bird Club have carried out some further work, they have now erected an hide at the feeding station. The hide is also wheelchair friendly, so at last the disabled can obtain pleasure from a visit. The feeding station was very active, we had all the titmice except willow tit, green, gold and chaffinch were enjoying themselves on the seed provided and tree sparrow must have reached double figures. On the ground beneath the feeders a moorhen and female pheasant were feeding away, accompanied by a small rodent, probably a wood mouse. All were gorging themselves fully on the seed provided, and good luck to them. A great spotted woodpecker could be heard but not seen, and a nuthatch made lightening raids.

Now for Scott Hide, we just about all managed to get in which was a change. Common tern were feeding young on the rafts in front of the hide, and I was surprised to see how large a fish the young would take, just a swallow, followed by a gulp, and they were ready for more. Scanning the dam Len picked out three common sandpiper, and a real telescope job these were, they were almost invisible through just binoculars. At this stage Roy took half off to visit the northern end of the reservoir, Len stayed with his half for a little longer. The mute swan flock was small by Blithfield standards, totalling only 51, and these all appeared to be adults which did surprise me. In the reed bed in front of the hide a reed warbler could be heard calling away, and the odd flicker of a reed could be seen, but no good view was to be obtained.

Len now prepared to move off, after a bit of gentle persuading, all left with him leaving me to my own devices. Shortly after their departure three duck came flying in very fast and as they landed up went their wings, a nice white wing bar showed, three gadwall, every other duck up to this point had been mallard. Working my way through the birds on the water I counted 17 great crested grebe, all moulting through from their summer plumage, many were looking quite white in fact, and a little grebe was calling from the reed bed in front of the hide, they have a lovely trilling song which I always enjoy hearing. Hirundines were not very numerous today which did surprise me, there were enough small insects on the wing, even I could feel them. Swifts were a little more evident as they came screaming through at a rate of knots. Time has caught up with us, I must make my way back to the car park to meet up with my friends, and as I left the hide I had the bird of the morning, a male hobby came hurtling through in hot pursuit of a martin of some sort, they vanished from sight behind a clump of trees so I never will know if the bird had caught his dinner or not.

A pleasant morning it had turned out to be nothing mega, but a few nice birds shared among pleasing company, you cannot ask for more than that surely! Tomorrow is not going to be one of my better days, three years ago, by the date, my dear wife Dorothy died, and the passing years have not eased the pain of losing a loved one, contrary to what people say. Dorothy was cremated at Sutton Coldfield Crematorium,

I chose Sutton Coldfield as this was where Dorothy was born, so it was as though I was returning her home. Each year since I visit the Crematorium, take a few flowers and spend some time in thought, and I have to admit, it does me good. I just hope Dorothy knows I am doing this and also knows how much I still think of her. Bye my love!

The 26 July has dawned, I did not sleep particularly well last night, and by mid morning I am on my way to Sutton Coldfield. I have a nice small bouquet of carnations with me, one of Dorothy's favourite flowers, yellow in colour, the colour she had chosen for her wedding bouquet some 53 years ago. Tucked away in a little corner of the 'Garden of Rest' lies a small pond and it was here Dorothy's ashes were scattered almost three years ago, a quiet, peaceful spot, ideally suited to Dorothy's temperament, and where I wish my ashes also to be scattered.. I laid my flowers on the grass, saying a few words as I did so and then sat down on a nearby bench, alone with my thoughts. I sat here for almost 45 minutes, deep in thought, the occasional tear rolling down my cheek. I could also hear the occasional bird calling, a robin particularly so, I thought he was going to land on the bench at times. A green woodpecker could be heard laughing away, a great spotted woodpecker also joined in on occasion and a buzzard was mewing away high above, but it could not be located. On the pond a moorhen had a family party of three young, these were very downy and I doubt if they were above a couple of day old. It was nice to see these, at a place associated with closure on life, we could also see a beginning to life, thank you moorhens, you have helped me today far more than you could ever realise.

I drove home in a contented state of mind thanks to a few birds, I was very pleased I had made the journey, and I will continue to do so for as long as I am able. Moments shared with loved ones, even though they are no longer with us in a physical sense, are to be treasured, and do not let any tell you otherwise.

This afternoon I have an appointment with my doctor but they knew no more than I, although he was going to make enquiries, but I suppose there is only so much your local doctor can do in these circumstances, after all it is not a case of life or death. Mind you, I feel I have now lost almost a year of my life while my problems have been investigated. He also decided to try me with a change in medication, something to help with my pain and discomfort, if this could be controlled I would feel a lot better. When I returned home I found my garden in a right state, collared dove feathers were scattered all over the garden, our local sparrowhawk had obviously been in and made a kill.

Thursday is going to be a day of mixed fortunes, not that I realised this early on. The post arrived somewhat earlier than usual and in it were two letters from the hospital, one confirming a date for my pacemaker annual check-up and the other, more importantly was a date for my for my hip replacement operation, 7 September. Although this was about three weeks earlier than originally quoted, I must confess I was not in very high spirits with the news, the 7 September seemed a long way from 30 June when I had my pre-op' assessment.

Imagine my surprise, when about 30 minutes later I receive a telephone call from the hospital asking could I come in for my operation on Thursday 10 August, a cancellation had just been reported. It did not take me long to answer that question! I was able to make arrangements for a blood test that was necessary prior to my op' and also arrange for my pacemaker check-up to be brought forward too, after the original gloom, the day had brightened up considerably. Then to put some icing on the cake, the surgery 'phoned in to let me know the blood test I had yesterday had proved negative so there were no problems there. All in all a very successful morning it had turned out to be, eventually. Due to all these comings and goings I was rather late with my work for the day, so any ideas I may have had for a trip out this afternoon were well and truly dashed. Never mind, I had the news I wanted, so any birds will now have to wait until tomorrow.

The post was nice and early this morning and in it was confirmation from the hospital with regard to my op', blood test and pacemaker check-up, very efficient I think. Roy has also 'phoned in, he is happy with the letter I have prepared advertising the Scottish trip, so this can be printed and distributed on Monday to all those attending the field meeting, which incidentally, is Chasewater. Margaret can then e-mail it to the reminder. We would like to get it put to bed by mid August, especially as with my being out of circulation shortly, I do not want it all to fall on Roy's head. The day has remained grey but the temperature is still perfect, so Blithfield here I come. I have a few words with a birder who has been here some time, he has seen little to get enthusiastic about, but as he is not a member of the bird club all his viewing has been from the causeway. I have a feeling the club is going to get one new member!

I open up, drive through, I had only travelled a couple of hundred metres of so, when a large gull caught my eye, it was having a bathe in the shallows. My first thought was herring gull, but I slowed down to have a better view, my window was already lowered which helps, and I was able to view the gull from about 20 metres or so. The gull stopped bathing and proceeded to groom itself, and it's yellow legs soon became visible, that knocked my herring gull theory on the head, they have pink legs, had we a lesser black-backed gull, they are the common gull with yellow legs. I concentrated further, no this was no lesser black-backed gull, it must be the yellow-legged gull, we did see one very close to this spot a few days ago. But I still was not happy, so I picked up my telescope to have a better view, and I was glad I did, this bird had dark eyes, not the bright yellow eyes of the yellow-legged or herring gull for that matter, here we had a Caspian gull, remember him from Norfolk in March, and a very nice adult too. I have a feeling this may be my first Caspian gull for Blithfield, a very nice bird to start the day with.

The gull became bored and took to the air, vanishing in the direction of the dam, leaving me to concentrate on my driving. I had not driven far before a large bird caught my attention, initial thoughts being great black-backed gull, but when I realised the bird was being harassed by terns, I became more interested. Stopping once again I quickly saw it was an osprey which was doing it's best to avoid the terns, but they could out-manoeuvre him any time. Fortunately, from the osprey's point of view, they quickly tired of the game and left the osprey to get on with what ever it had planned to do. Unfortunately for me, the bird vanished round the corner of Beech Tree Point into Tad Bay. Not that I was complaining, it had been an entertaining few minutes, I just hope we are as lucky tomorrow for Sarah, she has still yet to see her first osprey for the year.

I moved my attention over to the terns, there must have been over 20 of these and they were now busily flying low over the water off from the Beech Tree Point, taking, I presumed, insects off the surface of the water. At this distance it was impossible to tell exactly what they were, although one bird in particular caught my eye, it's flight was far heavier than the remainder of it's colleagues. I have a sneaky feeling this was a Sandwich tern, but at this distance we will never know the answer. Enough here to bring Sarah back for come tomorrow, although I doubt the Caspian gull will remain, but you never know.

Saturday dawned and Blithfield was very quiet, not a single car on either of the causeway car parks, it has been a long time since I last saw that on a weekend. We opened up the gate, drove in, and had not travelled very far before we spotted several terns feeding on the water just a little way ahead. We stopped and proceeded to study these closely, there were about a dozen birds, all looking like common terns but one caught my eye. This bird was performing just as the bird I saw yesterday, but today it was a lot closer, probably no more than 40 metres away, so I pointed the bird out to Sarah, telling her to try to get the bill colour, her eyes being far better than mine. Black with a yellow tip is what we are after, and the head needs to be squared off at the back.

The bird, eventually, comes in quite close and even I can see the bill is black with a yellow tip, we have our Sandwich tern, and for Sarah she starts the day off with a very nice 'Year Tick'. After a few minutes the birds drift off over the reservoir to become just mere specks of white in the distance, but we do not care. We now proceed further down the reservoir, and park up in Dairy House Reach.

A large flock of mixed lapwing and starling are out of the drying mud, feeding on insects that can be seen on the muddy surface, these look fairly large through the binoculars. The large flock of Canada/greylags are still in residence, there are well over 300 of these, and we must have 20 or so grey heron scattered along the shoreline, or what is left of it. While all of this is being taken in my eyes wander to a large tree in the distance, on this sits a large bird, and it looks too large to be a buzzard. Time for telescoping I think.

I point the tree out to Sarah so she can keep her eyes on it while I erect the tripod. Tripod up, 'scope focused, and at along last Sarah has her osprey. I quickly call her across to have a look, and we were very lucky, within a few seconds of Sarah looking at the bird it was up and away, over the woods to Tad Bay. Sarah was over the moon, she had her osprey for the year, it felt as though the pressure was off, her second 'Year Tick' in the matter of a few minutes.

As we still had some time we decided to finish off down at the dam. A tern was resting on a small buoy, so we stopped to have a clearer look, this fellow had very short legs, we had a juvenile Arctic tern in view. As we watched it an adult came down and passed over a small fish, which the youngster quickly swallowed. Arctic terns do not breed locally, so even though this bird was a young one it had probably migrated over 100 miles from where it was first hatched, and the adults obviously feed the bird in transit, this is something I have never seen before. Driving over the dam a flash of yellow takes to the air in front of us, a yellow wagtail, and as we slow down to enjoy the bird a further two are flushed from the grassy verge. You never tire from seeing yellow wagtails, they are delightful birds.

Time for my evening meal, along with a nice bottle of wine, tonight I think it will be a rich, smooth claret. Care to come round and join me? I may not be the best cook in the world, but my choice of wine is usually good!

127

The end of the month is nigh, and where to finish off is the question. I had thought of visiting some of the Derbyshire waters but decided to pop up to Tittesworth and probably finish with the moors. Tittesworth has the benefit of a nice café as you will probably remember and I can park close to the birds, thanks to my Blue Badge.

The River Churnet is now very shallow and in parts it is just about flowing: rippling over the stones is the best way to describe it. A couple of pied wagtails are seeking flies in these shallows and a chiffchaff could be heard calling. A movement above my head caught my attention, it was three spotted flycatchers, two adults with one juvenile, the juvenile was no mug, it had learned to catch flies very quickly, and was also very proficient at it.

It was a day of movement not song, and due to the leaf canopy clear views were not easily obtained. I thought I caught a sight of a redstart, but could not be sure, a fairly tame robin was no problem, however, and a mewing buzzard was easily identified by it's call.

I pulled in on the first car park, this gives a good view of the northern end of the reservoir and the island usually boasts a wader or two, but not today, the island was almost land locked, just separated from the shore by a narrow strip of water. The only waders were three lapwing, and due to the lack of water very few duck were evident. The gulls were enjoying themselves, someone had brought in a good supply of bread and a fair amount of this was still scattered along the shore. The majority of the gulls were black-headed in various plumage conditions, two or three lesser black-backed and as I was about to move on a small gull with very dark undersides to it's wings dropped in. What a treat, a nice adult little gull. As I have no doubt mentioned, probably many times, the little gull is very tern-like in flight and once you get your eye in they are quite easily picked out from among other smaller gulls.

Nothing new to finish the month off with, but it had been an enjoyable few hours, and I close on 203 for the year. No complaints there.

Map references:
Beeley Moors Triangle: SK 293677.
Slagmill Plantation: SK 303681 and SK 310688.
The Gas Plant and Wragg's Quarry: SK 285663.
Pitsford Reservoir –dam car parks: SP 761686 and SP 753693.
Pitsford Reservoir – Causeway: SP 786700.
Sence Valley Forest Park: SK 404118.
Kingsbury Water Park – Broomey Croft Entrance: SK 205969.
Cannock Chase – Coppice Hill: SJ 981193.

Chapter VIII

August

August has not come in as I would have liked. During the night I have been ill, having to get up a time or two due to sickness, so I was not able to enjoy my final day out with the troops. Not a lot of interest was seen this morning at Chasewater I have been informed, the open area of water and mud which was in the centre of the reservoir had dried out appreciably so obviously the dam repairs have not been completed and water is still being withheld from the reservoir.

My hospital day is now here, firstly I have a blood test, then this is followed up by my pacemaker test, fortunately I was able to arrange them for the same day. As things turned out, the wait for my blood test was quite lengthy, they were very busy, and when I arrived for the pacemaker test I was able to go in a quarter of an hour early, so I was home shortly after lunch time.

The following Thursday I have to stay in as I am due some healthcare products needed to assist my recovery from the hip operation, if these are delivered early enough I may get out. The spoonbill was still at Blithfield today, and a turnstone was also reported from Admaston Reach, and I believe Sarah needs one of these for her 'Year List'. Given the chance I will suss these out. I think a couple of hours birding is thoroughly recommended, and earned!

I was disappointed on my arrival to find workmen were busy working in Admaston Reach, they were putting out the floats of barley used in the control of green algae, so that was goodbye to any chance of finding the turnstone here. Never mind, I opened the gate and drove down towards the Shallows, with little visible for the first 50 metres or so. I picked up the odd oystercatcher, lapwing and black-headed gull, but there was little about. The odd cormorant flew through and in the distance great crested grebe could be seen, it looked as though disturbance had been greater than I first thought.

I was well into the Dairy House Reach before birds of any consequence were to be seen. Lapwing numbers were now quite high, four or five species of duck were scattered about on the surface of the water and down into the Shallows the large flock of geese were still to be seen. Working my way through the lapwings there were no other waders to be found, just several starlings, the turnstone was not tucked in among these. A slight commotion occurred, as two buzzards slowly circled above, but the duck soon settled down again, they had nothing to fear from buzzards.

Another heavy shower started so I turned and drove slowly back along the reservoir intending to go round to Tad Bay to see if the spoonbill was still in attendance. Pied wagtails were very evident, this would have been a good opportunity for novices to have got to grips with their various plumage states as we had adults, both male and female, and likewise juveniles, one or two of the latter could easily have been mistaken for white wagtails.

Tad Bay was full of birds, most of the swan flock had moved into this bay, plus more geese, several species of duck and 30 or so cormorants making up the numbers, but the bird I was looking for was no where to be seen, it looked as though the spoonbill has moved on. As I still had time to spare I made a quick trip round to the deep end to see if anything was to be found off the dam. Apart from pied wagtails the dam was very quiet, as was the drive round to Ten Acre Bay, very disappointing really, then we had that one short moment of pleasure, and the reason why the bay was quiet soon became obvious. A female hobby came hurtling across the bay, the speed of her approach even put two cormorant to flight, not that they need have worried, they were far too large for an hobby's interest. This certainly accounted for the absence of smaller birds, if the hobby had been round for some time all the smaller birds would have moved on to pastures new, and who could blame them?

Later in the evening I had a telephone call from Roy, there are now definitely eight of us who wish to visit Scotland next year, so we are going ahead with our plans.

Blithfield it is to be today, and on arrival the reservoir looks like a mirror, it is so calm, hardly a ripple disturbs the surface, perfect for birding. I pull up on the rough lay-by in the lane over looking Tad Bay, the last reported place for both the osprey and the spoonbill. It is going to be a telescope job the reservoir seems to be receding daily. I spent a good 10 minutes looking for the spoonbill, with no luck, and I was just about to move off when most of the birds on the water took to flight, they were in panic mode. A quick glance up into the sky showed why, gliding across came the osprey, and it was not interested in the panic caused, if it was hungry then fish would be it's prey. The osprey quickly glided out of sight and sanity returned to the scene. Unfortunately, no spoonbill was seem in the commotion.

As I open up the gate onto Admaston Reach I pick up a small wader running along the shoreline. The bird is a common sandpiper, and before I can get a good view it flies off up the reservoir. The Reach was very quiet just a few greylags on the shore but on reaching Dairy House Reach things brightened up considerably. A bird of prey came past at speed, flying very low, at first I took it to be a merlin, but it was too large, this bird was a hobby. A group of pied wagtails were foraging along the shore and these took to desperate flight, but one young pied wagtail has lived a very short life.

Most of the birds had flown out of Dairy House Reach after this performance so I drove on down to the Newton Shallows. I think we had better change the name, the Shallows are now dried land with vegetation springing up and sheep grazing there on. The geese were all congregated right down the bottom of the Shallows so it was going to be a telescope job to sort all these out.

My first pass showed up only Canada and greylag, but I decided to do a return run and I was pleased I did. Halfway through my sweep some geese commenced to climb up out of the River Blithe onto the dry ground and these birds had lovely grey backs, barnacle geese and 15 of them climbed up out of the river.

Not a lot more was picked up, and I did not find the common sandpiper so time to go down to the dam. The first bay after the Sailing Club is Mickledale Bay and as I drove into this I was surprised to see a great spotted woodpecker fly across in front of my car and land on a fence post nearby attacking it with relish, with my car windows down I could really hear it 'bashing' away, I just hope it was finding something edible after all this effort. Driving down into the bay I picked up four yellow wagtails, a nice little family group of two adults and two young. The next bay is Portfields Bay. Apart from a few pied wagtails this bay looked quiet until I noticed two dunlin were feeding away, these two were quite drab looking little birds, obviously two juveniles.

When Martin arrived he told us that as he drove through Kings Bromley this evening he thought he had seen eight little egrets, but once again traffic was heavy so he could not stop to confirm his sightings. After dinner, Sarah and Martin decided to pop down to Kings Bromley to check out the little egret situation, leaving me to finish the clearing away, I am sure the little egrets were secondary to escaping the work!

They were soon back, they had not seen eight little egrets but they did account for five, and more significantly, a green sandpiper was also in attendance, a very nice report this. Sarah and Martin duly placed these reports on the net, and when we go out in the morning it will be interesting to see if they are still there.

Kings Bromley still had it's five little egrets and the green sandpiper was also busily feeding away in the shallows. It was a very nicely marked bird still showing much of it's summer plumage, the little egrets were, unfortunately, just a little too far to be able to age these with any certainty, but in a group of this size I would presume there to be some juveniles.

On to Croxall Lakes. Things were very quiet, only one car in the car park so we were not going to be over-run by visitors today. It did not take us long to pick up the first greenshank, it was standing on a mud bank, on one leg, with it's head tucked back, presumably asleep. Working the far shore Sarah located the other greenshank, this bird was actively feeding away in water, which is why it has long legs and a long bill. While enjoying the greenshank two redshank came into view, these too were wading quite deep, except their legs and bills are not as long as the greenshank so they feed in shallower water.

As we had some time left we decided to pop down to the Haye, the turnstone may well have gone across to the lake there, a reasonable thought, but no, it had not. We did, however, have a nice grey heron and a common sandpiper to keep our interest going. Just as we started to move off a bird of prey came flying across at speed, a nice male hobby, probably only the second or third Sarah has seen this year, so she was more than satisfied with this sighting.

A circuit of the rough lane would just about finish the morning off nicely for us, and this turned out to be a good decision. Near the feeding station in the lane we saw about 25 tree sparrows, a tidy little flock this, and to really finish the morning off, in the tree near the micro-light landing strip we actually saw two little owls. They may not have been 'Year Ticks', but they were a cracking bird to end up with.

Sunday has been forecast as a day of bright periods with scattered, sometimes heavy, showers, definitely a day for birding from or near to the car, so Thornton Reservoir and Groby Pool it will be. I am taking a gamble on Thornton, but looking at the map and reading up a little it does look as though the whole of the reservoir can be viewed from the car park at the western end of the dam. It is comparatively small, 76 acres, easily within telescope distance I would say.

It was a pleasant run across, only taking me 45 minutes, and the weather certainly was to forecast, the only thing they had not mentioned was hail, this rattled off my car on one occasion as though someone had thrown a handful of grit over my car, it is only August is it not? This car park is the one at the westerly end of the dam, and although it is not large it does have half a dozen or so places reserved for the disabled, and these are in a perfect spot, right on the side of the reservoir with nothing to obstruct your view. At the end of each plot is a bench, perfect for use with a telescope and tripod, and from this point a good 95% of the reservoir is in full view. Parking is free, there are no facilities but just opposite the car park is a garden centre with a café, so I think it is safe to presume they would have full facilities.

The reservoir is obviously very popular with the locals with several family groups out feeding the ducks etc., two or three boats are on the water with fishermen employed thereon, and people can be seen walking the perimetre of the reservoir, not on the shoreline I hasten to add they are on a public footpath, so the birds are not unduly disturbed by their presence.

I start off by panning the westerly arm, little down here although I do catch sight of a tern, at this distance I will presume common, and on the water are tufted duck and the odd pair of grebe. A few Canada geese fly in but they are only interested in food. As I move along the shoreline in front of Brown's Wood two oystercatcher appear and start to feed on a muddy area, being harassed by a black-headed gull as they do so. Further along a smaller wader appears rushing along the shoreline, it stops and promptly bobs, this has to be a sandpiper of sorts. Zooming in I find myself looking at a green sandpiper, something of note at last.

The easterly arm is completely devoid of birds, so I start to work my way back along the dam. A few brown jobbies are flitting along the dam, I guess linnets by their actions and lack of colour, and then I stop abruptly, four yellow looking birds have caught my attention, another nice family group of yellow wagtails. They prove to be my last birds of any consequence. I shall be back to Thornton, this place has good prospects, and the viewing is most leisurely, which suits me. Time for lunch before travelling the short distance to Groby.

I have not visited Groby for a good 10 years or more. Dorothy and I used to visit this part of Leicestershire regularly, Sarah has also spent many an happy hour here. It is all adjacent to the Charnwood Forest area and includes Swithland Wood and Reservoir, Bradgate Park – if you wish to get close to deer then this is the place to come, Cropston Reservoir and nearby Beacon Hill Country Park along with the migration site of Deans Lane close by. You would need several days to cover the whole area properly, but by being selective you can really enjoy the area and all it has to offer on a daily basis. Anyway, back to Groby. This is one of the first places where Dorothy and I saw breeding mandarin ducks in the wild, we could not believe what we were looking at in those days, all well over 40 years ago I hasten to add. Another glamour bird breeds here on occasion, the red-crested pochard, another real beauty for you, so Groby has many a pleasant memory for me. Now it is the question of what will we see today. As far as people are concerned very little, only one other car on the car park, and the car park is free, but there are no facilities, and the majority of pathways are wheelchair friendly.

I drove on a short distance and spotted the entrance to a quarry on the side of the road, it was a Sunday and no one was working, so I would park up here, and bingo, right opposite where I parked I could see a bench and the pool, the pool, incidentally, is owned by Hanson Quarry Products Ltd, so it is probably appropriate I am parked up by their entrance! I understand this pool if the largest stretch of natural water in Leicestershire, by that I mean not man created. Today it is quite choppy and there are very few birds on the surface, but one bird who is persistently diving catches my attention, this was no tufted duck.

As I have mentioned quite frequently of late, many of our duck are now in the midst of their annual moult and this does not help us to identify them quickly. Behaviour helps a lot, we do not have a large number of diving duck at this time of the year, the majority of ones which do dive are winter visitors to us here so far inland, so I only had four or so to concentrate on. Eventually I got the view I wanted, this bird was a drake red-crested pochard, not at all as colourful as the illustration you are likely to see in your field guide. In this state it is quite drab, but fortunately it will not remain so for very long, in a few more weeks he will look his normal beautiful self, and also make identification a sight easier for us.

Two days remain before I go into hospital, and today instead of being out with the Rosliston Birders I have a few things to tidy up. I have just sorted out my clothing, anyone would think I was going on my holidays. I shall no doubt have a call or two later on to let me know how the days birding at Thornton Reservoir went on, be nice if they could get something a bit special. I just hope the weather has been a little better than I have experienced this morning, it has been very showery and blustery, not good birding conditions.

There will be very little birding for a week or two that is for sure, so I will have to hope that some excitement arrives in my own garden. This morning for instances, the sparrowhawk put in an appearance, I had not seen him for some time, although he had left his trade mark in the garden, piles of loose feathers, so he was obviously about.

I am home after my op', and I am pleased to say that things appear to have gone to plan, or so I have been reliably informed. I had my op' in the morning and was back in the Ward by midday. You hear lots of complaints against the NHS but all I can say is the staff at The Queens Hospital in Burton on Trent were first class, and I mean this at all levels of status. I just wish they could do something about food, why is it you can rarely get decent food when in hospital, it may be very healthy, it is just a pity you cannot enjoy the taste. I go back early October for a check-up, but in between it is now up to me and nature.

While I am home I will deal with a subject I have not touched upon yet, books, with field guides in particular. A good field guide is as important to a birder as their optics, and there are a multitude of such books available, and these go from the very poor to the exceptionally good, so to review the pick of these will be very useful I believe, and at the very least will supply you with a start: do not go mad, two field guides are more than enough to start off with. I say two because you may wish to keep one at home for reference, and the other to have in your car so you always have it to hand for when required.

The first book you will need is a Field Guide, as identifying the bird you are looking at will always be your number one consideration. There are basically two types of field guide, and this concerns their illustrations, photographical or art drawn, but the common belief is art always outshines photographical skills. A good artist, and there are many, will draw you to the more important features of a bird by the delicate use of his brush, a photograph, will rarely, if ever, do the same. So, biased though I may be, I shall be reviewing art illustrated publications solely.

The probable first thing you will notice when working your way through the various books to be found on a book shelf is size and weight, as with your optics, always remember you may well be carrying this book with you, especially in your early days. The book, therefore, needs to fit in a pocket or at worst be carried in a back pack, the latter is not the best place to keep it, by the time you have taken your pack off and got into it the bird will probably have flown and be gone for ever. It is very important that while you are getting hold of your field guide you memorise as much detail as possible just in case the scenario just described occurs to you. There are several slim-line guides available published by Collins and Mitchell Beazley which are very well presented, the only problem I find with them is that due to their size they sometimes lack the detail required. I consider they are of greater use to the more experienced birder, the starter needs more information.

If I was to buy a novice birder his or her first field guide you could do no better than starting off with an AA publication *Field Guide to the Birds of Britain and Europe*. The illustrations are clear and have a crispness about them, the information is concise, and believe me this is quite a change from some of the books I come across. The book covers the birds of Britain and Europe, including a selection of the rarer species and vagrants. 530 species are covered, there are over 1,250 illustrations with distribution maps for all except the rarest of vagrants. The last price I have available for the publication was £9.99, a snip in my opinion.

I am sure if you were to look on my bookcase your attention would be drawn to a very well thumbed book which has most certainly seen better days. It is a copy of *The Hamlyn Guide to Birds of Britain and Europe* by Bertel Bruun and illustrated by Arthur Singer, it is now 41 years old, and looks it, cellotape was a wonderful invention! You can still buy the book, do not ask me how many times it has been reprinted, and is frequently to be found in the end-of runs book shops where you can pick it up for £4.99 when I last looked. I still consider it to be the leader in it's field, there are better and much more expensive books available, but as a cheap and well presented field guide I believe it cannot be bettered.

The best of all field guides ever to be published, and here I am completely biased, is the *Birds of Europe with North Africa and the Middle East* by Lars Jonsson, and published by Christopher Helm Ltd. It was first published in 1992, and the only complaint I have is the fact it just about creeps in for size and weight. Definitely a back-pack job this one, although I do have one jacket where my paper-back version will fit, I then walk with a decided tilt to starboard so to speak.

We have some first class artists available today, but to my mind Lars Jonsson is the pick of the bunch, his illustrations fly off the page at you because here the guy is a birder too, you do not come across many publications where the author and artist are the same person. Due to it's size and weight my paper back version lives in my car so it is never too far away, and a hard back copy lies on my book shelf. I do not know the current price but if you only buy one book, it is worth every penny.

At the turn of the century, the most eagerly awaited field guide of all time hit the book shelves, *Collins Bird Guide*, by Killian Mullarney, Lars Svensson, Dan Zetterstrom and Peter J. Grant. The proud boast for the book was it would be the most complete guide to the birds of Britain and Europe ever published, and it quickly gained the distinction of being the 'Best Bird Book of the Year 1999', and it is one hell of a book. The book comes in two formats. The large sized version, slightly over A4 size. Not a book for the field obviously, but it is probably my most used book at home, it is always my first reference. The layout is superb and it all helps to make it a most easily used book. At £29.99 when I first bought my copy, it was a snip. For field use Collins have printed a much smaller version, an awkward size, too large for the pocket but much worse than that in my opinion, the reduced page sizes has also reduced the text and illustration sizes to such a degree I have difficulty in reading it. I do need spectacles for reading, but this is the first time I have experienced such difficulty, I frequently joke Collins should have provided a magnifying glass with each book sold.

Do not take my comments as gospel, do check out the book yourself. Any of the above will get you started and prove of tremendous assistance to you in your studies, and I do suggest you buy at least two of them, one for use at home, the other for the field. That way you can buy two separate books should you so choose.

Now let us take the next step of progression. You are now the proud possessor of field guide, binoculars and telescope, the next question is where to go to use them. I have already mentioned joining a club, society or even attending courses if they are available locally to you, plus I trust some hints from between the pages of this tome, which I hope have pointed you in the right direction.

The publishers Christopher Helm have produced a series of books which become a most necessary part of any birders' paraphernalia, and these are the titles to be found in their *Where to Watch Birds* series. The series starts with *Where to Watch Birds in Britain*, within it's 600+ pages a mine of information can be found. Alongside this are the whole series which covers the UK *Where to Watch Birds in Scotland, Yorkshire, West Midlands, East Anglia*, and so you can go on. Where ever you live your local area will be included among the pages of the book. I have most of them on my bookshelf, and I have just ordered two more to fill in the gaps. When ever I go on holiday the book of the area accompanies me, it is as much part of my packing as my toothbrush!

I will finish off this piece on books with a bit of fun. I was browsing through some second hand books at a NT house when I came across a book titled *A Field Guide to the Rare Birds of Britain and Europe* by Ian Lewington, Per Alstrom and Peter Colston, and published by Domino Books Ltd, the book was priced up at £5.00, although the list price had been £14.99 when new. The book was in as good as new condition, so a fiver was quickly handed over. This book has been a constant joy. Ian Lewington is an artist of note so the illustrations alone make it a book of pleasure. Field guides by their very nature, cover the common and regular species of their area, with the rarer species sometimes getting a mention. When you consider the 300-odd far rarer species which irregularly reach Britain and Europe from North America, Asia, Africa – some even from the subantarctic and Antarctica itself – a guide to assist in the identification of these had long been awaited. The wait ended in 1991. It is a book dreams are made for, you can browse through it's pages and just wish some of the birds would fly into your patch, they are unlikely, but if they do you may at least have the book which will help you to identify them. It has worked for me on more than one occasion, it helped me identify a northern waterthrush down in Dorset one year, and a pied-billed grebe in Northumbria on another, the field guides I had at that time were of little use, I was pleased I had brought my copy of the 'Rarer' with me on holiday.

Today, as it so happens is Friday 19 August, to give you some idea of just where we are, and normally I would be out doing a bit of reconnaissance work for Sarah, but this I am unable to do not being allowed to drive until six weeks after my op'. Although it is probably early days to talk about my progress, things do seem to be a little better, so I am just keeping my fingers crossed. As far as my wound healing is concerned that appears to be going to plan, thanks to the two arm-crutches I have been provided with I am able to move about without too much discomfort, my worst problem is changing my anti-thrombosis socks.

On Saturday we decided to visit JCB and the temperature had reached 17 degrees by the time we set off, a very pleasant figure as far as we were both concerned, neither of us being sun worshippers'. We just managed to park up at JCB, the pleasant weather had brought out several family parties so the local ducks were not going to starve that is for sure.

We had hardly got out of the car before the first nice bird of the day came sailing past, a smart looking female mandarin who was sporting a full set of primaries. Some children provided bread for the ducks so a melee was soon taking place into which crash-landed four red-crested pochard, a female with three fully fledged juveniles.

I had by now walked about 200 metres, which may not sound a lot, but it is the most I have done for about 10 days or so, as a bench was near by I decided to make use of it, leaving Sarah to walk the second part of the loop herself. As I sat down a large goose came flying in, calling loudly as it came, before it crash-landed on the lake, not a very elegant landing I am sorry to report.

Looking closely at the bird I was surprised to see it was a free flying swan goose, some books refer to it as the Chinese goose, so take your pick. I stopped to think a little, in all my years of birding I had never seen a swan goose in flight before, so this is one I can count, my 'Year List' has now reached 204, and this is the first movement on the list since 15 July, progress is very slow.

Not very elegant birds at the best of times, and a pair of black swans were not impressed with it's arrival so they promptly chased it off further down the lake. At this point a goldeneye drifted into view, a nice duck, was she part of the collection I wondered. No matter how hard I tried I just could not get the angle of view I wanted to see if the bird was pinioned or not, so I shall never know the pedigree of this bird.

Two Egyptian geese swan walked out onto the grassy shore, making their way towards where some duck were being fed. They were not the only birds interested, a group of about a dozen semi-domestic 'Heinz 57' varieties also joined in. The Egyptian geese were not too amused with all of this so they set about the domestics with such vigour they actually drove them off. This was followed by a victory dance of sorts, with much wing beating, this showed them to be fully plumed, so they too could go onto today's list. While all of this was going on the smaller duck were still busily feeding away, I think they had their priorities right! Collections can be interesting places, you have all the foreign species to enjoy and most collections have a few native species among them, here we have eider, pochard, ruddy shelduck, pintail, teal, and gadwall to name but a few, and as they are part of a collection they do come close in for food. This provides marvellous opportunities to really study the bird and home in on their finer detail which may hold good for when in the field.

At this point Sarah returned she had seen several family parties of great crested grebe which was nice and had seen a common tern close enough to be positive over it's identification. Just as we were about to move off a whistling call could be heard, and walking along the shore line came a white-faced whistling duck, needless to say not a native to the British Isles. They are to be found in either South America: Argentina, Paraguay and Uruguay etc., or South Africa: Angola, the Transvaal and Madagascar. No ticking this one I am afraid, he was clearly pinioned. Tick-able or not, a nice bird to end the day on, and we do have a bird or two to report, so at the very least the bird line will know I am still a live.

Wednesday has come in most pleasant, plenty of broken cloud and a light breeze make conditions almost perfect for a walk, pity I cannot accomplish this at speed, actually completing it is was what matters to me. Goose Green lies alongside the River Swarbourn and is regularly covered with water from the river so consequently it has a very nice range of flowers and insects. Growing in the corner by the entrance is a nice tall and straight conifer, I am rather proud of this, I planted it. It must be almost 50 years ago when we used to buy live trees for Christmas and as this one was a particularly nice shape it was decided to plant in on the Green. The Green was then private land, although villagers had free access to it, and the landowner, who I knew well, was only too pleased to have an additional tree, and it has done us proud. The land now is council owned but I am pleased to say it is still well maintained.

The entrance lies at the bottom of Town Hill, which has a particularly attractive bridge, just a nice height to lean on. The river here runs fast and clear being just at the bottom of a weir, and is usually a good spot to see trout, and so it proved today. In the clear water nine brown trout could be seem, three of them about half a pound or so in weight I would have guessed, two on a plate would have made a good supper of that I am sure. They were safe from me, I prefer to see them swimming free rather than grilled.

Moving over to the Green I made my way along the river, several banded agrion damselflies were on the wing, as were both large and small white butterflies. A couple of very dark butterflies, almost black, flew rapidly by, peacocks no doubt, and from the wooded slopes behind me a nuthatch could be heard calling away. A few rooks were hanging around at the rookery, very silent for a change, although the odd jackdaw called out, and a sparrow hawk flew through and the nuthatch promptly stopped calling, and who can blame him. I will try to increase the distance walked each day, as I have been told this is as good a way to exercise my hip as any.

It is now Friday and in my walk today I intend to include the Swarbourn Meadows, although there are no laid down pathways the area is regularly cut so walking should not be a problem. Unlike Goose Green, the Meadows is the area where dogs are walked regularly, why this should be the case I do not know, probably because the entrance is directly opposite a road from the estate, so it is obviously the most convenient.

A lady was walking a couple of dogs as I entered the Meadows, both were on the lead I am pleased to say, we passed the time of day and I made my way down to the river. The Swarbourn is a very clear river, almost reminiscent of those seen in the Dales, here it is lined with alder and willow and during the winter months tidy mixed flocks of titmice/finches are to be seen, at this time of the year it is remarkably quiet, just the odd chaffinch calling away and the inevitable robin singing away most merrily.

I find the bench and take the weight off my legs. Close to the bench is a small but very thick patch of Himalayan balsam, and this is full of bees, no matter what we may think of this evasive foreigner, the bees are more than happy with it. Not a plant for butterflies, however, the flower shape suits a bee which just climbs inside for it's feed of nectar, a butterflies proboscis is not so suited.

I had intended to walk up to Goose Green, but I decided instead to go down to Bond End Bridge, where there are good views of both up and down steam from the bridge, and considering it is less than 100 metres from my home this is the fist time I have been here this year. From the bridge there are some delightful walks, one of our favourites was the walk to Whychnor, but I have not attempted this since Dorothy died. The bridge is hump-backed, and is not a road bridge, it just joins up the farmland and has not seen a tractor in years, just carries a public footpath. I stood on the bridge, leaning against the new wall which was built recently, once again enjoying the view of trout beneath, when something swimming towards me caught my attention, had we a moorhen? No, this was a mammal, and quite a sizable one too. Focusing up my binoculars I was thrilled to bits to see the mammal was a water vole and I watched it swim under the bridge and then followed it down stream until it vanished from sight. In the clear water it showed up nicely, and I must confess whenever I see a water vole I am always surprised by it's size, you tend to think of voles as being mouse like, and they are much larger than that.

It is many a year since I saw a water vole in the Swarbourn, must be nearly 40 years ago, it is just so nice to know they are back with us. I shall have to report this one to the Staffordshire Wildlife Trust as they are logging records of it's recovery. Many years ago they were relatively common, but pollution decimated them in recent times, so to see them again does at least show the Swarbourn is a nice clean river.

The Rosliston Bird Study Group had been to Carsington last Monday and I understand they saw a few nice species, greenshank, green sandpiper and common sandpiper especially so, their trip was obviously worthwhile. This Monday, the Bank Holiday, the Rosliston Birders are at Croxall Lakes NR, Roy has said he would pick me up. We are hit with typical Bank Holiday weather, overcast, intermittent rain and a cool wind, definitely no sunbathing today I am afraid. Fortunately Croxall does have hides so we will be able to escape the worst of the elements. 20 souls have turned up, could it be they all wanted the opportunity of seeing me again? The overnight rain has filled in all the pot holes in the drive up, and worst of all from our point of view, the scrapes are all covered with water so it is not going to be a good day for waders. The hide will not accommodate us all, but a place is kindly sorted out for me. Part of the group under Roy's guidance make their way East Side, Len and the remainder pack into the hide. At first there is little to see but a snow white bird drifts across the lake, a little egret, his yellow feet trailing, brightens up the gloom. The bird lands on the far side of the lake very close to a grey heron, a chance here to compare sizes of these two birds, and the grey heron looks at least twice the size of the egret.

Duck numbers are low, I doubt if we have above 30 birds in total, and the pick of the bunch are three shoveler, drakes in eclipse, four gadwall and a juvenile shelduck, the remainder being just tufted and mallard, quite disappointing really. Even gull numbers are low, seven black-backed and two lesser black-backed, if it had not been for the little egret things would have been very drab indeed.

Roy and his band of merry men came back so Len moved on. Roy had done better, they had seen a nice greenshank along with redshank on the East Side pool and a couple of oystercatcher had provided them with a flypast of sorts. At least the little egret and greenshank were birds of note and would have to be reported.

Normally when visiting Croxall as a group we usually finish off with a quick trip down to Whitemoor Haye, today things would be a bit different. I had learned of a pectoral sandpiper being seen over at Branston Pits, and the directions for seeing this bird had been quite good. Although I would be unable to go to see the bird, the walking distance being too much for me at present, some of my friends were going to have a stab, and who can blame them. Roy gave me a call, they had drawn a blank with the pectoral sandpiper, but as compensation they had seen a black-necked grebe. Either of those two birds would have been a 'Year Tick' for me so I am a little bit envious that two such birds have been in my patch, and due to circumstances beyond my control I have been unable to chase either. I think they call it frustration, but if you are going to become a serious birder, then frustration is something you have to become accustomed to.

Wednesday 31 August is nigh, and I am halfway through my 'No driving penance'. From a bird watching point of view August has been a bit of a none event, well from 10 August to be more accurate, and my total for the year was only increased by one, the swan goose/Chinese goose, and that bird was a bit 'iffy' to say the least. I now stand at 204.

Map references:
Thornton Reservoir – East end of dam: SK 475072.
Thornton Reservoir – West end of dam: SK 470074.
Groby Pool – Car Park: SK 525078.
Yoxall – Goose Green/Town Hill: SK 143187.
Yoxall – Swarbourn Meadow: SK 143186.
Yoxall – Bond End Bridge: SK 142185.

Chapter IX

September

I had a look on the net this morning and I am missing one or two good birds within the county. Today the following had been reported, red-necked grebe, black-necked grebe, curlew sandpiper, whinchat and redstart from one or two locations and the first movement of wheatear have been reported. They are one of the earliest of the returning migrants and one of the earliest to depart. While talking about departures, I have not seen a swift since I went into hospital, and that was on 10 August, have they all gone? I shall have to keep my eye on things, you never know come Saturday we may be able to chase one of these, it just depends where they end up.

A letter from the Ecological Records Coordinator for Staffordshire, Craig Slawson arrived today. My letter to the Trust regarding the water vole, had been forwarded on to him, and the information has now been passed to the Biological Records Centre. I was pleased to note it was his first record for the Swarbourn, a very important sighting in his opinion. He now intends to contact Nick Mott at the Trust to see if he can assess the population. Fortunately I had left a message for Nick so once he returns from his holidays this should not come as a surprise.

Individual sightings, such as this, can help build up a fuller picture, and with regard to the water vole, it is of vital importance, should the animal I saw be one from a group, this could easily be another important piece of the jigsaw for it's survival, nationally.

Summer looks as though it has terminated, today has dawned grey with a slight hint of dampness in the air, although I do not think this will stop us going out for an hour or two. I have already had a look on the net and there is nothing of interest been reported locally so I think it is safe to presume Branston Water Park it will be.

We called in at the Kings Bromley lay-by to see if the little egret was about, it was not, but when Martin came through later in the afternoon it had reappeared. We were first aware of the bird late 2010 and since that time numbers have varied between five and one. There is an old quarry working nearby, from what I remember of this place it has many wooded areas, so they could easily and safely roost up there. Many years ago I used to regularly visit the quarry, but it has changed hands several times since then and the current owners declined to grant me permission to visit due to health and safety requirements.

We did not make Branston due to the weather, but we did at least have a bit of excitement at home. Sarah called my attention to a large dragonfly which was sporting itself about over my garden pond, it was a lovely female southern hawker, quite a common dragonfly of gardens. After a short while it became obvious she was depositing eggs either directly into the pond or attaching them to some pond vegetation. She was active for about 15 minutes before she flew off and was gone.

I had a look on the net this morning and I almost wish I had not. Blithfield had a curlew sandpiper in Admaston Reach for most of the afternoon, the black-necked grebe is still at Branston Gravel Pits, and I picked up a report from Stanford Reservoir which was most impressive, and once I am fit and able I shall definitely make a visit. The reservoir is quite interesting for other reasons apart from birds, the county boundary between Leicestershire and Northamptonshire runs through the middle of it, and all of yesterday's reports were from the Leicestershire side, very little was reported from Northants'. The reservoir is probably only an hours run from home in normal travel conditions, I really must put the place on my itinerary.

My daily mission has been accomplished, I have completed my walk as planned and I am pleased to add I do not feel too badly, my legs are telling me I did it, but not as painfully as they did a few days ago when I walked less. Time heals, or at least so they say, and I must confess I am beginning to feel the benefit of my operation. I have just 16 days remaining before I can drive again and those days cannot pass quick enough, mind you, knowing my luck, all the interesting birds will have moved on to pastures new, and I shall be left with little of excitement.

Today, Tuesday 6 September has dawned damp and miserable and I was very disappointed to find two dead birds in my garden, both juvenile greenfinches, one was clearly a diseased bird but the other looked very clean, it may well have been a victim of a window strike. While clearing the dead birds up I was conscious of the garden suddenly going very quiet, what few birds had been about had made a mass exodus, and the reason why was soon apparent. Sitting out on a branch of the laurel tree under which I was standing sat a male sparrowhawk, I hardly dared to breath, he was barely five feet above my head, and was staring straight at me.

I do not know if you have ever been close to a bird of prey, but if you have one thing I am sure you will have noticed is their eyes. All of the birds I have been close enough to really study have bright eyes, normally yellow, orange or red, and these are clear and cruel looking. This sparrowhawk certainly had these, they were so brightly yellow I almost thought they were studying me as a possible next dinner, I was staring directly into the face of a killing machine, and what an incredible looking beast. With the majority of birds of prey the male is smaller than the female, and this bird was probably no longer than 28–30cm, but every centimetre was feather covered muscle. Their bill is quite small really but having said that it is sharply hooked and it's talons were sharp and quite long, you could see these well wrapped round the slender branch on which the bird sat. While taking in a much detail as I could, the moment was gone, he launched himself into the air, almost catching me on my head as he flew directly over me, I felt the wind of his passing that was for sure. What a magic few moments, the memory will stay with me forever. It just goes to show you do not always have to travel far to see wonderful things, they are all around us if we just take the time to look.

Thursday is again a dull start, I hope it bucks up as Sarah and Martin are off to Stratford for a dose of Shakespeare, this time they are seeing *A Mid Summer Nights Dream* which I am sure they will enjoy. By a remarkable coincidence this is the last Shakespearean play that Dorothy and I saw together, I hope they enjoy it just as much as we did.

Although the morning has started off dreary there is no actual rain and the forecast is for a better afternoon, and the forecasters have got it right! I decided to walk round Bond End Bridge which was very quiet, just a moorhen fluttered down stream and a couple of rooks over flew. So I head over to Swarbourn Meadow. Here I did not have it all to myself, a dog walker was out exercising his two dogs, and they were enjoying themselves, judging by the noise they were making. The net result for me was no birds, although I did see several speckled wood butterflies plus large whites, so it was not a total disaster. At Goose Green the nuthatch I have heard on previous visits was still calling away, moorhen could be heard but not seen and a party of lesser black-backed gulls drifted over. A few rooks and jackdaws were still in attendance at the rookery, and a pair of wood pigeon were cooing away on a nearby bush.

I headed towards the small pond and was pleased to see a southern hawker dragonfly heading in the same direction, this was a male, a nice glossy blue, and he proceeded to hunt over the rushes of the pond. While enjoying the dragonfly I heard the call of a bird of prey from overhead, so I stopped to have a look. At first I could see nothing, but the bird called again, and judging by the volume of the call the bird was quite low, so I gazed in the general direction I believed the call had come from. I was thrilled to bits to realise the bird was a red kite, not a bird I hear calling all that often, and it just drifted across, no more than 20 metres or so high, to slowly vanish in the east. I few moments of sheer bliss, red kite are a bird I have not seen all that frequently.

A nice bird to end up on, so I can now make my way slowly back home, and another walk in excess of half a mile accomplished. I am beginning to believe I am getting there, so I will just have to keep my fingers crossed.

Today, Monday, has certainly come in breezy, the winds to be honest are more than breezy, some of the gusts almost blow you over. Many bird watchers will be viewing this with interest as they are very likely to bring something in with them. Many birds of north America will have started their migration south along the east coast, particularly waders and waterfowl, and some of these will be picked up and blown off over the Atlantic.

Tuesday 13 September. The bird rush has commenced and the 'Twitchers' will already be off. I had a look at the net this morning and the unusual species were already being reported, not a lot, but certainly enough to start an adrenaline rush for many, and the place to go appears to be Cornwall.

Today, on my walk up to the church a movement high up in the yew caught my attention. Two very small birds were flicking about, one of them flew out and hovered for a second or two before plunging back into the security of the yew. I had seen all I needed to see, these two birds were a pair of goldcrest, our smallest bird. They were probably calling away as they performed, but unfortunately, over the years they have slipped from out of my hearing range and I would have to be very close to hearing them call.

Saturday is nice and bright at present, with nothing new on the net, Blithfield Reservoir it will be. At least coming here does seem like real birding. Driving across we experience the first of the promised showers, so birding today is going to be done from either in the car or near to it.

We concentrated our efforts on the reservoir, quite a few gulls were flying over the water, all black-headed as far as could be seen, with cormorant, great crested grebe and mallard on the water. We walked across the roadway to have a look north, here the picture was much the same except Sarah picked up three little grebes which were swimming close in to the shore. Turning back, to walk towards the car, a buzzard drifted overhead, promptly to be chased off by a pair of carrion crow, there are times when it is not much fun being a buzzard, big as you are. Time to drive on over the causeway to the western side of the reservoir.

Here again we had the car park to ourselves, although it was not long before another car drove up, two more birders to join in the scene. A large black cloud was drifting overhead so we decided not to move away from the car, we may need to get back in it rather quickly. A large gull caught our attention, the bird was flying high, and from it's size it just had to be a juvenile great black-backed gull. While studying this bird another large bird, flying above the gull, caught my attention, this bird was no gull. I drew Sarah's attention to this bird and we watched it slowly circling round, when it closed it's wings and made a sudden swoop earthwards. This was only momentarily, it quickly assumed it's slow circling flight. In the time of it's swoop we had seen all we needed to see, the bird was an osprey.

Looking along the shore line in Admaston Reach, there was a nice long drift of waders, 25 or so. I had not brought my telescope with me so we made our way over the road to get a closer look. There were at least six dunlin, double figures of plovers, both ringed and little ringed, plus the odd common sandpiper. Not a bad little collection.

We crossed back over the causeway to view down the reservoir towards the dam. A large bird came up off the water, the osprey, and it was carrying something in it's claws, obviously a fish it had just caught. For a few moments the bird busily struggled with it's claws to get a firmer grip on the fish, but it was no good, it let go and the fish crashed back into the reservoir beneath. The osprey had to go with out it's dinner, and the fish may well live to fight another day.

Come Monday my constitutional took in the Swarbourn Meadows where I could sit on my usual bench, I do not know who positioned it here but I am extremely pleased they did. In the alder, above my head, a family party of long-tailed tit were busily feeding away on the catkins I had mentioned earlier, and judging by the calls there are a few blue tits among them. Over head a buzzard could be heard calling but not seen due to the thick tree cover, and a robin was singing away quite happily. The afternoon was nice and bright and several butterflies were evident especially the lesser white, they had obviously had a very good second brood. Along the river banks speckled woods were also quite numerous which is always pleasing to see they are always a busy and fussy butterfly.

Today's walk was accomplished without any difficulty, I did not have to take a rest at all which I was very pleased about, although I knew I had done it once I did sit down. My car is also collected, it was very pleasing it started straight away, after being left idle for six weeks it is probably a good test for just how good your battery is! Coming back with the car via Kings Bromley I was pleased to see the little egret was still about, this morning Sarah saw two as she made her way to work.

Tuesday has come in very dull with persistent rain, but I had my trip across to Blithfield anyway, travelling through a very heavy shower in the process, my wipers would hardly take it. I drew in by the sailing club car park initially to have a quick look along the dam, only mallards and black-headed gulls, so I drove my way slowly round the shoreline into Mickledale Bay. Here it was also quiet save from further black-headed gulls, but as I was about to turn round and retrace my footsteps a large gull flew in and landed on a buoy. I stopped, this bird had a bright black back, and due to size it was it could only be one thing, a nice adult great black-backed gull. While enjoying the bird a large bird came gliding across the dam in a direct line for us, our 'resident' osprey was putting in an appearance. I turned to watch it's slow progress down the reservoir, before it vanished after crossing the causeway. This bird has been at Blithfield for some time, and I must have been fortunate to see it on a dozen or more occasions, so no one is complaining here.

Time now for the causeway, pulling in on the Watery Lane car park there was little to be seen apart from the black-headed gulls once again. I was the only vehicle here, the poor weather had certainly kept the 'day trippers' in, so I crossed over the causeway to park up in my usual spot over looking Admaston Reach The picture here was not much better, and I was thinking of moving on when an old friend of mine drove up, Bernard Smith. He had seen the osprey in Tad Bay, but had little else to report upon. We were having a nice little chat, we have known each other for about 40 years, and while we were doing so in flew a small flock of waders, which landed quite close by in the Admaston Reach. There were two distinctly different sized birds within the flock and after a little while we got the views we wanted, we had 15 dunlin and seven ringed plover, not a bad little haul really.

Thursday 22 September looks as though it is going to be a very pleasant day, so I decided early to make today my day for Stanford Reservoir, so by 10.00 hours I had my lunch packed and all my gear ready for the day ahead. I have never been in this part of Leicestershire previously, and I found the countryside very pleasant. Access to the reservoir was not going to be easy, and I had difficulty in locating the first reasonable viewpoint, but on a minor road out of South Kilworth I found a suitable spot where I could pull over to view the eastern arm. There was a car park here but it was locked up although I noted it belonged to the Northamptonshire Wildlife Trust so members may have a key. The River Avon feeds the reservoir at this point, and it has formed a nice small lake prior to running over a weir and into the reservoir. The pond was full which is more than you could say for the reservoir. In the small hawthorn trees round the pond seven grey heron were sitting out and as I leaned over the bridge a nice male grey wagtail flew from underneath.

I crossed the road to view the reservoir, but due to the conditions it was all dried mud with just duck and gulls sitting out in it, with open water being some distance away. Now to find the dam, apparently you can park near here and obtain permission to bird watch off the dam. This I was unable to do, due to locked gates once again, so I drove on. After a 100 metres or so I found a suitable spot, although the reservoir was at least 300 metres distance but even through binoculars you could see a number of birds, so it was up telescope.

Gadwall were well represented as were mallard, tufted, a few shoveler and on the far shoreline, which incidentally is in Northamptonshire, even though I was still standing in Leicestershire, were three little egrets. Closer in, this time in Leicestershire were three green sandpiper, that was two very nice birds for the day. While enjoying the view I ate my lunch and then it was time to make up my mind what to do with the rest of the day, I decided upon Blithfield once again. Part of this road must have been a drive to Stanford Hall as it lime tree lined, and very imposing it looks, and these trees produced my bird of the morning. From a tree on the right hand side of the road, a lesser spotted woodpecker flew and landed on a bare branch of a tree opposite. I was able to stop and for about 30 seconds watched this bird climb up the branch until it vanished into the leaf canopy, to see a lesser for 30 seconds is a once in a year event, believe me. This alone was worth the journey.

The journey back to Blithfield took just about an hour, so I had a full afternoon ahead of me. It was quiet, only one wind surfer on the water, he was not going to be a real nuisance, so on towards Mickledale I drove. In the bay were several black-headed gulls, lapwings and a couple of great crested grebe which were looking quite wintery, very pale. A nice mixed flock of linnet and goldfinch were feeding on seed heads, must have been about 50 in total, and a cormorant flew across.

Two terns were sitting on a launch out in the bay, at this time of the year they are always worth a second look, so out with the telescope. These birds certainly had short legs and a closer look at their wing length convinced me they were indeed Arctic terns, so I was pleased I stopped to view. As I have mentioned before on the Arctic tern the tail streamers are longer than on the common, I could not see bill colour at this distance, but I was happy enough with my 'diagnosis'. Off now to the causeway, you may remember a couple of days ago there was a nice mixed flock of waders in Admaston Reach, so a second go at these would not go amiss.

I had the car park to myself, so I quickly got my 'scope out to survey the shore line and I was pleased to see waders present. I slowly worked my way along them, quickly realising there were far more than I saw previously. Today we had 43 ringed plover, a wonderful number by any ones standards and 18 dunlin. A small fracas developed between two of the dunlin, and I had the surprise of my life, one of them showed a bright white rump, this was no dunlin, it was a curlew sandpiper, a bird I had been moaning about missing. It just goes to show you can never be too careful. I must confess I went back through the flock more studiously, was anything else hiding away? I am pretty certain not, but I am not complaining, my first 'Year Tick' for the month is now in the bag, number 205 to be precise.

After trying new ground yesterday, the bug had bitten, so as nothing near home had been reported, apart from my own records from Blithfield, I decided to try pastures new again. King's Mill Reservoir, at Mansfield in Nottinghamshire had picked up the odd good bird recently, the pick of which had been a grey phalarope, and as I have never visited the site, although I have driven past it on many an occasion, I thought I would give it a try. The reservoir is called King's Mill for a very good reason, it was created to store water for use at many of the mills once operating in the area, and is well worth a visit not only for the birds but also anyone interested in industrial archaeology.

The car park is free with just a couple of Blue Badge parking lots, but this is no problem. The Visitor Centre is close by and serves refreshments and has the necessary facilities, and the reservoir, which incidentally is 1.5 miles round, has very good pathways, quite suitable for wheelchair use, but do take a soft cushion as the roots of a few trees have pushed up the pathway's surface in places. The terrain is flat so I decided I would attempt to walk the distance myself as I had been assured there were benches in abundance.

I made the mistake of walking the wrong way round, I should have looked at the direction of the sun, so do check on this when you visit. I have never seen so many coot as a percentage of water surface in all my life, the reservoir is very much a medium sized stretch of water, 70 acres max I would think, but the coot numbers were phenomenal. I would think this place is the coot capital of the UK! Among the numerous coot I did manage to pick up a few different birds, there were several mute swan, a single Canada goose (how often can you say that?), just a handful of mallard, the odd moorhen and a few black-headed gulls. The edge of the reservoir is tree lined which can be a bit of a nuisance for clear viewing, but in the right conditions this should be alive with small birds, not today however. As I turned the eastern corner of the reservoir I quickly realised my error, I was full face onto the sun and all the birds were in silhouette, lovely and warm, but not good for birding. I traversed this section as fast as I could until approaching the western end of the reservoir where viewing conditions vastly improved, and here I could start to add species to my day's list, as this certainly appeared to be the area of the reservoir which attracted many of the birds. It was far more natural and work has obviously been done to improve the habitat, there are areas of reed and rafts of plants floating on the water which makes the area far more attractive to wildlife. Here I meet up with my first tufted of the day, and I was thrilled to bits to see a ruddy duck, only one, a female. This lady had escaped the gun, and good luck to her.

The trilling song of little grebe broke the silence, he was quickly located and I was pleased to see a family party of five, two adults and three young. While enjoying these I suddenly realised I had not seen a great crested grebe, there should have been a pair or two on a water of this size. I wonder if the antagonism of the many coot had made life for the great crested grebe just plain intolerable, they are a fairly docile species.

On two of the plant rafts several lapwing were rested up, and it was nice to see a good selection of juvenile birds among them, and on two of the rafts coot were still nesting, no wonder there are so many.

I was now approaching the end of my walk, and I must confess I had used many of the benches, and they were not exaggerating about the number, and had reached the sailing club when I came across the first bird watcher I had seen all morning, he was sitting on a bench enjoying his lunch. He looked up as I approached and I commented about the fact things were quiet, he smiled, and pointed. Not 10 metres out on the water sat a black-necked grebe, and I had talked about it being quiet! I had nearly missed out on a 'Year Tick'. I sat down, and thanked him accordingly, the bird had first been seen yesterday apparently. I am sure that had not this birder been sitting down where he was I would not have noticed the bird, it was among a flock of coot and could so easily have been missed, talk about luck, and what a perfect note to end the day on.

Nothing on the net this morning so I will have an hour or two over at Blithfield this afternoon, take a drive down the shoreline which is something I have not done for some time, since previous to my op'. The Newton Shallows have been producing a few birds of late so I hope things continue, mind you with the luck I have had over the last couple of days I should not expect too much, after all I have just had two 'Year Ticks'.

There was a little more activity at Blithfield today, four birders were at the car park on the western side of causeway, all known to me. Apparently the osprey had been showing well a few minutes before I arrived on the scene, but a small group of waders were in Admaston Reach, 18 ringed plover to be exact, so they were compensation. After a bit of a chat I moved on to go down to the Newton Shallows, moving cautiously so as not to disturb the ringed plover, which I managed.

While driving down I became conscious of a large flock of geese flying in, and judging by the calls most of these were greylags. I stopped to look at them and was amazed at the number, there must have been over 300 birds and the majority were greylags, I do not think I have seen so many locally.

I began to realise I would not be going down as far as the Newton Shallows as the water level was very low, I would be doing my birding from Dairy House Reach. As I drove along I picked up the heads of five duck, they were just raised above the shore, I stopped promptly, these were goosander. I watched them for a few seconds before enough was enough and off they flew up the reservoir, their white wing bars showing well.

I started to look along the river track, the river now was just a narrow strip of water, and a wader caught my attention, this bird was quite greyish but had a decided dark patch round the eye, a juvenile grey plover. This was totally unexpected as I had seen no report of the bird and while I watched the bird commence to bath another walked in, so I now had two juvenile grey plover. I was not grumbling about these, I may have seen them previously this year, but you can never have too many.

A decent number of hirundines were flicking over the water, swallows and sand martins, and the way they were performing there must have been a good supply of flying insects low over the water. In the nearby vegetation, which was mainly thistles, a nice mixed flock of linnet and goldfinch were very active, which was not surprising as the thistles were covered by seed heads, they were not going to go hungry. As I was about to move off I picked up a large gull flying in, it proved to be a juvenile great black-backed gull, but a nice enough bird to sign off with.

After overnight rain the day is gorgeous, so I now have an incentive to get my chores done and then I will be able to have an hour or two out this afternoon. It was lovely to drive off in just a short sleeved shirt, the weather was so comfortable. I had Croxall to myself, no birders no dog walkers, as I drove down the Canada geese decided to all take off and for a few minutes the sky was full of geese accompanied by a real cacophony of sound. At times I get fed up of Canada geese, but to see over 200 birds take off with such a volume of sound is quite spectacular.

As I arrived at the hide I could see a number of waders on the scrape area, was there going to be something of interest hidden away among them? I quickly got into the hide and put my telescope up to slowly work my way through the birds, I was going to be disappointed, all were lapwings, 74 of them actually, so I turned my attention to the lake. I need not have bothered, very little was visible here either, so I turned my attention back to the scrape, and at very moment a little egret walked into view, it had been hidden behind some vegetation. The water was so shallow where it walked it yellow feet and ankles could be clearly seen.

While enjoying the egret a small wader flew in to join up with the lapwings, egret quickly forgotten I swung round onto the wader, it was a nice, clean, juvenile dunlin, two interesting birds in a matter of a few minutes, this is one of the joys of birding, the whole spectrum can change in the wink of an eye!

I stopped to have a look over the lake, this was very quiet, a few swans and mallard seemed to be the lot, so I took myself off down to the rough lane. Driving slowly I flushed a small flock of birds from the hedgerow, I stopped to watch them settle a little further ahead, tree sparrow, seven of them in fact, I always like to see tree sparrows.

I stopped opposite the little owl's tree, not hoping for a lot I must confess, but surprise, surprise, sitting out in full sunlight, sat the little beauty. This was too good a chance to miss so I gently opened my car door and put up my telescope, and quickly found myself looking straight into the face of the bird. Whether it was due to the bright sunlight or not I do not know, but the owl's eyes were just narrow slits as it stared in my direction. I enjoyed the bird for a few moments more before I slowly moved off, not wanting to disturb the bird further. That proved to be my last bit of excitement for the day, but no complaints, three birds to be reported and nice memories of the owl, what more could one ask for?

Today I had a dentists appointment which went well, and as it was still a very nice day I took the opportunity to nip out, for a quick visit to Blithfield. Little did I realise just how good my trip would turn out. I pulled in on the eastern side of the causeway and initially there was little to see, so I crossed over to view down the north side of the reservoir. I was about to move off when I noticed a dark looking duck diving off Yeatsall Bank. Fortunately I had got my 'scope with me, so I quickly focused up on the bird. I had hit the jackpot with almost my first bird of the day, I was looking at a juvenile, female scaup, or greater scaup as most new field guides call it. What a start to my afternoon, and this bird was a 'Year Tick' to boot. I watched her for a couple of minutes before she vanished round a piece of headland.

I drove across the causeway, opened up the gate and drove into Admaston Reach, parking up after a short distance, several waders were scattered along the shore line, another telescope job. Initially they all seemed to be ringed plover and dunlin, but as I carefully went through, counting as I did, I pick up a small wader, the little stint was still here, and near to the little stint was a slimmer, greyer looking bird, I had the juvenile curlew sandpiper, what a super collection, and there were 27 ringed plover, 13 dunlin, 1 little stint and the curlew sandpiper. You could not ask for much more than that.

I drove on down towards Dairy House Reach, not expecting a lot after the birds recorded so far, but my day was not over. On the shore line stood a solitary juvenile grey plover, remember we saw two a few days ago, and close by was a wagtail, a pied I initially thought, but something about it caught my attention. Although it was not that far away I decided to use my scope as I wanted to see as much detail as possible, and it was a good job I did, pied it was not, white wagtail it was. Yet two more cracking birds. I now have eight birds to put on the net, they will think I have been a busy lad. You do get days like this, they compensate for the quiet times.

The nice weather was continuing so I decided to visit the Chase. I made my way to the Cadet Camp the tracks here are nice and flat so walking with sticks is not a problem. I made my way towards the ranges, and was rather surprised to find the Chase so quiet, I would have thought other people would have been taking advantage of the good weather.

Things on the bird front were very quiet, a couple of magpie were chattering away nearby and a carrion crow could be heard calling in the distance. My attention was caught, however, by a sudden movement in a bracken patch nearby, out popped a lovely male stonechat, and he sat on the top of the bracken just looking straight in my direction, and for a few seconds we just stared each other out. A little further on a female was also sitting out, stonechat are never ones for hiding their light under a bushel fortunately.

I was about to get into my car when I heard a 'chip, chip, chip' from above, I looked up realising I was hearing crossbills flight calls, and overhead three crossbills flew. As I still had time I decided to call in at Blithfield for a few minutes, just to have a look to see if the waders were still in Admaston Reach, Sarah could do with the curlew sandpiper and the little stint.

As I had been out for a walk I only had my binoculars with me and initially I could find no birds whatsoever, then a couple of heads popped up right on the shoreline, and two birds quickly became about 20. There was another birder here today and I pointed these out to him, he had a telescope and he had not seen them. Looking through the birds we had 11 ringed plover, seven dunlin and the single little stint, obviously part of the flock has moved on. For pointing out the waders he was able to show me a wheatear which I had not been aware of. A nice female was busily hoping along the fence posts, dropping on to the ground to catch an insect, and then flying up to eat it, normal wheatear behaviour. A fair exchange.

Thursday has dawned with the Indian Summer continuing, the temperature could reach 28 degrees today, that is starting to be too hot for me. Mind you, come tomorrow we will be on the coast near Boston, should there be a nice cooling sea breeze conditions could be well nigh perfect.

Blithfield is far busier today than for some time and the ice cream vendor is doing a roaring trade, not that I am stopping, today my interest lies on the far shore. I drive in and close the gate and start to scan the shore line. A couple of black-headed gulls land in and they do me a favour, the waders are all disturbed and move to the waters edge, one thing is quickly obvious, the numbers are much reduced on previous. I start to count, 9 dunlin, 8 ringed plover and 1 curlew sandpiper. As I drive down the wheatear pops up onto a fence post, she is still around, but on arriving down Dairy House Reach I find very little, not a wader in sight, not even a lapwing. Even the goose numbers are low today and you cannot say that very often. On my return journey things really do hot up. I notice a very pale looking buzzard roosting up in a tree in Mickledale, so I slowed down to have a good look at the bird, little realising what I was going to see.

My initial thoughts were it was just a pale common buzzard, you do get them, but as I approached the bird took to flight and flew directly overhead, this generated a prompt adrenaline rush, I could not believe what I was looking at. As I said the bird was pale, it had white leading edges to the wings with very black carpal joints, black heavy markings on the belly and a white tail with a dark terminal band. This bird was no common buzzard, it was in fact a juvenile rough-legged buzzard, and here was I, on my own, with no one to share the experience with. Rough-legged buzzard are very rare, I doubt if I have seen 10 in all my years of birding, and they are the last bird I would look for on my own patch, this bird has probably come down from Scandinavia just to see me, needless to say I thank him.

When putting my reports on the net I noticed a long-billed dowitcher had been reported from Freiston, I hope that bird hangs on until tomorrow, I have only seen one in all my years at the game, and I am sure for Roy and Len it would be a 'Lifer'. The long-billed dowitcher is a North American wader not too dissimilar to our greenshank, keep your fingers crossed for us.

Len was his usual prompt self and we drove off at 07.30 hours as expected, and left with Roy at nearly 08.00 hours. Roy, as always, had mapped out his route doing his best to avoid early morning traffic as we had Nottingham to negotiate, and this he did very well, so much so we made Frampton with time to spare. We were meeting Jane and John here for the day, they were coming from their home near Norwich, so between us we had a fair amount of birding experience, and little did I know it was going to be required.

In many respects today was a sort of 'Twitch', we hoped to catch up with two rarer species, the pectoral sandpiper and long-billed dowitcher, as well as enjoying other choice species associated with The Wash estuary. We popped into the Visitor Centre to check up on the pectoral sandpiper, it had been seen early on from the Reedbed Hide, so using the Visitor Centre's facilities we were off on a bird hunt. There were only a small number of birders in the hide and the unfortunate news was the sandpiper had flown off a few minutes prior to our arrival, the times you hear that! There was, however, much for our attention on the lagoon in front. Ruff numbers were very good, I would estimate in almost three figures, large numbers of wigeon were in and their delightful whistle-like call sounded especially attractive on such a bright sunny morning. A dark bird standing among the Canada geese caught our attention, it was a Brent goose, a juvenile in fact, not a bird we see in our neck of the woods very often.

Len drew our attention back to the ruff, he had picked up a smaller bird moving through the vegetation, could this be our sandpiper? No it was not, it was a little stint which eventually came into view, and this one quickly became three. Time to move on to the next hide, the 360 Hide, so called because you have all round vision, a full 360 degrees.

Conditions here were not very good as part of your view was directly into the sun putting the birds into silhouette, which does not help with identification. A few bar-tailed godwits could be identified and little egrets were scattered almost everywhere, there must have been well in excess of 30 of these, the largest number I have seen for some time. We decided it was time to move on when Len stopped us. He had been checking up the local bird situation on his mobile, and the pectoral sandpiper had just been relocated a short distance from the Reedbed Hide, we were now off in 'Twitch' mode and made our way in the direction required, passing a few birders who could confirm the bird was still there. I sent my friends on, they were far more mobile than me, and for some of the them the bird was a 'Lifer'. I made it, eventually, and the bird was still behaving itself and showing well. The bird was a juvenile, which is to be expected really, and the dark streaked neck and breast was quite noticeable. It is due to these markings the bid is so called, this dark area terminates at the pectoral region.

Before we leave Frampton, here you have minimum facilities, the Visitor Centre has toilets and you can obtain a warm drink, not that warm drinks were called for today. Outside the Visitor Centre is a picnic area, which is where we lunched. The pathways are all wheelchair friendly as are the hides, and for those who walk, but slowly, there are benches, mind you not too many of them. Entrance and parking is free. Above all, Frampton is a 'wild place' with much to enjoy.

Freiston has no facilities apart from a car park and hide, and the car park is rough ground, there is at least one Blue Badge parking spot, which luckily for us was vacant, every other spot was full. According to the latest reports, the dowitcher has been favouring the bottom corner of the lagoon, up against the sea wall, a walk of about 100 metres or so, the corner was just tucked away out of our vision so walking it would have to be. The pathway looks in good condition so wheelchair access is available. The hide is about halfway down the track, so we visited this and I was able to have a sit down. The hide has a ramp I was pleased to note. There was little to see from this point, three oystercatcher and two black-tailed godwit, so time to move on.

As we left the hide two birders came along who were able to confirm the dowitcher was where expected and was showing well, that enabled us to walk on with renewed vigour, well almost. We could see several birders a little way down the track, and when we reached them there was our target in full view to all. We put up our telescopes, although they were not completely necessary, but as this bird was a 'Lifer' to all but me, everyone wanted as good a sighting as possible, and this gave us the opportunity to age the bird. The bird turned to face our direction and the head markings could be clearly seen. The bird has very distinctive white supercilium, (white line over the eye), which join up over the beak and form a white 'V', identifying the bird as a juvenile. On the evidence of this bird they are a very energetic feeder, with a long, straight bill, which they probe into the water with almost a non stop effort. Although not being as large as a godwit, they look a very heavy and stocky bird. I was lucky as there was a bench handy so I could sit down and enjoy the occasion.

As we now only had half an hour or so to spare before moving off, we walked up the sea wall to have a view over the shore line, the sea incidentally was not visible. We could just about make out a group of golden plover and several curlew could also be seen and heard. Ah well, we may as well make our way back the cars we thought, when a small brown looking bird flew across the salt marsh in front of us, it had a decidedly up and down flight motion and was continually closing it's wings, very woodpecker like, and dropped into the dank vegetation. My first thought was wryneck, so Roy, Len and John walked up towards where the bird had dropped, Jane and I just stood and watched them.

After a few minutes they put up their telescopes so they had obviously located the bird, and we awaited a verdict. John turned and waved at us 'We need an expert up here' he called, Jane and I looked behind us, no one else in sight, John must have meant us! We made our way as quickly as possible and I had a look through John's telescope, and a beautiful sight met my eyes. The bird was obviously a juvenile pipit of some sort, but all I knew was I had never seen a bird like this. The head markings were so distinctive, the flecking or speckling down the breast of the bird were very pronounced against a nice buff back ground and these vanished before you reached the flanks – what on earth had we here?

Early on I mentioned the range of experience between us all, so jokingly I mention this and suggested they proved me right, so out came their field guides and we started some serious work. Thanks to our collective experience we were quickly able to delete the four pipits we were familiar with, juvenile tree, meadow, rock and water pipit look nothing like the bird we were studying, then something hit me. Only two pipits seen in the UK have so distinctive an eye ring, and these are Richard's and red-throated pipits, so I mentioned this and we concentrated our efforts on these two species. We quickly deleted Richard's pipit from the equation due to other plumage differences visible, now to concentrate on the red-throated, and bingo, we had it. The illustration in both Len's and John's field guides could have had our bird as the artist's model, identical in almost every detail, what a bird to find.

We carried out further checks and we most certainly had made the correct identification, and we had found the bird, there had been no record previous. This bird will most certainly have to be reported so it gets onto the national bird lines, and I just hope Freiston can accommodate the possible influx of birders tomorrow! We could now go home feeling very smug.

Red-throated pipits are not regular migrants to the UK, they are instead what we class as a vagrant, and they are here purely by accident, their migratory route does not include us. I have seen red-throated pipit on two previous occasions in the UK, but both were adult, winter plumage birds, hence my initial problems when we first sighted this bird. They originate from the near Arctic and northern Norway. Dorothy and I were on a cruise to Norway and Spitzbergen, way up into the Arctic Circle, and North Cape was on our visiting list. We were right in the breeding area for the pipit, and we were fortunate enough to see a couple, I must admit they are not that common up there. I am sure Dorothy would have loved to have been here today to experience this little beauty.

When I first commenced this journal I mention the fact a waxwing would be my bird of the year, this was based on emotional feelings. It now has competition, both on the emotional front and the sheer simple beauty of a rare little bird. A magical day over, three reports on the net, and come tomorrow I shall be having a bird-free day, I am looking for a new car, I now believe an automatic car would be of benefit to me.

September now comes to a close, after a slow start I have knocked up several very nice birds which were not anticipated, my final figure is now 211.

Map references:
Eastern Arm View Point of Stanford Reservoir: SP 612812.
Western Arm View Point of Stanford Reservoir: SP 593805.
Kings's Mill Reservoir: SK 515593.
Frampton Marsh RSPB: TF 357389.
Freiston Shore RSPB: TF 397424.

Chapter X

October

My new car hunt turned out to be unproductive, plenty of 4x4s on display but few which were automatic or in my price range. Later on I did at least have a reason to get out my binoculars. Sarah is a bit of an astronomy buff and likes looking at the stars, and apparently Jupiter has been in view very nicely over the last few night, so tonight we spent a little time seeking it out. It was so bright it took little time in finding, and through the binoculars three of it's moons could be seen, and to think we were looking at something which was light years away. I can never get my head round that fact, we are looking at stars etc, which are no longer there probably, it is just the fact their light takes so long to reach earth. If you do not mind I will stick with ornithology, that is difficult enough at times.

I shall at least do a little birding today, I have not made my mind up where, but due to the fact the hot weather is continuing I will not journey far.As events have turned out Blithfield it was, and I had a most enjoyable couple of hours. In transit I stopped at the Kings Bromley lay-by, and here I had a very pleasant surprise, it was not one little egret, it was six, the highest number I have ever had the pleasure of seeing here. A cracking start to my trip out.

I arrived at Blithfield Reservoir and decided to view the deep end first, so I drove down the eastern bank towards Mickledale and Portfields Bays. In Mickledale a large gull was sat out on a buoy, this was either a great or lesser black-backed gull, so I stopped to use my binoculars. Legs were pink, this denoted a great, a lesser would have had yellow legs, but you know all of this as I have discussed this several times. Portfields was very quiet so off now to Admaston Reach. The car park was deserted so I had Blithfield to myself, or at least the western bank. I opened up the gate and let myself in, pausing to study the area of the Reach, not a bird in sight. Gate closed I slowly made my way down the Reach. After about 100 metres or so I picked up a few small shapes working the waters edge, I had some waders. I approached slowly so as not to disturb them, and managed to park up relatively closely. It was a very nice little group, 8 dunlin, 3 ringed plover, 1 curlew sandpiper and finally a little stint. You will recollect these birds have been here for some time, although the overall numbers do seem to be reducing. As I started to move off a movement from the fence nearby caught my eye, it was the wheatear, she has been around for three to four days.

I made my way to Dairy House Reach and here I parked up as this was going to be telescope time, so I was having to get out of the car to see the birds for the first time today. Scanning the mud there at first appeared little to see, until a small bird dashed across a dark muddy area, and this bird showed a nice area of white. Focusing up I had a ringed plover, and working the complete area one was soon 13, so some had stayed behind, not all had left for pastures new. Out of the river, or ditch as it now looks, came a dozen or so waders which I had not been aware of, they had been hidden by the bank. Dunlin, 11 of them as it so happened, so here again we had further waders who were staying put for some time yet.

Not too far away a small group of nine black-headed gulls had been sitting out on the mud, and I had hardly given them a cursory glance, when they suddenly got up and started to walk about, and among these white gulls were two very brown birds and they were not juvenile gulls. Telescope time again. The two birds were a black-tailed godwit and a ruff, and I had nearly missed these, the two birds of the day really as far as Blithfield is concerned.

Today, 4 October, would normally have been a day for celebration, not me wandering off on my own, it would have been our 53rd wedding anniversary and I think birding would have taken a back seat. However, it suits me to go off on my own where I can share my memories with the birds I now love, I know Dorothy would not mind this at all.

Duck numbers had started to build up, teal must have been in three figures, 20 or so wigeon, some you could hear whistling, and a good number of mallard. Work as hard as I could I had no joy with the mandarin which had been reported, she must have moved off, but while working my way through all the birds I had a very pleasant surprise, I came across three pintail. All of these being in eclipse needless to say, although one had the rich brown neck colour coming through, denoting this to be a drake. They are probably my favourite duck, just look in your field guide at the male in full plumage, he takes some beating in the beauty stakes.

Len 'phoned me earlier, he has confirmed he will be going to Norfolk with me for a weeks birding, so I shall be onto the Pheasant Hotel tomorrow to book us in. I will send a round robin to members of the Rosliston Bird Study Group to see if anyone else would like to join us. What could be better, good company, nice food, comfortable hotel, the odd bottle of wine and plenty of birds. We are going to the Pheasant on the 7 November for the week.

I have really cracked on with my chores this week as I was leaving tomorrow free for a day out. I intend to visit Carr Vale Nature Reserve at Bolsover in Derbyshire. I have never visited this site previously but it has the reputation of being the 5th best birding location in Derbyshire, this is some accolade. There are no hides so there is little or no cover available. Therefore, pick the days to visit, the last thing you will want is rain or snow. The journey up took just an hour and as I approached Bolsover I noticed a sign pointing to the Pools Brook Country Park, if I have time I will call in on my return journey. I parked up on the Peter Fidler Reserve car park, it is free, and made my way into the reserve. The footpaths are all firm and suitable for wheelchair users, although there are a few gradients so it may be useful to have some one to push on occasion. For the rest of us there are adequate benches, almost every 100 metres or so.

I picked out the short route and set off. Birds were very quiet, but this is the case at this time of the year, the only bird you are likely to hear singing is a robin, and it was only when I reached the Reserve Pond, this was originally a fishing pond used by the miners of Bolsover, where I saw birds. There was a bench nicely adjacent so I sat down to view the pond. Five grey heron stood in the shallows by the reed bed, several mallard were swimming about almost lazily and the most common bird on the water was gadwall. Looking at this pond I believe this would be a good area for breeding reed warbler.

Walking on I made my way towards the Mound, this is a piece of high ground with a viewing area over the Middle and Meadow Flashes which are usually the most productive areas on the reserve, and so it proved to be today. There were many gulls, mainly lesser black-backed and black-headed, a fair number of geese and swans, along with teal, mallard, gadwall and wigeon, the later could be heard whistling. While enjoying the panorama, I picked up two white birds coming in to land, two little egrets, you know how much I like these birds, and they, very obligingly, landed just in front of the Mound.

The weather looked as though it was closing in so I made my way back to the car park, stopping at a small feeding station on the way. It was only a tray nailed to a post but several species of titmice were feeding on it, so I paused to watch, the birds fortunately did not seem at all interested in me, they were probably used to people. Two rather drab titmice came in, grabbed a seed and flew off quickly, what had we here, marsh or willow tit? I settled down to watch, their visits were very quick, a dash in and a dash out, but I managed to get the view I wanted, two willow tits. Not a bad bird to finish up on. Time now for my lunch and a quick visit to Pools Brook.

Pools Brook Country Park was only about 10 minutes away, and was useful: on more than one account. Here we had a café and full facilities, Carr Vale has none of these, and car parking was once again free. It does have an area for Blue Badge holders, but it is not large and today was full, the main car park however is close by.

This area has the reputation for being good for winter gulls and regularly clocks up a few of the rarer species, even a Bonaparte's gull on one occasion. I went out for one last look over the lake, large numbers of geese, the usual Canada, greylag and Heinz 57's you get at these places, being fed by several grandparents with their young grandchildren, a marvellous way to get kiddies interested in birds and also showing them how to be kind to them. A couple of great crested grebe were way out, both looking very white as they had moulted into their winter plumage, and the odd tufted and mallard were to be seen, not as many as I would have thought on a water where they are regularly fed.

While taking all of this in a large gull came drifting in, first thoughts were herring gull, but for some reason I picked it up in my binoculars, and I was glad I did. As the bird came in to land on the water a pair of bright yellow legs were dangling down, I had nearly missed out on a yellow-legged gull. I know I have seen several this year, but I never fail to be attracted by them, it is only in recent times they have become the slightest bit regular. A nice bird to end the day on.

Saturday has come in rather drab and grey, our summer may well have departed, but autumn is looking very colourful. Yesterday I noticed the colour in the trees particularly so, the various hues looked beautiful. I think I will have another day visiting pastures new, I just intend to get out my map, Sheet Number 128, Derby and Burton upon Trent, my local patch, and see if I can find somewhere which looks hopeful, and fits the Blue Badge criteria. After a while my attention is drawn to a selection of locations near to Moira, not an area noted for it's birding. I have located two parking areas which are identified as picnic spots, both of which are next to water and woodland and close by is a lake at Willesley which looks visible from a nearby road.

I must confess it was not too successful, but one of the location at Oakthorpe could be a site for the future. Saltersfield Picnic Area has great potential I believe. It is a nicely wooded area with water features, one of which you can walk round by use of a board walk, ideal for wheelchair users. Although little was seen today the water was surrounded by a decent reed bed which I am sure would be home to reed warblers during the breeding season, and the thickish undergrowth would suit many a different warbler. The second lake is much larger and here a few duck could be seen, plus a pair of great crested grebe. Car parking is for free, but there are no facilities.

Willesley was my next venture, and here I was very disappointed, The lake is a nice size, surrounded by woodland, but it is obviously a major angling location. What birds were visible were way out in the middle of the lake and these only appeared to be black-headed gulls, mallard, coot, moorhen and great crested grebe, and apart from the gulls I doubt if they numbered 20. Access is not very good unless you are fit and active. I do not think I will visit again.

Sunday has come in far brighter than I expected after a night of steady rain, mind you it is only 08.10 hours so anything can happen. I have decided a visit Clumber Park is in order. Clumber Park is National Trust, although it is surrounded by free access areas, but for visiting the area round the lake membership is required to avoid car parking fees. As it is National Trust it has all the usual facilities, including a café. The journey is uneventful and I arrive well before 12.00 hours, and Clumber is already heaving with people. I made my way down to the lake, which was the principal reason for my visit, and I found a bench to sit on and slowly worked the water in front of me. Large numbers of Canada geese were out of the water, being fed by the many families here, with several mute swans and mallard among them.

I was not here for the 'tame' variety, my reason was to try to find the mandarin which are reported as becoming more frequently seen on the lake. With all this activity going on I very much doubted if any would be on open water, they are a very secretive duck at times, so my best chance was to work the several small tree covered islands dotted about. Mandarin are a tree duck after all, so they are likely to be roosting up until things quieten down. I must have spent a good half an hour before I became lucky, and I located three greyish looking duck on a branch over the water. Focusing up more critically, I had my bird, three female mandarin, not as dashing as the drakes, but three ducks is far better than no birds at all. The reports are obviously true, and I am sure there were others hidden away.

Time now to go searching for my other quarry, another Clumber speciality, the hawfinch. Years ago, whenever Dorothy and I wished to see hawfinch, Clumber was the place to go. It is only in recent years I learned about Cromford, which is my first choice nowadays. From past experience the area round the Chapel was always the best place to see them, but with all the noise and activity of today this was not going to be easy.

I found another bench to sit on and concentrated on sound, could I possibly hear a bird with all the background noise, doubtful. But having said all that I could hear a nuthatch complaining away as only they can, and a party of long-tailed tits could be heard as they moved through the holly above where I sat. I was just about ready to give up when I saw a movement in a nearby yew tree, I sat studying the spot when out popped a male hawfinch who promptly flew off to vanish in another yew. At least they are still here so should things ever change at Cromford, I will know where to come.

Monday has come in very windy indeed, not at all the sort of day to be out on open marshland, but I am off to Doxey Marsh, near Stafford, with the Rosliston Bird Study Group. The journey across was nice and easy so we arrived a little early, but by 10.30 hours nine of us had turned up so it was not a big turnout, but not to worry. Three of my colleagues were interested in the Norfolk week, so we may yet have a decent number. So off we went, suitably wrapped up for the wind and anything else the weather may have to throw at us.

Our first stop was at the Cresswell Flash, a medium sized piece of open water. Several geese were to be seen so we concentrated on these, and it was a good job we did. What we at first thought to be all Canada, turned out to be Canada and nine barnacle geese, and for one of our new members the barnacle were a 'Lifer', not a bad start. A couple of snipe gave us a quick flypast, too quick for some of us, and a grey heron was stalking the lake fringes.

We moved off making our way towards the Boundary Flash, this is usually the most productive, not today. It was receiving the full blast of the wind and all we could see were three Canada geese and a single black-headed gull. The wind was fierce here abouts so we quickly made our way towards the Tillington Flash, and as we approached Len pointed out a small duck swimming in the ditch. Our first thoughts were female teal but as we approached she took to flight, and fortunately flew directly past us so we had a good view of her wings. I was pleased to have Len here today as he was able to confirm my impression of the two white wing bars, the trailing edge was broader than the forward wing bar, here we had garganey, if it had been teal the opposite would have applied. One small detail like this is where positive identification frequently lies.

We were very pleased to have an hide to go into at Tillington, were we could all sit and be out of the wind. The Flash was well shrouded from the wind so we had many birds to see and enjoy. Canada again predominated, but tucked among these was a solitary barnacle goose, so that made 10 for the day. A large flock of lapwing were roosting out on a mud bar, they must have been in three figures, and among the duck were teal and shoveler, an interesting selection, and seeing the teal gave us an opportunity to compare with our memory of the garganey before it took off.

Doxey Marsh is always open as it has a public footpath through it, unfortunately being close to a large town such as Stafford it does suffer the odd outbreak of vandalism, and hides have been burned down in the past. Dog walkers and cyclists are regularly encountered, but in the main they are acting responsibly. Car parking is free but there are no facilities, and the majority of pathways are wheelchair friendly, just be careful on the odd occasion. The reserve is managed by the Staffordshire Wildlife Trust and has a warden. During the summer months it is a wonderful place for warblers and water rail, the latter are probably the highest count regionally, wintertime is good for wildfowl. It can be approached from the Sainsbury's car park, but here you have to pay, but you can at least use their toilets if you wish, just look like a shopper! Just a final point, if visiting Doxey Marsh for the first time, do not head for Doxey, you are the wrong side of the river. Take the Eccleshall Road, the A5013, off the A34 going north of Stafford. The map reference, needless to say, is to be found at the end of this chapter.

Tuesday is showing all the signs of being a miserable and grey day, still with a strong wind. In the afternoon I decided to pop across to Blithfield and call in at Kings Bromley on the way back to see if the great white egret which had been reported was about. Due to the wind the reservoir resembled the North Sea, waves were crashing up against the dam, and apart from gulls, birds were none existent. I concentrated on the gulls, you never know what strong winds may have brought in, but nothing exceptional, although there was a nice, clean, adult great black-backed along with a first winter bird, so it was not all gloom and despair. I drove to the causeway and down to Dairy House Reach to see if any waders were still hanging on. Needless to say I had the reservoir to myself, and here, for some reason, the water was much calmer and quite a few duck were bobbing about, mostly mallard and wigeon.

I drove down to the Reach, flushing an oystercatcher while in transit, and pulled up to survey the mud. Every time I come down here the water levels are receding and more mud is being exposed, if we do not get some rain soon I can see us having water supply problems.

Initially I could not see a lot apart from the foresaid ducks and a largish group of gulls, black-headed and lesser black-backed, and then a sudden movement on the waters edge caught my eye. Waders, and it did not need the telescope, they were close enough for binoculars, which is probably why I did not see them earlier, I was studying at distance. I counted 10 birds which initially looked all dunlin, but on closer observation one turned out to be a curlew sandpiper, presuming this is the same bird it has been here for a few weeks now, I just hope it hangs on until the weekend for Sarah.

On the lay-by there is snack caravan for most of the day, Mr Choppy as it is known, and when I arrived he was just packing up for the day. I stopped some distance from his van to have a look along the river. The little egret was still in residence and as I was enjoying it down came 'Mr Choppy' to speak to me. 'Was I after the bird' he said, I replied in the affirmative. He proceeded to tell me he saw the bird most mornings when he arrived at first light to set up, and this had been going on for about three weeks. He had no idea of what he was looking at but by coincidence a birder called in for a cup of coffee and he was able to tell him all about it That is when it hit the net last week, and since then whenever you pass the lay-by there are birders about, admittedly only me today. Needless to say, he had seen the bird this morning but it was no where in sight now. Having seen two previously this year I do not think I will be getting up at the crack of dawn in the hope of seeing this one.

On Wednesday I decided to have a trip down to Croxall Lakes NR, Whitemoor Haye, Barton Marina and a quick look in at the lay-by in Kings Bromley just in case the great white egret decides to put in an appearance.

Croxall was totally deserted of people, I had the place completely to myself, not that I minded one little bit. It enabled me to drive up close to the shore without the fear of upsetting anyone should I flush the birds, which I am pleased to say I did not. This was useful as it had started to drizzle, so I could keep my equipment dry and view from the car. I started by viewing the scrape area, many birds were in attendance. Working my way through these all turned out to be black-headed gulls, lapwings and starlings. In an small area of water I spotted a medium sized wader, I had missed this on my first pass, focusing up it turned out to be a redshank.

I then put up my telescope to scan the far shore, not a lot was happening until I picked up four pure white shapes standing on the shore, little egrets. They were all at rest, with their heads tucked in, just a dumpy ball of white on long legs. Continuing round I picked up a few great crested grebe, all now looking very white as they had moulted into their winter plumage and at this point I realised I had not seen a goose, this is most unusual at Croxall. I swept back and as I approached the little egrets once again I caught sight of what looked like a large white bird moving behind them, but my view was obstructed by trees. I drove forward slightly to get a better angle, had I found the great white egret was my first thought. I had not. What I had seen was the white front of a grey heron, I had the right size and family group, just a case of the wrong bird. Excitement over. I then decided it was time to go and as I moved off a small bird flicked up onto the top of a nearby teasel, a female stonechat, she was a surprise. Stonechats were not on my hit list for today, and this year I have not seen all that many, whether they had suffered with the bad weather last winter I do not know, so she was a very welcome visitor.

Off now to the Haye. Stopping to have a look at the lake I quickly found out where the geese had gone, they were all here. There must have been in excess of 300 birds here, mainly Canada with just a smattering of greylags. Of more interest to me was the sight of a nice flock of pochard on the water, must have been about 50 of them, they have arrived nice and early. We usually do well here for pochard, but I normally anticipate seeing them from November onwards, not mid October. Is this a sign of a bad winter as the pundits are forecasting? The pochard all seemed to be in full plumage, they had obviously moulted early, before they set off on their migration to us. Although pochard do breed in the UK, they are not a common duck, it is the winter when we really see them in number, as it is the case with most of our duck.

Off now down the rough lane to see if the owl is in his tree, if he was he was not showing himself. Further down the lane there was a lot of activity at the spot where someone feeds the bids regularly, so I drove down very carefully. Stopping a short distance away I was amazed at the number of tree sparrow I saw, they were very active so an accurate count was not possible, but there were certainly in excess of 25, plus a few reed bunting and yellowhammer.

Now let us see what Barton Marina has to offer. I tend to visit Barton Marina during the winter months as it usually has a nice flock of wigeon who seem to get used to visitors to the marina and are not easily scared off. Unfortunately today, as far as wigeon were concerned, there was not one. A few Canada, mallard, tufted and coot was it.

Thursday started drab, but as the morning progressed so did the weather, and by late morning the sun was out. My only chores today were to look after a load of washing, once this was done the day was my own. Little had been reported on the net, so I decided I would take a trip across to Chasewater. I understand the repairs to the dam have now been completed and they are allowing the reservoir to fill up again. This will not happen overnight, apparently it will take nearly three year. I call in at the Kings Bromley lay-by in transit, the great white egret had been reported yesterday, I do not need to tell you it was not here today, but two little egrets flew off upstream as I arrived, their yellow feet trailing, so they alone worth popping in for.

Chasewater was quite busy today, the unexpected sun had brought a few people out. Water levels were lower than last seen, vegetation had sprung up in various places which normally would have been below the water level. On what water was available it was mainly gulls, tufted, mallard and coot, with two or three great crested grebe and two cormorant.

On the way home I again call in at Kings Bromley, no egrets of any type here on this occasion. But on getting home I see the great white was reported again, and only half an hour before I first arrived before lunch. So, I decided to pop out again to have an hour looking for it. I pulled up on the lay-by, opened my car window and sat down to study the meadows on the western bank of the Trent. I had only been there for about 10 minutes, when a large white shape walked across a farmers field about 300 metres away, it just had to be the egret. I had not brought my telescope with me but even through my binoculars you could appreciate the size of the bird, unfortunately, within a minute the bird had walked out of sight.

A few birders drove up, so now there were five of us working away. We must have spent a good quarter of an hour when I spotted a large white shape in flight, it was our bird, but just where was it flying to, fortunately everyone saw it. The bird landed on the river bank some 100 metres away, in the open, so we now had very clear views of the bird. Even through the binoculars you could see the large yellow bill which denoted the bird was a none breeding specimen, and while we were enjoying the occasion it again took to flight, this time landing in a field directly opposite where we stood. No sooner had it landed when a couple of grey heron, who were also in the field, flew across to chase the bird off. The egret was having none of it, it stood it's ground.

When you look in your field guides, they say the egret is almost the size of a grey heron, in the field the egret looked much larger and with a more powerful bill and a thicker neck. To see the two birds side by side was marvellous, and we all just stood there enjoying every minute of it. I was about to move off when one of the other birders said a little egret was coming in to land in the same field, and he was right. We now had great white egret, two grey heron and one little egret all within a few metres of each other, if anyone had a camera, what a picture it would have made. This has to be one of the outstanding moments of the year for me, and it was all happening within about a mile from home, I just wish Sarah could have been here with me, she too would have appreciated it all.

Today, Friday, we are off to try out a new car, a 4x4 automatic I have seen. As the car is much larger than my current vehicle we are going to drive it home to make sure we have the space necessary. I have test driven the car myself and I am happy with it, now it is just a question of will in fit! The deal is done, come next Wednesday I will be the owner of a Kia Sorento, 2.5 diesel, auto, 4x4, due to my leg I really did require an automatic gearbox, I am lucky it is my left leg which causes my problems. It is rather nice just to sit in a car, put it into gear and drive off. I have a feeling I am going to enjoy my motoring once again, and with the car being higher off the ground I can now see over the tops of some hedges and walls.

Saturday has come in quite brightly, blue sky and weak sunshine at present, but it is early. Kings Bromley and Blithfield it will be, on a chase to see if we can get Sarah a new bird or two for the year. We pulled in on an empty lay-by at Kings Bromley and as we got out of the car the great white egret was there to see. On the meadow directly opposite the lay-by stood our prey for the day, much in the same place as I last saw it, and it was again in the company of a little egret and a grey heron. For Sarah this was her best view ever of the great white, her only one previous record had been at distance and partly hidden by a dense reed bed, so she was thrilled to bits with today's view.

To say Blithfield was quiet is the under-statement of the year, there was hardly a bird in sight, and although we drove down to the end of the water level, not a single wader was to be found. A few gulls, one or two duck and a handful of greylags was our lot. Realising we still had time available we drove round to Tad Bay, but instead of walking down to the hide we decided to drive on to Beech Tree Point, and park up there which should provide us with a good sweeping view into Tad Bay. This area is only open to key holders unfortunately.

Due to the low water levels we were able to walk out some distance which gave us a very good view down the bay, and lighting conditions were well nigh perfect, and here the telescope came into use.

On the shore line I had seen four small waders mixed in with the lapwings, so it was back to finding these. First impression was dunlin, but one of the birds looked a lot paler, almost greyish, so I would up my zoom to 60x magnification, and I was glad I had, this bird turned out to be the curlew sandpiper. Quickly calling Sarah across to have a look, she did, and what do you think had happened, the bird had moved off. Time for some more hard work, but relocate the bird we did, and Sarah had her second tick of the day, the other three birds by the way were dunlin.

Back now to the water to try and find the other birds which had raised my interest. It did not take long for number one to appear and this was a lovely adult, male, pintail, a mega duck in the beauty stakes. Sarah's ears pricked up at the mention of pintail, I did not realise this was going to be her first of the year. I quickly moved over for her to have a good look at the bird, she thinks as highly of pintail as I do.

In the afternoon I decided to visit JCB at Rocester to see if anything unusual had joined in with the collection birds. I just managed to park up, due to the nice weather quite a few family parties were out feeding the ducks and eating an ice cream or two. I was sitting on a nearby bench watching all this activity, when a call was heard from above, and in came two Egyptian geese, and they scattered many of the smaller duck as they crash-landed. Two duck were swimming on the periphery of all the activity, and these caught my attention, they were both red-crested pochard ducks, not the glamour puss drake, and I realised these were not collection birds, they both were fully primary equipped, free flyers in fact. These are the type of species I call in at Rocester in the hope of seeing, wild birds which are attracted in by all the feeding activity that goes on here, and the same thing could easily be applied to the Egyptian geese.

Time to return home for a relaxing evening in, and I have a bottle of wine to accompany me tonight. I have finished a course of medication which did not allow you to enjoy a drink, so I will celebrate tonight, and due to Sarah seeing her curlew sandpiper this morning she has chosen a bottle of Sandpiper Carignan-Shiraz, from France.

Although it is quite early, Sunday looks as though it could be another pleasant autumn day, and after a quick check up on the net, Daventry and Pitsford Reservoirs it will be. The grey phalarope was again reported yesterday from Daventry and the ferruginous duck from Pitsford, so I will give them both a go.

The journey across to Daventry went very well and it only took me about 80 minutes. The country park in which the reservoir is situated was well sign posted so I had no trouble in locating the right spot. The reservoir is a canal feeder for the nearby Grand Union Canal and was constructed as long ago as 1804, which must make it one of the oldest in the country. The whole of the country park, to give it it's correct title 'The Daventry Reservoir Country Park' looks a very interesting area, and the bird list for the location is very impressive, a very good reason for further visits. Blue Badge parking is available, although the area is not too large, but wherever you park as long as you display your badge, it is free. There is a warden on site, café, gift shop and full facilities, the pathways I walked on were firm shale and would be suitable for wheelchair users.

I made my way to the dam, and not knowing just how far this was I did not take my telescope with me, as looking at a map the reservoir is not large, so I hoped my 'scope would not be required. As things turned out the walk was not far and the 'scope was definitely needed. After a good half an hour I was becoming more frustrated, with the suns glare all the water looked silvery and trying to locate a small white and grey bird was very difficult and tiring. I had just decided to go back to my car for my scope when a young lad, in his early teens I would guess, accompanied by his mother, arrived on the scene, and he was carrying a telescope. He asked me if I had seen the phalarope, to which I obviously replied no. Bless the lad, he offered me his telescope so I could have a good look. Initially I could find nothing until a small pale bird caught my attention near to the shore line, I wound up the zoom as the bird could easily have been a small gull at this distance, but no, it was our prey. I quickly handed the 'scope back, and my new young friend and his mother had a 'Lifer' to enjoy. I was able to give them some facts about grey phalaropes which up to today had only ever been a picture in a book for them both.

Now for Pitsford and the ferruginous duck, if we are lucky. I set up my 'scope to scan the water, and I had a shock. I have never seen so many tufted and pochard together, and many were female or still in eclipse and they are very difficult to split at this distance with the ferruginous duck, all three being brown jobbies. The birds must have been 250 metres away, and as I started to work my way through them I began to realise my task was well nigh impossible. There were several female moulting tufted duck who all showed the white under the tail which is characteristic of the ferruginous, and at this distance other important features were not visible, the bird will have to wait for another day.

I decided to work the near shore as I had noticed waders along the water line. I was panning my way through these, which incidentally were all lapwing, when I picked up a small brown bird running among them. The bird was quite upright, and focusing up more critically I was pleased to find myself studying a rock pipit, not a bird I see a lot of, so I spent a few minutes enjoying the bird. It was not a 'Year Tick' but it did help to compensate for not finding the ferruginous duck.

Time now for making my way home after a most enjoyable few hours. Passing through Kings Bromley I pulled into the lay-by, my car almost pulls in here automatically. Looking downstream I was pleased to see a little egret doing his stuff in the shallows, and as I pulled off him something white on the river bank caught my attention. It was the great white, sitting there, all hunched up, looking grumpy as only heron and egret can.

My work load went very well this morning so I shall be able to have a couple of hours out later, a quick visit to Blithfield will fit the bill. Driving over the dam I saw a large gull flying over the water. As no one else was on the dam I was able to stop, this bird was big, and when I picked it up again it was easy to understand why, it was a first winter great black-backed gull, and as I have said before, they are big. The only other birds I saw as I crossed over were two pied wagtails, they were really being blown about with the strong wind.

As I drove into Mickledale Bay I spotted a small group of waders busily feeding in some newly exposed mud. I managed to get fairly close and sat back to study the birds. There were only six birds in the group, four were obviously dunlin, but what were the other two, one being smaller the other larger? Due to the glare from the sun I needed to change my angle of vision. The small bid was quickly identified, a ringed plover, but the larger one was not co-operating and kept vanishing up a small channel of water. Eventually I got the view I wanted, and I was very pleased to see the bird was a knot. They are not a rare bird, but they are a bit special so far in land, and especially at this time of the year. I can only presume it had drifted in on the winds of late, I was more than happy to see it.

The collection of my new car went smoothly and I was able to have time to give it a little run so I could get used to the controls, they were very different from my Fiat. I came home via Kings Bromley were I, needless to say, pulled in at the lay-by to have a brief look along the river. No great white but two little egrets were feeding in the river downstream from the lay-by, and as I was watching these a small bird flew rapidly across the river. What on earth had I got here, but I could no longer see the bird which had vanished into the bank. A short while later out it flew and proceeded to hover over the river, I had me a kingfisher, the first I have seen here for many a year, and it confirmed Sarah's sighting of one a few days ago. We will have to keep our eyes open when stopping here, it obviously is not just a case of egrets, there are other, more colourful things to see.

My Thursday morning chores were completed on time, so I have decided to go across to Staunton Harold Reservoir. It was a pleasant run across and I arrived nicely in time for a bit of lunch. It was warm enough to sit out in the picnic area which also gave me a nice view across the reservoir. Initially there was not a lot apparent, Canada geese, various common duck and several black-headed gulls, two of which were persecuting a great crested grebe which had caught a small fish, mind you the grebe was having none of it. A family party came down to the shore with a large plastic bag of bread, soon as they scattered this about the gulls gave up and went after more easily obtained food. The geese and ducks raced up from the water, I did not know they could move so fast on dry ground, they must have been starving! This left the grebes to get on with their own business without any duress.

A movement on the far shore caught my attention, four small waders were running rapidly along the waters edge, focusing up my telescope, these turned out to be four dunlin. Something of real interest at last, but they turned out to be all I was to see.

Never mind, off now to the Calke View Point Car Park which over looks the southern end of the reservoir. Water levels were very low and the bay in front of Spring Wood was almost devoid of water, to compensate a little, there was much activity at the feeding station, so I concentrated my efforts here. I was quickly rewarded with several tree sparrows, I would estimate about 10, but they were in and out so quickly it was impossible to count accurately. A marsh tit kept popping in: because of a loose feather in it's wing I knew it was only one. While enjoying this activity I noticed two white birds flying down the reservoir towards me, so I spun round to study these, and was rewarded with two little egrets, who landed on the shore line of Spring Wood, the shallow water suited them.

Nothing else of interest caught my attention so I decided to drive off and pop into Rosliston Forestry Centre to see Kate and organise the next term of bird study for the Rosliston Bird Study Group. They have got away with it nicely this term due to my problems, so they have some serious catching up to do, not that they know it yet. I also arranged details for our Christmas Bash which we have each year, Heather will shortly be giving out her instructions to us all regarding what we have got to provide.

Leaving Kate to get on with her work I drove off to Croxall Lakes NR, I thought I would finish off here. The road to Croxall passes through Walton on Trent and just south of Walton the road borders the River Trent, it is here where we have seen goosander in the past. Driving past I picked up a small bird on the river, which I initially took to be a little grebe. As I drove past the bird turned, it showed a white face, the bird was no little grebe, we had either a black-necked or a Slavonian grebe, I just had to turn round to have a second look. Fortunately there was a farm near by, and I managed to turn round and retrace my way. I parked up, but initially could not find the bird, then up it popped, and it was a juvenile black-necked grebe. In all my years of bird watching, this is my first record of the bird in flowing water, I have always seen them on lakes or in the sea.

A new day and I have decided to pop up to Old Moor today, an RSPB reserve near to Barnsley, noted for it's winter flock of golden plover. A very well appointed reserve, wheelchairs can be hired and all the pathways and hides are obviously wheelchair friendly, and it has a cracking café if required. I was on my way promptly this morning and my journey up to Old Moor was very pleasant, I must admit I found an automatic gear on the motorway most enjoyable. Just north of Derby you cross over the River Derwent and as I did so a little egret flew down the river, a nice start to the day. I was surprised by the number of cars parked up at Old Moor, but on entry it was not as bad as first thought I made my enquiries regarding a jack snipe which had been reported regularly, but not today it seemed. It was last seen from the Bittern Hide, so nothing for it but to make my way to that hide.

There were only three other birders in the hide and the news about the jack snipe was not good, no sign of it at all so far. Still I am here now and I could do with sitting down. Bird life was quite thin on the ground, a pair of swans, the odd mallard, coot and moorhen was it.

After a good half an hour I was about to get up when one of the birders shouted 'Water rail', and flying across a corner of the lagoon was indeed a water rail. This more than compensated for the lack of the jack snipe as I had not seen a water rail before this year, a nice, and unexpected 'Year Tick'. I could now move on with a smile on my face.

I slowly made my way back and proceeded to walk on to the Family Hide, which is positioned in the corner of the largest stretch of water, the Mere. Here very good numbers of waterfowl could be seen. Large numbers of gadwall, it is a very good spot for this duck, a nice flock of shoveler all looking very smart, the drakes anyway, mallards were well spread and a very large population of coot covered the water. On the meadows surrounding the Mere were large numbers of Canada geese and a few greylags, and lapwings were well scattered. I then moved across to the nearby Field Pool West Hide, a hide I have always found to be very quiet apart from snipe, who tend to favour this spot. But not today, there was not a snipe to be seen, just a few teal, shoveler and pheasant. Looking up the marshy area I was pleased to see a very large flock of golden plover/lapwing flying, there must have been in excess of 800 golden plover. I know who will be interested in this, my friend Andy Toman, photographer to this tome, he will want to test his skills with these birds, so I must leave a message for him.

Old Moor is a delightful reserve, with plenty to see on the bird front, I have been a little critical today, as apart from the water rail I have not seen anything new, but having said that the golden plover were a bit special to say the least, we do not see them in those numbers in my local patch. It is worth the visit just to experience those, especially for the first time. There are several other interesting bird watching locations locally so you could well spend a day or two in the area, I have in the past. Three in particular are Broomhill Flash, Wombwell Ings and Edderthorpe where a large expanse of subsidence water collects, map references will be provided as usual at the end of this chapter.

Tomorrow is going to be a quiet day on the bird front. We will not be having or usual morning out, as Sarah has just had two days holiday, she has work to do, and in the afternoon I am taking a friend of mine over to Blithfield to meet another friend who has a pair of binoculars for sale, to see if they can do a deal. The three of us met up as planned, and went off to use the binoculars, they had belonged to my old friend Mike Dix who recently died, so I knew they would be a good quality binocular and have been well looked after. Evelyn, who was buying them, was able to give them a very good workout and she was completely satisfied with them, as I thought she would be, so the deal was done.

Now for a bit of the serious stuff, searching for birds in trees, with leaves still on the bough this was not going to be easy. A small flock of birds was flitting about in an oak right above our heads, and a couple flew out and proceeded to hover, just the clue we needed, goldcrests. The odd blue tit also appeared and as we were watching these I heard a 'Chip, chip, chip' call from the larch trees behind us, I quickly shouted 'Crossbills', as we swung round to look.

Our luck was in, sitting right out on the top of a larch were three of them, unfortunately sitting right in the sun, so we only had them in silhouette, but with their shaped bill there was no doubt over identification. Within seconds they were up and away chip, chip, chipping off into the distance. That is the story with crossbills at times, just a fleeting glimpse or a distant call is all you get, we had done well, and for Evelyn a nice christening of her new acquisition. As yet I have no idea of what I will be up to tomorrow, but I do feel like somewhere new.

For the last few days a white-rumped sandpiper and an American wigeon have been reported from Rutland Water, in Leicestershire (or should that now be Rutland?), as I have not seen a white-rumped sandpiper for over 20 years, I decided to have a trip over. My last white-rumped, my only one ever, was a bird I shared with Dorothy, and I must confess I receive a great amount of pleasure when I see a rare species which I can associate with memories of my wife, so if I am successful it will be a double celebration. My journey to Rutland was a shocker, road works everywhere especially in Loughborough, I will not go this way again, but eventually I arrived. Rutland Water Nature Reserve is managed by Leicestershire and Rutland Wildlife Trust in partnership with Anglian Water and provides one of the most important wildfowl sanctuaries in Great Britain, regularly holding in excess of 20,000 waterfowl. It is also a Ramsar site and is relatively new as the reservoir was only created in the 1970s.

A charge is made for entry, but if you are a member of a Wildlife Trust you get a 10 per cent discount and concessions are available for senior citizens, students, disabled visitors and their carers. Car parking is free, there are toilets in both the car park and the Visitor Centre, and if you are disabled I would suggest you use the Visitor Centre's facilities. An electric buggy is available for hire at Egleton, but do book it in advance. 17 of the hides are adapted for wheelchair users, there is a gift shop and drinks are available, the only complaint I have is the limited number of Blue Badge holder car parking spots, only room for three.

Enough of the advertising on behalf of Rutland, let us get back to birds. I checked up on the two I was particularly interested in and both had been seen during the morning, the only problem for me was the fact they were at the furthest point on the reserve, a round walk of probably a mile or so. I had not come here for nothing, so a walk it was going to be, the buggy was already in use.

The pathways were very dry and level so progress was not too bad, and the Lapwing Hide was my destination, it was here all the action was being reported from. I was rather disappointed by the small amount of benches provided, so by the time I arrived at my destination I was really ready to sit down. As I approached the hide I met up with two birders who were just leaving, they told me I may be in for a long wait as a peregrine had just flown across and flushed all the waders. Not the news I wanted to hear.

Upon entering the hide I was greeted by a birder I knew from way back and he had the sandpiper in his scope, what an arrival! I had a quick look so I could relocate the bird myself, and found a place to sit down, I really did need to rest my leg, but felt the effort was well worth it. The bird looked to be a juvenile, which is what I would expect for a bird from North America, it should not be here it should be in South America, the fact we have so many vagrants from America is obviously due to the cyclones and storms recently experienced on the east coast of America. Juveniles especially have just been driven across by fierce winds, they lacked the experience of adults to combat such conditions. I spent some time enjoying this bird, it was quite accommodating really, continuing to feed quite close in.

Time now to find the other Yankee, the American wigeon. The hide was facing due east and the silvery sun was casting a silvery sheen over the water so most of the duck were in silhouette, which was not helping things at all. After about 20 minutes of hard graft I just gave up and concentrated my efforts on the mud, as I had been aware of wader activity. I was pleased I did, there were ringed plover, ruff, dunlin and redshank feeding on the mud, and a curlew gave us a nice flypast, very vocal, now there is a sound for you! A birder at the side of me suddenly commented 'I think I have the American wigeon, could I have a look to confirm it?' I did not need a second invitation, and a quick look confirmed he had indeed found the bird. The news spread like mad throughout the hide so most swung round to look for the bird. The birder was thrilled to bits, he was a novice and he had located the bird everyone wanted, this was a day he would probably remember for the rest of his life.

I had my two birds, although, needless to say the white-rumped sandpiper was the one I really wanted, if only for memories, very happy memories I may add. Now the pressure is off, time for a bit of general birding, so I made my way down to the Shoveler Hide, if my memory serves me correct, this is the hide for the gadwall, which to me is what Rutland is famous for.

I was not to be disappointed, gadwall were in three figures, and they looked truly magnificent. They are a very elegant duck in my mind, not at all precocious like some duck, they just have a most special merge of greys, white and black, and the female of the species is not too bad either. Most of the duck were looking quite special, most appeared to have completed their moults so the drakes were all looking exactly as your field guides illustrate them, especially the teal and shoveler, and above visual experiences the soft, melodious whistle of the wigeon could be heard, a perfect situation. While soaking up all this atmosphere, three little egrets flew in and started to hunt right in front of the hide, and one of them quickly located a worm-like object which it swallowed with much relish. To see birds going about their business like this is what birding is all about.

A quick look at the feeding station in front of the Visitor Centre provided tree sparrow, reed bunting, chaffinch and a very agile rat which was climbing up to a seed feeder. I presume this was the brown rat our native species, but I am not a mammal expert so I stand to be challenged on this. All I can say is this mammal was a master at it's game, and good luck to it. I know rats are an enigma to many people, but it is only due to our untidiness they are so prolific. I personally think they are an incredible creature who has learned to live off man.

Monday has dawned bright and crisp, I do not think we have had a frost, but there is a noticeable wind chill. Ten of the Rosliston group have joined us today, Roy was unable to do so but Len is here with me so we should be able to spread our time round nicely.

The main lake at Croxall still had the large flock of pochard in attendance, Neil counted them, 72 he reckons, not that anyone was going to challenge him, and while complimenting him on his maths, David drew our attention to an unusual looking bird in the midst of the pochard flock. Although being the same distinctive shape of a pochard this bird was very pale, almost white, compared to a pochard's delicate grey, but this bird did not look like an albino.

I had not brought my telescope with me today so I moved over to use David's. The bird was definitely pochard like, it had the brown head and distinctive profile of the bird, but not the correct body colouring. It then hit me, we had an hybrid, a cross between a drake pochard and a female tufted duck. I have seen hybrids the other way round, drake tufted/female pochard, but this is my first ever pochard/tufted. Whether these bird are fertile or not I do not know and should they breed they may produce even more unusual looking offspring. Although not being a true species I will record this in my yearly bird list as something most unusual. A very interesting end to a pleasant morning.

As there is little being reported locally, apart from a great grey shrike on Cannock Chase who is proving rather elusive, I have decided to visit Blithfield Reservoir, primarily for a bit of off-roading. I can drive round over half of the circumference of the reservoir on some quite rough surfaces, so it will give my car a good test of it's 4x4 capabilities. First of all I must call in at the Staffordshire Wildlife HQ at Wolseley Bridge, I have lost my key for Croxall Lakes NR. I obviously had it yesterday when we visited, but what has happened to it I do not know. Fortunately they had a few spares so I now have a new key, I had better take good care of this one.

Driving back to Blithfield you pass Bishton Private School and as I drove past I noticed a flock of lapwings on the school playing fields. As you will by now know, I rarely pass a flock of lapwing without studying them closely, so I pulled over to study these. I was pleased I did, I counted 17 golden plover scattered through the flock.

I pulled in at Admaston Reach, opened up the gate and drove slowly round the perimetre of the reservoir. Not a lot to be seen, so I reached Dairy House Reach and at this point a police helicopter chose to fly, low over the reservoir, and almost every bird from further down Blithe Bay took to flight, thank you!

Fortunately once the 'chopper had vanished they started to return, so I speeded up a little to get into position for the full return, my car, by the way, was handling very nicely. I parked up, wound the window down and waited the bird's return. The return was slow initially, but once a large flock of Canada/greylags flew in, sanity returned very quickly. The duck were mainly teal, wigeon and mallard and the gulls were a mixture of black-headed and lesser black-backed, until three very large gulls drifted in and landed right on the shore in front of me. Great black-backed, two winter adults and a second winter bird, and from my position they showed up very well indeed. A smallish grey looking duck caught my attention, as it swam in closer I realised it was a female mandarin, one had been reported a short while ago, not that I was able to find it on that occasion, she was obviously hanging on.

I slowly returned back along the shore and as I reached Admaston Reach I spotted four small waders feeding along the waters edge. They were close enough for binoculars, so I stopped and focused up, three dunlin and a ringed plover, not mega by any means, but it was at least nice to know we still had a wader or two about.

As I still had some time I drove round to the dam, and on into Mickledale Bay. A nice flock of linnet and goldfinch were in the bay feeding on seed heads, there must have been in excess of 60 birds here, but they were so active counting was impossible. I was about to move on when I noticed a large gull roosting on the mast of a small launch anchored in the bay. It had a pale grey back, first thoughts herring gull, until I realised the head was a brilliant white in colour, most herring gulls by now are getting a bit of grey on their heads. Through the binoculars I could not be sure of leg colour, so it was a case of up telescope, and I am sure you by now know what I was looking for, were the legs pink or yellow. They were yellow, we had a nice winter, adult, yellow-legged gull, not a bad bird to end up on.

The morning of 26 October has come in beautifully, and after I have completed my weekly shop I intend to have the afternoon out birding. As conditions are well nigh perfect for viewing over distance I have decided to go to Blithfield and view down Tad Bay, from Beech Tree Point, as Sarah and I did recently, to see if there has been any movement on the duck front. I set up my tripod and panned down the bay. Before I really got started a bird flew up the bay which I at first thought could be a juvenile black tern, but as it got closer it was obviously a small gull, and by it's behaviour a little gull. The bird was performing exactly as the books say, flying low over the water with occasional darts at the waters surface to take small insects, and the diagnostic black 'W' on the upper wing surface and black tip to tail could be clearly seen. A perfect example of the bird.

Now back to the duck, and there were plenty. The far shore was lined with mallards and teal, wigeon were in the far distance but their call could be clearly heard, and small flocks of pochard and tufted were scattered over the water. I was very pleased with the numbers of shoveler to be seen, and while working through these I became aware of a female pintail up-ending, she quickly became four: three duck and one drake. A dark duck which dived close by was the next bird to concentrate my efforts on, this turned out to be a female goldeneye, and she was joined by two others, also females.

At this point a heron came in to land and it chose to land right among the lapwings which were roosting on the shore, they took off in blind panic and I became conscious of some smaller waders flying among them. Fortunately sanity returned very quickly and the birds came back in to land. Telescope time again. Working my way through the lapwings I started to pick up the odd dunlin. This had turned out to be a very pleasant afternoon, with five birds to report.

When I drove off I noticed a friend of mine driving down, so I stopped to tell him about the little gull, and he was able to tell me he had just been over the Chase and the great grey shrike had been showing well, plus a hen harrier had been reported. The shrike which was on the Chase last winter, nearly drove me mad with many wasted journeys, maybe this year this bird is more affable, we can but hope. When putting my reports on the net I noticed two firecrest had also been seen on the Chase, and quite close to where the shrike has been reported. Adding the hen harrier to these two makes a visit to the Chase more desirable by the minute, two would be 'Year Ticks' for me, all three for Sarah.

Friday, I was up before first light and was pleasantly surprised to see a star filled sky after the dull and very overcast day we experienced yesterday, among these stars was a very sparkling yellow star which I am informed is the planet Saturn, I will have to have my telescope ready tomorrow just in case it is still visible to see if I can see the rings.

I will have a stab for the shrike and anything else that may present itself in the hope they stay around for Sarah tomorrow. I drove across to the Chase in lovely sunshine, it was almost like a springtime day, and arrived at the Cadet Camp car park for about 11.30 hours. Quite a few cars were on the car park and a few had bird club stickers on their windscreens, so I was not the only one out hunting for the shrike.

I had not walked far before I could see two birders gazing intently into the distance. I made my way towards them and as I got closer they waved me over, they had the shrike in their telescopes, this was birding made easy. We spent several minutes chatting away before they moved off to try to find the firecrests which had been reported, when I realised how far away this was I contented myself with further study of the shrike which was very active and at one stage it chased after a blue tit, fortunately for the blue tit, without success. Several times it flew off completely, what it was chasing I could not see, but each time it returned to the holly tree: obviously the bird's favoured post. This augurs well for tomorrow when I shall be bringing Sarah across to see the bird.

I have promised to meet my friend Evelyn at Blithfield, she wishes to buy a new telescope as she is dissatisfied with the one she has, so before she does so I offered to have a good look at her present model just to make sure she is correct with her diagnosis. To give it a good test we went down to the entrance of Tad Bay, from where I had the little gull, here we had the full expanse of the bay to look over, any problems would soon come to light in these conditions. We set both of our 'scopes up, I had brought mine so she had one to compare with her own, and after just a few minutes I found she was quite right with her thoughts. So now we knew what she had to do, we settled in for some birding.

Tad Bay was very busy, the shoreline was covered with lapwing and as I moved through these I came across both golden plover and dunlin, to be precise 42 golden plover and 15 dunlin, not a bad little haul that. Working my way through the many gulls which were just roosting up I managed to find our little gull, it was just sitting on the mud, asleep by the looks of things. Moving onto the larger gulls, there were 50 or so lesser black-backed and three herring gulls, but as I moved off these one of the herring gulls turned it's head and I realised we were in fact looking at a Caspian gull. This is probably my third this year, they are becoming slightly more regular, like the yellow-legged gull, a close cousin. Moving on to the open water, large numbers of teal and wigeon were to be seen, the whistling of the wigeon was delightful, and while enjoying this three dark birds flew down the bay, goldeneye, three ducks, probably the same birds we had a few days ago. Working on, two pintail came in to view, both up-ending as they fed away, once again ducks. I worked hard to try to find a drake, but was unsuccessful, but females will always do.

Although I was up bright and early to have another look at Saturn, I need not have bothered, the sky to the east was cloudy and no stars nor planets were showing through this. Saturn's rings will have to wait for another day. This astronomy lark can be as time consuming and frustrating as birding, so I will stick with what I know.

It is still only 10.00 hours and nothing has appeared on the net so far, so shrike hunting it is. The sky has brightened up considerably. Parking at the Cadet Huts car park is quite light, being the weekend I had expected more visitors after the shrike.

Walking across we meet a birder who informed us he had just seen the shrike sitting out on his holly tree, so things look good. Arriving at the same spot I chose yesterday we found only two other birders, a father with his young son who told us the bird had been on it's tree a few minutes ago, so I erected my telescope and we set in to wait. Within a couple of minutes the shrike flew in and landed on a silver birch, before I could get the 'scope on it for Sarah, it flew off. After about five minutes back it came and this time it landed right on the top most point of his favourite perch, the holly tree. While Sarah was looking at the bird I swung the 'scope round so she could see it better. This bird is a right poser, it just sat there enjoying every minute of our attention, I say his, as I am now convinced it is indeed a male, the colours are so bright and crisp.

Then we experienced two memorable moments. Firstly the bird flew off it's perch straight in our direction, and then proceeded to hover no more than 10 metres away, it did not find any foods, however, so back to his holly bush. Then the bird darted down from the tree to land in the bracken beneath, to return to his perch with a large insect in it's bill. With a toss of his head, the food went down. This holly tree is probably about eight metres high and the angle of his dive down must have been an overall distance of 15 metres, how did he see it at that distance, they must have incredible eyesight.

Time to move on, and at this point Sarah raised the question of how many birds have we seen this morning? Thinking about it the only other bird we have seen, well heard really, was a magpie. I have rarely found the Chase this quiet, but our visible bird was slightly mega, so we were not complaining. When I put my report on the net I noticed a squacco heron had been seen at Attenborough, so I decided I would have a trip across this afternoon. I need not have bothered, no squacco heron had been seen since early morning, it serves me right, I should not have shot off for a 'Twitch'. I did see an Egyptian goose!

When I checked the net last night, the squacco had been reported twice during the afternoon, but on both occasions some distance from the Visitor Centre at Attenborough, so I could not have seen the bird had I even known of it's whereabouts, I could not have walked the distances required. I shall be taking no further interest in this bird unless it moves to a new location. One has to appreciate one's limitations, and as my old friend Ivor is always saying 'They are only birds!', and as I usually add 'There is always tomorrow!'

I will have a trip out in my local patch: Kings Bromley, Croxall, Whitemoor Haye and part of Blithfield, be interesting to see if the rain has brought anything in, it frequently does, but I did not realise just how interesting today was going to be. First off, the little egret was perched up in a tree at Kings Bromley, a very nice start to the days proceedings. Croxall looked very busy, but when I entered I found only a couple of dog walkers in attendance, I can only presume the other cars belonged to walkers. As I drove up the track which had numerous pot holes full of water, it had certainly rained well last night, I spied two dark birds on the water, so I stopped and wound down my window, two juvenile drake goldeneye. A largo flotilla of Canada geese were streaming up the lake, although I worked my way through them I could not find anything else among them.

The far shore was lined with teal, there must have been in excess of 50 spread along the waters edge, mallard and a few wigeon were on the water, a large flock of lapwing were standing out on the scrape area, nothing hidden among these either. Continuing my panning of the far shore I picked up a snipe, and this sighting coincided with the sun breaking through, which was fortunate for me. I had moved on when something hit me, the bird had a very dark central strip to it's crown and the stripes on the wings were yellow not pale cream. I swung back to the spot where I first saw the bird, hoping it was still there, pulse racing a little, this bird just had to be a jack snipe, had I missed it. No, it was still standing in the open area of mud where I had first come across it, to see a jack in the open is quite a rare event, and I had nearly missed out on this one. No doubting what I was looking at here, a totally unexpected 'Year Tick'. After a short while it moved back into the denser vegetation where it completely vanished from view.

Time to move on down Whitemoor Haye. Near the old farmhouse a small bird of prey was sitting on a tall pole, what had we here? I stopped, just as the bird flew off, it was a lovely male merlin, another nice and unexpected bird for the day. On my return journey I called in to have a quick look over the lake, a small group of about a dozen lapwing were feeding on the shore, but more interestingly, three golden plover were with them.

A nice finish off for the morning, now time for Blithfield where I will have my lunch. The eastern shore was very quiet, there was much activity on the water, boats everywhere, plus the odd loud announcement over the sailing club loud speaker system, there was no doubt a sailing event taking place, so I quickly drove over the dam. The western shore was going to be a lot more peaceful both with people and birds. I drove the full length of the shore without hardly a bird, until I was in the last bay, St. Stephen's Hill Bay, and out on the water were three female goldeneye, they just about saved Blithfield from being a waste of time.

Late yesterday evening, my friend Ivor gave me a call, he had been across to Attenborough to see the squacco heron and had very good views. He was able to tell me where to park up and shave off a bit of distance, so today I am off on another 'Twitch'. I just managed to park up where Ivor had told me, taking the very last place available. A tarmac road ran alongside the railway line for about half a mile or so which terminated at the sailing club. Here, where the railway line ran over the River Erewash, was the spot where it is claimed the heron feeds. In the distance a group of birders could be clearly seen, there must have been 30 or so, and as I past a few returning birders they all said the same thing, it was still there and showing well. I strode on as best I could, there was a very useful low wall alongside the road on which I was able to rest occasionally.

I arrived and was greeted by a cheery 'Hello Brian, come and have a look, it is in my scope'. Andy Russell, a birder I have known for some years, was the guy with the 'scope, and I was only too pleased to take up his offer. The bird was standing at the bottom on a concrete bridge support, over which the railway ran, not a particularly attractive location for the many photographers who were in attendance, but that was their problem, I was delighted with the closeness of the bird. It was a juvenile, and it does just beg the question, where had it flown in from? I would guess Holland, not that it's nationality worried me that much, I was just pleased to see the bird, my second only ever in the UK.

The patience of these birds is quite amazing, it stood completely still for several minutes, even though the odd fish jumped out of the river quite close by, until he slowly moved one leg forward and made a lightening stab with it's bill, and down it's throat went a small fish. I stayed to watch the bird for about an hour and it hardly moved at all during that time, even though there must have been as many as 50 birders studying it's every move during that time. The bird was completely oblivious to us all.

That is another month put to bed, and after a slow start in some ways it has proved to be a very interesting month, with a squacco heron being the perfect way to put it to bed, it being my 218th bird of the year.

You will have noticed that I have not given map references for some of the parts of Blithfield Reservoir, like Tad Bay, as an instance. The reason for this is that to visit parts of Blithfield you need a permit and a key, these are only obtainable through West Midland Bird Club membership. The areas open to the public have had map references provided earlier in this work. For those of you who live local, membership of the WMBC is recommended as they have other reserves equally as interesting as Blithfield, you can obtain information by going to www.westmidlandbirdclub.com. They have several groups scattered through, Staffordshire, Worcestershire, Warwickshire and the West Midlands County, where field meetings and indoor meetings are regularly held. Where ever you live you should find a bird study group locally to you, and as I have said before, membership will quickly introduce you to the best areas for bird watching.

Map references:
Carr Vale NR – Peter Fidler car park: SK 463207.
Carr Vale – car park near to sewage works: SK 461702. I did not use this but it is closer to the Mound.
Carr Vale – the Mound viewing platform: SK 458698.
Pools Brook Country Park – Visitor Centre: SK 438736.
Saltersfield Picnic Area: SK 322137.
Willesley Lake: SK 338146.
Clumber Park – Visitor Centre: SK 622742.
Doxey Marsh: SK 904254.
Barton Marina: SK 198182.
Daventry Reservoir Country Park: SP577642.
Old Moor RSPB Reserve: SE 422022.
Broomhill Flash: SE 414028.
Wombwell Ings: SE 416035.
Edderthorpe Subsidence Pool: SE 415068. View from lay-by.
Rutland Water – Egleton Entrance: SK 878073.
Attenborough NR – Visitor Centre: SK516339.

Chapter XI

November

The 1 November has come in very wet, with heavy overnight rain and the sky looks full of it still but by mid-morning the weather had passed over and we now have bright blue skies and a very pleasant temperature for the time of the year so I will nip over to Blithfield, calling in at Kings Bromley for some bird food supplies in transit.

I made straight for Tad Bay, where I parked up near Beech Tree Point, I am beginning to enjoy the panoramic view of Tad Bay but I would not recommend this vantage point in poor light conditions; on a lovely bright and clear day like it now is, even birds at distance can be seen well, as long as you have a decent telescope that is.

Wigeon and teal numbers are really on the up, there must be at least twice as many as I saw when last here, and the pochard numbers seem to be creeping up nicely. The bottom shore was full of lapwings once again, so I started to work through these. I quickly located golden plover, and as I panned more appeared, we certainly had experienced an influx of these delightful waders. Time to try to count them, so back to the start I went. Working my way through them very carefully and slowly I reached a count 174, my largest local flock for some time.

Whilst concentrating on the plovers I also picked up the odd dunlin, nine in fact, so a few of these were still hanging on. Great crested grebe numbers are steadily increasing, it is not unusual to have these exceed three figures spread all over the reservoir, Blithfield is a real meeting place for these magnificent birds.

Now to concentrate on the water. Five pintail were quickly found, three ducks and two drakes, and a little further on four goldeneye, all ducks. Two ruddy ducks swam into view, but as you by now know, I do not report these, I do not want the 'rent a gun mob' in. Incidentally, both of the ruddy duck were drakes, and they did look smart.

As I was enjoying these many of the birds took off in panic, and I quickly understood why, a peregrine came flashing through at speed. The peregrine was not staying, however, and it quickly vanished from sight, allowing sanity to return. So I returned back to the water, I wanted to have a good look through the gulls, of which there were many. Lesser black-backed numbers are steadily increasing, black-headed are now well into three figures and even the common gull is up to about 20. Herring gull are still low in numbers, but that will change very quickly I am sure. Four very large gulls are sitting it out on the bank, great black-backed, all adults, and they really dwarf the local gulls.

Last evening, when putting my birds on the net I noticed a black redstart had been reported from the Wheaton Aston area, apparently it had been seen for four days, this is just about a 40 minute drive from my home, so I decided once I had finished my weekly shop I would pop across to see this bird.

Black redstarts are not common birds in the UK, I doubt if I have seen above 20 in all my years of bird watching. Abroad, especially in countries such as Switzerland and

Italy, they are relatively common, and Dorothy and I have enjoyed their company on many an occasion, they were one of her favourite birds. When walking the Alps in Switzerland, Dorothy could always pick them out by their song a long time before I did, much to her amusement and my annoyance.

Instructions were very good and I soon located the spot on my Ordnance Survey Map, so I arrived without any hassle. Two other birders were already in situ, but their reports were not good, no sign of the bird while they had been there. Another car drove up, Joyce, she lives locally and she had seen the bird yesterday, so we were at least in the right spot. The four of us then spent a frustrating two hours searching hard for the bird and to no avail. We had goldfinch, greenfinch, chaffinch and house sparrow a plenty, even a great spotted woodpecker, but not the bird we came for. By 15.00 hours I decided enough was enough so I drove off intending to have a few minutes at Blithfield Reservoir on my way home.

Blithfield has a very good gull roost each evening, and I had not watched them fly in for some time, so I thought half an hour or so just enjoying this spectacle would be time well spent. The gulls just drift in, groups varying between a few to a few hundred, and when the roost is complete you are talking of thousands of birds which roost up on the water during the winter months. We are not quite up to those numbers as yet.

A group came sailing in quite close to where I had parked up my car and I was casually watching these when I realised one of the birds had white primaries, put your brain in gear Brian. The bird was an adult Mediterranean gull and I had nearly missed it. It does not do your ego any good when this happens, fortunately I was on my own. That bird at least made up some of the disappointment of missing out on the black redstart.

Time for home. Tomorrow I am unlikely to do any birding, the gas man cometh to carry out my annual service of all things gas. I have a slot of between 12.00 and 14.00 hours booked, but on past experience it will take far longer than two hours to look into everything, but with winter not far off I like to have confidence in my heating system.

Early this morning I was awoken by torrential rain falling, for about 15 minutes we experienced a really heavy storm, and my garden is now covered with fallen leaves, so a session of tidying up is required, except the forecast is for yet more rain. But the weather has bucked up considerably, so I popped over to Blithfield and drove down Admaston Reach for a short distance to find my way blocked by workmen, they were filling in the many ruts which littered the track, and I could hardly ask them to move all their equipment so I could drive past. I am sure the many anglers who drive down here in their saloon cars will be pleased with the work, for me it spoils the fun of off-roading in my 4x4. I then drove round to the deep end to visit Mickledale and Portfields Bays, here several anglers were fishing from boats and birds, in consequence, were few and far between. Nothing else for it but to drive to Whitemoor Haye to see if any owls were about, barn or short-eared being the species I was hoping to find here.

As I drove round the rough lane I noticed a white van parked up, I became very concerned at this stage, were they fly tipping as we get a lot of this along this stretch of lane. I need not have worried as I approached the van I could see, clearly printed on the door, Lichfield District Council. When I reached the van the driver was peering into the ditch, camera in hand, photographing something in the ditch.

I walked across to see what was doing, he turned out to be an employee of the Environmental Department who was actually out collecting litter, my first thoughts could not have been further from the truth. In the ditch lay a large dead rabbit, he had seen an animal dragging the rabbit and he wondered if it had been a mink. I told him I doubted this as the River Tame is nearly half a mile from here, and mink do not roam far from water. He then told me the animal had a black tip to it's tail, problem solved, he had seen a stoat. I told him the stoat would return to find it's dinner so just leave the dead rabbit where it was, the stoat had used up a lot of energy in catching the rabbit, so do not let us deprive it of a meal. We said our farewells and I drove off to the little owl tree, and here I had my reward, the owl was sitting out right in front of it's hole, no doubt contemplating whether to go hunting as yet. A quality bird at last, in what had otherwise been a quiet afternoon.

'Bonfire Night' has come in grey and drab, but on our way through we obviously called in at the Kings Bromley lay-by and we were rewarded by seeing our little egret who was feeding upstream. A nice start to the day. On arriving at Croxall we found we had the reserve to ourselves; driving up the track we stopped to admire a goldeneye, a female, who was swimming close in. She soon spotted us and dived, never to be seen again.

From the hide it was very noticeable how high the water level had risen due to the heavy rain we have recently experienced. The scrape was completely submerged, so it was not going to be day for any waders. While I was working the far shore Sarah spoke up, 'A little egret has just walked out of the channel from the river' and continued to work it's way along the far shore, continually stabbing at the water as it walked. From where we sat it was impossible to see if the bird was actually catching anything.

Time to move off to Whitemoor. The pochard flock was still on the lake plus the odd wigeon, tufted, mallard and great crested grebe. As we were about to move off Sarah called my attention to two birds of prey which were on the ground in a nearby field of winter rape, for a short time I thought she had found a couple of hen harrier, but they were not, they were buzzards. After the overnight rain the ground is obviously soft and worms are likely to be either on or near the surface, and many a bird of prey will eat worms if the opportunity presents itself.

Sunday has come in a beautiful morning, slightly misty, but a blue sky over head, a good day coming along I think. Swimming in the bay at Blithfields was a second winter Mediterranean gull, which was quite accommodating, and swam by quite close in so identification was no problem. Nothing else of interest was to be found so I took myself off to Tad Bay, going into view from Beech Tree Point once again. Firstly scanning the water I located three pintail and five goldeneye and while enjoying these a party of seven goosander flew in, no complaints with any of these. Turning my attention to the shore line I quickly found the lapwing flock, but today there were no golden plover among them, although I did find five dunlin.

Now for Norfolk. The journey across was very good and we arrived nicely in time for lunch. Len had done his homework on the net and found a cattle egret had been reported from Blakeney over the last two days. Before Blakeney, we intended to have half an hour at Stiffkey Marsh, an area noted for birds of prey and owls, and I was after a short-eared owl, not having seen one for some time. Not today, however, no birds of prey nor owls of any description, but plenty of other birds to concentrate the mind on. Pink-footed and Brent geese, shelduck, little egret and a small party of five thrushes flew into a nearby bush, three fieldfare and two redwing, my first of the winter, both Len and I were happy with the latter especially.

Driving down into Blakeney we found the hotel and a spot to park up quite easily. The instructions were quite clear, the bird was being seen from a field east of the hotel, so telescopes set up, we commenced our search. For about 10 minutes we were finding very little, and then a white bird flew in and landed behind a hedge, time now for patience, the bird just had to walk out from behind the hedge. It seemed like hours although it was just minutes before the bird came into view. Len was at a better angle than I was, it has a yellow bill he shouted, bingo we had our bird and what a start to our holiday, a 'Year Tick' for us both. Len commented it was a shame there were no cattle in the field for the bird to associate with, and he was right. A truck came slowly over the field followed by about 20 cows, they were obviously being fed, and within moments the bird flew in to join them. For a good 10 minutes or so we were able to watch the bird going about it's business as per the text books. Several times it appeared to be dodging the feet of the cattle as it searched for a tasty bite or two, a dicey way to obtain a living.

The bird then flew off and vanished from sight, but what a memorable time we had experienced, this was only the fourth cattle egret I had ever seen in the UK, it was Len's third. My first was way back in 1994, Dorothy and I were on holiday on Anglesey, when we met up with a birder who told us about a cattle egret seen along the coast near to Rhyl, so we decided to have a go for it, a 'Twitch' if you like. The bird had been seen near to a holiday camp, which was easy to find and a group of birders were standing on the roadside gazing into a field nearby. In this field, among cattle, was our prey for the day, a magnificent cattle egret, our first for the UK. Dorothy and I have frequently joked about this as the field was adjacent to the holiday camp, and round the camp pool were many bikini clad young ladies, and we were sure many of the telescopes were not focused on the bird. Needless to say I was concentrating on the cattle egret, after all, Dorothy was standing right next to me!

We had some time left so we drove down to Salthouse which is a good spot for snow bunting and turnstone, not today however, no snow bunting and only a fleeting view of the turnstone, so to the hotel we went.

When I was last here in March you may remember my mentioning Rob Chidwick who works at the hotel part-time, Rob is the local birding guru, and I have known him for many years. This morning he presented Len and myself with a list of the best birds seen recently. We would start off at Kelling Heath for Dartford warbler, then onto Glandford for black redstart, then Cley for a sea watch and finally finishing up at Stiffkey for the raptor watch. .

Thanks to Rob's map and instructions we located the warbler spot without too much difficulty, I just wish the bird had read the script. We could hear a bird calling, but could we find him, could we heck! This bird was only to be an audible record, but that is better than no record at all.

Our next stop was to be Glandford for the black redstart and we found the location without any problem, would the bird be found so easily? Shortly after our arrival another birder arrived on the scene, he had seen the bird only minutes previously and he was of the opinion there were two birds not one. We spent several minutes searching without success, during which time other birders arrived on the scene, we were now in double figures, birders I hasten to add not black redstarts! After a short while a shout went up, 'There it is', and a lovely male black redstart was showing, standing on the mast of a boat, these boats were just lying up in a field nearby, obviously being stored up for the winter. Len then commented, there is another bird on a post nearby and he was right, as was the birder who originally thought there was more than one, we had, in fact, a pair, both male and female, what a turn up for the book. The Dartford warblers may have been shy in showing themselves, the black redstarts certainly were not. They gave us all wonderful views, so we were able to move on very happily.

Hunger satisfied, down to Cley Beach we go, and I was a little disappointed to find Len and I were the only birders in evidence, had all the birds which had been reported actually past through?

The sea was relatively calm, so viewing conditions were very good, any birds out there should be clearly seen. We found a couple of upturned boats to sit on, and our telescopes were set up, telescopes are a necessity if sea watching, birds can be easily half a mile or more away.

In the far distance the odd gannet could be seen and several species of gull were flying through, including the odd great black-backed gull, our first report for the week. At this point another birder joined us and he brought our attention to a bird he found on the sea, Len and I quickly focused up on he bird, and we were very pleased he had, it was a black-throated diver, which pleased the birder as he had never seen one before, he had only just taken up bird watching as a hobby. Whilst we were talking to him two other birds took off from the sea, we had not noticed these and I was pleased to see these two were red-throated divers, for me a 'Year Tick', for our new friend another new bird, I think he was pleased to have found us.

Out at sea several gannets could be seen, the odd one being very dark, some of this years youngsters, but they had quickly learned how to go about their business. Several gulls were passing and one caught our attention, a herring gull type, but this one was a Caspian gull, a bird our friend had never heard of and could not find in his field guide, so we explained it all to him.

Len then hit the jackpot, he gabbed my arm in his excitement 'I have a little auk'. I quickly moved over to his telescope, this was a 'Lifer' for Len, and to have found it himself made it all the more special. A 'Year Tick' for me and a special bird in many ways. The last little auks I saw were in Spitzbergen, while on a cruise with Dorothy some years ago, there we saw thousands of them as they streamed past our liner looking like black and white bees, their wings whirring away so fast you could hardly make them out. A superb little bird, I doubt if I have seen above a dozen in the UK, and what has made this one so memorable is the fact it is the very first one I have seen without Dorothy sharing the event with me, I had to fight back a tear.

Moving on, a line of black looking duck were flying low over the water, obviously scoter but as I watched them I noticed one had a bold white wing patch. I quickly called my friends attention to this bird as it was a velvet scoter, not one of your common stuff, they are a bit special to say the least. If it had not been for the white wing bar we would not have picked it out at this distance, another 'Year Tick' for me, a 'Lifer' for our new friend.

We were about to move on when a large, dark brown bird, came flying along the tide line, initial thoughts were a juvenile gull, but as the bird got closer my opinion started to change, I knew of no gull this dark, my thoughts now started to think skua. I mentioned this to my friends so we could concentrate on detail. As the bird gave us a fly past my thoughts proved right, the bird was in fact a pomerine skua, a first winter juvenile, for my friends the bird was a 'Lifer', for me a 'Year Tick', so we were all happy.

Len and I wanted to have a brief look further up the coast so it was time to drive off, our new friend was sorry to see us go I think. We did not see a lot so we drove back to the Cley Visitor Centre for a coffee and our last look over the reserve. The weather had brightened up slightly, the sun actually put in an appearance, and this obviously livened up the marsh harrier, we enjoyed seeing five put on a few breath taking displays, they are very elegant birds of prey. We had one male, two females and two juveniles, a super ending to the day.

Tonight Roy Hood and Neil Kelly are arriving for three days so we have company for dinner and our next few days birding. After a very enjoyable meal and wine we sat down to plan our day. Jane and John Hobson who live near to Norwich were also joining us for the day so we planned to visit Strumpshaw Fen for bittern, Horsey Mill for crane and calling in at Happisburgh for a melodious warbler, if we make all three it will be some sort of a miracle.

Wednesday morning, or Day Three of our holiday did not look a bad day as Len drove off, (I must admit I am finding being driven everywhere most enjoyable, thank you Len). We arrived at Strumpshaw just after 10.00 hours to find Jane and John waiting for us at the Visitor Centre hide, we had just missed a bittern by about three minutes, was this to be the story of the day?

We booked ourselves in, had a chat with the warden about what was in; a good chance for a few holiday ticks presented itself, gadwall, great crested grebe, bullfinch, common gull and jay could be seen, and then the scene erupted. From out of the reed bed to our right came the bird we had dreamed of, the bittern. A bittern does not fly about for all to see, they should sulk away in a dense reed bed, taking full care not to be seen, and if you are seen, making it as difficult as possible for the onlooker. Today has given me probably the best view ever of the bird, and I have been seriously birding for over 60 years.

Jane and John who now have this as their local reserve suggested we had a quick look from the Fen Hide, here the kingfisher is regularly seen, so off we went. Initially things were very quiet, a possible water rail in the reeds and just a couple of mallard, then a flash of red and blue flew across and landed on a stump in the water, we had our kingfisher. Whenever I see a kingfisher I think of the people who have said to me we do not have any really beautiful birds in Britain as say the tropics. All I can say to them is to get yourself out and have a look at a kingfisher, he would compare with any bird in the world, and he is not on his own among British birds, we have many other beautiful specimens, believe me.

As we walked back we were abused by several Cettis warblers, I have not heard so many from one place for many a year, and as we approached the Visitor Centre we saw a pair of stonechat. Jane and John were particularly interested in the latter, this was their first sighting at Strumpshaw this year, so these had to be reported.

Horsey Mill was quiet, but the gift shop come café was open, which was what I was interested in, requiring some light sustenance and a coffee. The manager was interested in our reason for the visit as the mill was open for visiting. We told him, nice as the mill was we were here for the cranes and he very helpfully told us to go to the top of the mill and out on the balcony as the cranes could be frequently seen from there. Roy and Neil volunteered to go up and they were rewarded with two cranes, there was no way I could climb up the mill, so we had our lunch and then drove off to try to find a suitable spot for viewing the cranes, we were unsuccessful I am sorry to say.

So Happisburgh here we come for some serious melodious warbler hunting. We reached our destination, found the cricket pitch near to where the bird was being seen and joined about another 30 or so birders who were also keen to see the bird. The news was not good, the bird had not been sighted for over two hours, so many were leaving disappointed. Only 5 minutes later the bird was back on the top of a nearby garden hedge. As quickly as we picked it up it went to ground, but at the very least we knew the bird was still here.

The bird kept on making fleeting visits which some times we caught, others we did not, but we were struggling for the view to confirm what we were seeing. Along the hedgerow a small Christmas tree was growing and the bird suddenly favoured this tree as a launch post to catch flying insects, anyone would have thought we were looking at a flycatcher not a warbler. As if to celebrate the occasion the sun even came out, the bird was indeed a melodious warbler, a juvenile bird, but age was immaterial to us. We were all too busy celebrating a 'Lifer'.

A black redstart had also been reported from here so we decided to have a look at the local church, a magnificent structure. Roy and Len, almost as one, picked up a male on the tower and as we looked at this bird it became two, as with our previous encounter with the species, it was a pair. While we were enjoying these birds two other birders came up wondering what was holding our attention, we showed them and in return they told us about a Pallas's warbler and a yellow-browed warbler which had been reported from Trimingham, 20 minutes or so from where we currently are, and also on our way back to base. Unfortunately Jane and John had left for home so we could not tell them about it.

Roy, being navigator for the day, quickly sorted out our best route, and we were on our way for a 'Twitch'. If these birds were to be found I had another 'Lifer' to look forward to as well as another 'Year Tick'. We quickly located the spot and several birders were milling around, neither bird had been seen for some time, so we joined the throng. After probably 20 minutes or so up went a shout, 'We have a Hume's', this bird had not been mentioned previously, so we joined in the rush back down the track.

I now realised we had joined in a group of birders among whom were a few of Norfolk's top birders, these people are out of the premier league, so we could learn something here, as well as see a super bird if we were lucky. Depending upon the age of your field guide this bird will be referred to as either a Hume's yellow-browed warbler or a Hume's leaf warbler, both being the same bird. Apparently the person who had first identified this bird had done so by it's call.

We congregated round the birder who had first identified the bird, and awaited further information. After what seemed ages, but really was only a few minutes, he said 'There it is, can you hear it calling?' I could hear a call but there was nothing very striking about it and I doubt if I will recall it at all, it just sounded like a dozen other birds to me. Someone else then commented 'There it is in that small sycamore tree'. I could at least identify a sycamore tree, so I felt a little more in control of my own destiny. The bird was small and was just a dark shape at the top of the tree and how anyone could make an accurate identification in these conditions I do not know. As if to resolve the problem, after but a few seconds the bird vanished into the thick ivy which surrounded the tree's trunk, never to appear again. There is no way I can accept this as a record. The call was insignificant, and the bird itself was just a small brown blob.

We had now reached the end of a most interesting day, and although not everyone had seen everything, Roy and Neil being the exception, we all made our way back to the hotel in a happy frame of mind.

Jane and John are among the most reliable of people I know, so off to Kelling we go. Unfortunately the conditions were as previously, grey and miserable with a bit of drizzle in the air, but nothing ventured, nothing gained. We were rewarded by superb views of stonechat, both male and female, but Dartford's were proving to be more elusive. We did, however, finally hear at least two calling, so the visit was not wasted.

Margaret Keep was joining us today and she 'phoned in as she had made good progress, so Len and I arranged to meet her at Titchwell at 11.00 hours. Driving over we really did strike lucky. Near The Lowes, Kelling, we had a juvenile rough-legged buzzard fly over the road directly in front of us, a magical bird to start off with. A first of the year for Len. When we arrived Margaret had beaten us to it, so we decided to have an hour or two birding prior to a spot of lunch. We were able to add several birds to our Norfolk list including a nice water rail which Margaret located and a Cetti's warbler which Len and I can claim credit for.

As we had some time to spare, after lunch we drove down to Blakeney to see if the cattle egret was still about, in transit we stopped off at the Burnham Overy Staithe view point for the rough-legged buzzard. Here Len proved his worth, he located the bird sitting out on the top of a bush, a smart, adult, winter plumaged bird, which it was nice to compare with the juvenile of earlier. The cattle egret, however, was no where to be seen, so the Greens here we come.

I must say I was very impressed with the Greens. In an hour or so we saw several marsh and hen harrier, both male and female, a merlin, many little egrets and a peregrine, although I must confess I missed the later. Definitely a spot for further interest.

Friday is our first day out with a full compliment, although Jane, John, Roy and Neil will all be departing after lunch. To say the day was a complete disaster may be a slight exaggeration, but only just. Flitcham, no owls, Sculthorpe Moor, no golden pheasant, sea watching at Cley useless and no snow buntings anywhere. Days such as this are not unusual, although in Norfolk they are. Margaret will only be with us tomorrow morning so we just have to find something of interest for her, otherwise she will wonder why she joined us. Fortunately she has a sense of humour, which believe me is required in this game at times.

Saturday has come in very pleasantly, so off to Salthouse we go. There are already a few birders there although none have any news of interest, so we make our way up the shingle bank to view the sea. Within a few minutes a flock of small birds fly in off the sea, as they fly past us some show a very bold white wing patch, I shout to my friends 'Snow buntings, seven of them'. Before they could pick them,up they had vanished, but at least some were about. Len then drew my attention to a bird on the sea, which initially we both thought to be a diver. It was some distance out and only had it's back to us. Then it turned side ways on and gave us the view we wanted, the bird was in fact a winter plumaged red-necked grebe, a 'Year Tick' for Len.

As we were enjoying the grebe another flock of small birds flew in off the sea, this time between 50 and 60 birds, many showed bold white wing patches, we certainly now had snow buntings. These birds came to ground near to us and we were able to fully appreciate them. Many of the birds were full winter plumaged males and they looked superb. This morning we had hit the jackpot. Just as we were about to leave Len picked up two auks on the sea which he identified as guillemots, Len's first experience of them in winter plumage, as they were for Margaret.

Time now for Cley proper. Cley Marshes NR is probably the premier birding site in north Norfolk, and to not visit it when in the area is a cardinal sin! We checked into the Visitor Centre, found out what was about, had a nice cup of coffee, paid out entrance fee and made our way onto the reserve. Cley is well organised for disabled visitors. It has Blue Badge parking and a lift up into the centre, the pathways are all wheelchair friendly, although due to distance a motorised chair would be favourable. As I was walking a few more benches would have been appreciated, but we made the hides.

From the Avocet Hide we had very nice views of ruff, dunlin, black-tailed godwits, and marsh harriers kept on flying through which put most of the birds to flight, giving quite spectacular views. Of the duck the wigeon and teal were looking quite splendid in their full plumage, and a couple of drake pintail were not going to be out shone.

Now for Dawke's Hide. Not a lot of change from Avocet as Dawke's overlooked Avocet so we were looking at he same birds. Things quickly changed, however, a female Marsh harrier over flew the lagoon and put many of the birds to flight. This interference at least showed just how many dunlin and black-tailed godwits had been on the lagoon.

Moving on to the Teal Hide, and it was easy to see why it was so named, there were discussion among the people already in the hide. Some where claiming rock pipit others water pipit. We were asked the question 'Were we any good on pipits?' Just how you answer a question like that without sounding arrogant I do not know, but Len solved the problem by just asking where the bird was. Clever old Len. It was obvious the half a dozen or so people in the hide were novices so here was chance to help them along the way. We quickly located the bird and it was easy to understand their difficulties. The bird was a meadow pipit but it was a juvenile bird moulting through, and not many field guides go into this type of detail, well not field guides which fit your pocket. We explained the whys and wherefores, and then settled down to our own birding, but this was not to be. Our 'new' friends obviously thought they had three experts in the hide and the questions came fast and furious.

We spent the next half an hour or so identifying little gull, ruff, Bewick's swan and snipe, the one bird we did not need to sort out was the avocet, they all knew that one. We had a nice time really and hopefully everyone went off with a little more knowledge and an increased love for birds.

Time now for a spot of lunch and wave goodbye to Margaret, at least after the disappointments of yesterday, she had seen some nice birds today. Len and I were off 'Twitching', we were after a desert wheatear at Holme, this would be a lovely bird to land. From the car parking area the bird was about 300 metres away, a walk along the shore or through the pines, not wheelchair country I am afraid although with willing helpers it may have been possible. I took my two sticks and walked the shore. I sent Len on, he had never seen the bird, I had, albeit only twice. In the distance the birders could be clearly seen, about 30 of them, I must admit I expected more, the bird was a bit unusual to say the least.

I arrived to find Len had the bird in his 'scope, and what a bird it turned out to be. It was a winter adult male, just have a look in your field guide, an absolute cracker. To make things more interesting, nearby was a northern wheatear, (sometimes referred to as just wheatear, depending upon the age of your field guide), so it was nice to get a comparison.

While enjoying the wheatear we heard of a hoopoe being seen on the reserve. You do not take the chance of a hoopoe lightly. We joined about 50 other birders looking for the bird, although we spent a good hour searching all to no avail, we were not despondent, the desert wheatear was more than compensation.

For our final day we decided to go straight to Cley Beach for an hour or so sea watching. The weather was gorgeous, almost like a spring day, so I took my stool with me so I could sit on the shingle and just enjoy myself. Sea watching is a funny old business and at times can turn out to be very frustrating, today the sun shone and the birds came by, so we had a great couple of hours. As we dove down to the beach a small flock of birds flew across the lane in front of us and Len was able to pull up so we could have a good look at them. As we focused they took off but one swiftly returned to perch quite near to us, I could not believe my luck, I was staring straight into the face of a female Lapland bunting, my first of the year, the omens looked good.

We settled down to sea watch and many gulls were travelling eastwards and the majority of these were little gulls, I have never seen so many in my life before. While I was enjoying these Len picked up four guillemots, and as I swung round to look at these I located three black-necked grebes. Len did not know which to look at first. He chose the grebes, but as he turned to view all three dived. Len turned to have another look at his guillemots, they too had vanished.

Fortunately another bird caught his attention, a great northern diver came sailing by. Although it was in it's winter plumage they are still a magnificent bird. Out at sea gannets were diving for fish, a very spectacular bird they are too. A bit further out I found two more divers, before I could identify them they took to flight, but this turned out to be to our advantage, their bills could be clearly seen, they had an upward tilt which instantly shouted out red-throated.

A grebe came in from the east, quite close in shore, we did not need the telescopes for this one, you hardly needed you binoculars, a red-necked grebe which was still showing some of it's summer plumage as the neck was quite dark. Another diver came into view, the bill on this one was quite straight and dagger-like, this time we had a black-throated diver. This bird meant we had seen all three of our native divers in less than an hour, I have never seen all three on the same day previously, let alone at the same place. As we moved off Len picked up a small party of linnet and it was not until he commented about them that I realised they were our first of the week, and I was ready to dismiss them as being nothing.

Time now to move on, our next stop being Wells Next The Sea, there are some marvellous mud flats here so we should be able to knock up a wader or two for our week's list. As it a Sunday the café was open so would have a place to get a bite to eat once we had finished our birding. The tide was well out with acres of black, oozing mud exposed. A veritable paradise for waders and the like, and there were many to see. The odd seal was lazily swimming in the channel, it was almost as though he appreciated the warmer weather, making the day an ideal day for a swim.

Before studying the mud, three duck caught our attention. These turned out to be red-breasted merganser, a duck we do not see all that often in the Midlands, so we always welcome the chance to spend some time enjoying these. On the mud a large number of godwits could be seen, now which are they. I have a simple theory that bar-tailed stay in salty conditions, i.e. the shore, black-tailed prefer fresh water locations, now to put my theory to the test!

What we needed to see to be absolutely certain was their tails and wings. I may have mentioned this before, but it will not hurt to repeat it. The black-tailed has a black end to it's tail and a bold white wing bar, the bar-tailed has barring across the tail and no white wing bar. Simple if the birds raise their wings, eventually a few woke up and started to preen, and bar-tailed they most definitely were.

Oystercatchers were plentiful and vocal, as were the many curlew out on the mud, turnstone were actively feeding on the shingle, and out on the mud several golden plover were standing. A group of smaller waders caught our attention so we concentrated on these. Most were dunlin but several slightly dumpier waders were among them, these just had to be knot, one of my target birds for the day. Up 'scopes once again, and knot they most certainly were, another nice holiday tick.

Nothing new was to be seen so went back for a spot of lunch and then drove down to the lake at the bottom of the car park just for a quick scan, a little grebe popped up, unbelievably our first of the week. Our next location was Holkham Hall, but things did not work out to plan, the hall grounds were closed to vehicular traffic, only cyclists and walkers could gain entry, so we took ourselves down Holkham Gap for a stroll in the woods. There are Blue Badge car parking places right at the bottom of Queen Anne's Drive, but you still have to pay, we were staying for two hours and the cost was £2.50. There are no facilities, but you can find these at the café near the entrance to the driveway to the Hall.

As we drove down Queen Anne's Drive we came across a large flock of pink-foots in the field alongside the drive, and one of these had a metallic band round it's neck. It would have been interesting to know where this had been applied as it was obviously fitted as a means of tracking the bird. We did not attempt to count the pink-foots but I would estimate close to four figures.

Once again, due to it being a Sunday, and such a nice one too, Holkham Woods were very busy so although the walk was pleasant it did not produce many birds, although a nice party of long-tailed tits flew past us, and a marsh harrier was flying over the marshy meadows in front of the wood. So we cut our loses and decided to have our last trip to Warham Greens in an attempt to find me a short-eared owl, needless to say we again failed but both hen and marsh harrier put on a show, this is certainly a good spot for them. We also saw merlin, curlew and vast numbers of geese over flew as they were returning to their roosting haunts. Whilst enjoying the geese I heard a call with which I was not familiar, obviously goose, but which one? Fortunately they flew overhead, they were five white-fronted geese, so I need to remember the call for future use!

As I needed to get back to the hotel for a talk with Carolyn about the hotel we called it a day. The hotel are carrying out some work at the end of the year as they wish to make the hotel more accessible to the disabled. At present they only have four rooms kitted to meet these requirements, although access to and from the hotel is very good and where there is a slight difference between levels there is a ramp as well as steps for the more agile. Their intention is to have a further 10 rooms converted early in 2012, and I am hopeful of receiving confirmation of their progress before the year is out.

Our holiday was drawing to it's close. It had been a marvellous week, good company, fine food and drink and some wonderful birds, what more could one ask for?

During the evening Len went onto the net and we were very interested to see cranes had been reported at Guyhirn, in Cambridgeshire. Guyhirn is on our route home so we studied the information rather intently. The description of where the birds were last seen appeared to be clear enough but the attached map did not, it was not showing the Guyhirn I knew. As we got closer we pulled over allowing Len to make a late check on the crane situation, there was no update so now it was a case of 'Lady Luck' helping us out, and didn't she just. As we approached a café which had been mentioned last night we saw a sign for parking, so we pulled off the road into the lay-by. We knew we had to look to the south, and this we did. The land here is very flat so you can see quite a distance, so Len started to work from the left, me the right.

After just a couple of minutes Len called out 'I have two', I swung in his direction and exclaimed 'You haven't, there are five'. In a field with cattle, a good half a mile away, five majestic cranes were going about their business. They are the tallest bird which breeds in the UK, long legs, long neck with a large bustle which makes them look almost Victorian. I was now very pleased I had not tried to climb the mill at Horsey. We spent several minutes enjoying these two birds, passing motorists must have wondered what was going on, two people looking through telescopes by the side of a major road, not that we were bothered. I had at last got myself a crane on my 'Year 'List', and we both agreed, what a way to end our holiday. Len may have seen the cranes when we were in Norfolk in March, but today's view was superb, you could see every detail of the bird.

My week's list closes at 120, with 13 'Year Ticks' and one 'Lifer', my 'Life List' now stands at 408 and my 'Year List' at 231, so I am not doing bad at all, thanks to this holiday.

My first venture forth has been to take Evelyn and another friend, John Hall, over to Focus Optics, at Corley, near Coventry, to purchase new equipment. Tim, the proprietor, is a most helpful man. Evelyn is now the proud owner of a new telescope and John new binoculars as well as a telescope.

The opportunity to try out their new equipment under field conditions, for the first time, came with a Rosliston Bird Study Group field meeting on Cannock Chase, we were after the great grey shrike. Only a few of us had a glimpse of the shrike, the majority, including myself did not, and among the 'did nots' was Evelyn and John, but they quickly made up for this.

A group of crossbills came out and put on quite a display. It was a flock of 11, and for over half an hour they flew by us, landing in trees close by, where they could be seen in all their glory. Their colours showed up beautifully, for some they were a first ever, and for many, the best views ever. They flew right over our heads 'chip, chip, chipping' away, and the light conditions were perfect, a bright and clear sunny day. Missing out on the shrike no longer mattered.

They were not the only colourful birds of the morning, we saw both green and great spotted woodpecker, jay and a superb buzzard, not a bad morning, and Evelyn and John were delighted with their purchases.

That meeting brought November to a close, and thanks to Norfolk it had been a bumper month for the time of year, and as mentioned previously, I have now reached 231 for the year. Whether I can improve on that remains to be seen, but I am more than happy. We will just have to wait and see what December can provide.

Map references:
Strumpshaw Fen – RSPB: TG 340068.
Horsey Mill – NT: TG 457223.
Happisburgh: TG 380312.
Trimingham: TG 280388.
Burnham Overy Staithe: TF 853440.
Warham Greens: TF 948438.
Guyhirn: TL 377030.
Focus Optics (just in case you wish to visit): SP 298852.

Chapter XII

December

The year is now slowly drawing to a close, and Sarah and I do not have many more mornings out to look forward to, but at least Saturday 3 December is one we can enjoy. The swan flock is steadily building up at Whitemoor Haye, so I have been reliably informed, so we decided to give that a try in the hope the first of the wild swans had put in an appearance.

I do not know about slowly building up, there must have been at least 200 swans in the field near to Sittle's Farm, so it was a case of up telescope and start to work through these. A birder we knew came up and told us that six whooper swans had been seen yesterday, so that gave us something to really concentrate on. We must have spent nearly an hour going through these birds, without success, just mute's as far as we could see. We were just about to move off when Sarah caught sight of a large bird of prey, which she did not believe to be a buzzard. I turned to look at the bird just as it passed through the sun and promptly lost sight of it in the suns glare, it took several seconds to relocate, and I was pleased when I did. Sarah was smack on not believing it to be a buzzard, the bird was a female hen harrier, a ring-tail as us birders call it. The bird was a 'Year Tick' for Sarah, and only my second local one, you may remember I saw one at the Alrewas Arboretum a short while ago. Harriers are majestic birds with a very elegant flight, nothing brash about them. Well done Sarah.

We drove back along the rough lane, seeing about 20 tree sparrows at the feeding station, and as a final special touch, even the little owl was sitting out in his tree. Not a bad start to December.

On Monday 5 December, the Rosliston Bird Study Group visited Attenborough, but we experienced a quiet day. One or two managed to get a glimpse of a water rail, I failed, and probably the most exciting birds we all saw were four Egyptian geese, plus the odd snipe. On the credit side the weather was lovely and the reserve does boast a nice café, which several of us made use of.

My week has been rather busy, and it is now Friday, the day for a recce on behalf of Sarah. Blithfield was exceptionally quiet, both birds and birders being almost non-existent. The best I managed was a nice small group of five drake goldeneye, a fly past by a buzzard and a couple of cormorant suddenly popped up on the surface. At Whitemoor Haye the lake was equally as quiet as Blithfield, a few gulls and a couple of grebes was all I could find.

So off down the rough lane, would this be better? A few tree sparrows were at the feeding station and three magpie were lurking close by. Approaching the corner I could see into the field near Sittle's Farm, and once again it was full of swans. At last something to get my teeth into. The number of swans looked far in excess of what we saw a few days ago. I worked my way through the flock looking for any wild swans, the light conditions were not good, I had a couple of 'maybes', but I could not be sure. On my way home I made my customary pull in at the lay-by, two little egrets were feeding in the river, so that at least brought a bright conclusion to the afternoons venture.

Saturday has come in bright and crisp, very crisp in fact, we have had a good frost, and as I am typing this up at 09.45 hours it has yet to start to thaw off. It is obviously going to be a day for woolly hats and gloves. Nothing on the net, so we have decided to visit Croxall Lakes, calling in at Kings Bromley to see our old friend the little egret, and it was there to see us. Croxall looked very quiet, only a single car on the car park, and they were dog walkers, both dogs on the lead I am pleased to say.

We made our way to the end of the reserve, where the River Tame borders the reserve, not an area we visit all that frequently. Initially it looked very quiet but a train came along and the noise and disturbance it created put many birds to flight. Fieldfare and redwing were in quite decent numbers, how we had not seen them before I do not know, but more interestingly a largish flock of small birds also appeared. These flew over the river to land on vegetation bordering the Arboretum. As they flew some colour was picked up, so goldfinch were included in the group, but the majority of the birds looked very plain. Initially I thought they were all linnets; goldfinch and linnets do flock up together, so this was the likely conclusion. The birds had gone deep into the vegetation so views were not clear, until a few came up onto the tops, and I then had the shock of my life. I was looking at three twite, a bird totally unexpected, and a 'Lifer' for Sarah. What a turn up. We spent several minutes enjoying these birds, and came to the conclusion we had at least seven twite in the flock, there may even have been more, but they were very edgy, every time a train came past they took to flight.

Time was on our side today so we popped into the hide. A little egret was standing still on the far shore, and a female goosander swam slowly past. Sarah then picked up a nice flock of eight goldeneye, and while she was enjoying these I found another group of six. That is probably the most goldeneye I have seen together for a long time, they are a delightful duck. A large flock of Canada geese flew in, very noisily needless to say, and they scattered the duck all over the place. A flock of 200 geese or so certainly know how to make an impression.

Sunday is not a very pleasant looking day at the moment, rain is likely. I am leading a walk at Croxall for the Staffordshire Wildlife Trust, so it will be very interesting to see how many people turn up for the walk, I have already had one telephone call from a lady who cannot make it, and just how many people have booked places I do not know. I just hope we do better than my last effort when only one person turned up.

10 people turned up for the walk, two of them were members of the Rosliston Bird Study Group, which meant eight were new to me. Unfortunately bird numbers were down on yesterday, only three goldeneye, the little egret was still to be seen, but the mixed flock of linnets, twite and goldfinch had obviously moved on. Fieldfare and redwing were well represented, and among the small lapwing flock two golden plover could be picked out. For several of the members of the party this was a new bird for them, so they were more than pleased.

Later on a few small flocks of geese flew in, noisily as ever, and one flock had five greylags with the Canada's, so this was another bird which brought some pleasure. Just as we were about to finish, down came the rain which had been promising all morning, so we were very fortunate. In talking to some of the people they asked if the Trust could organise a walk next year when we could look at bird song. With the nice range of warblers we get at Croxall this sounds a good idea, so I will have to suggest it to the Trust.

Monday has come in cold and crisp, a morning for thawing out cars, but not to worry, it is after all December. Today the Rosliston birders are off to Brandon Marsh NR, near Coventry. This is the HQ for the Warwickshire Wildlife Trust and it is a very interesting reserve. It lies just off the A45, south east of Coventry, and is probably Warwickshire's premier wet land site. It covers 228 acres, has 10 main pools and a bird list in excess of 220 species of which 60 species regularly breed. It has 3km of pathways, most of which can be walked with care, including the Onyx Nature Trail which is accessible to wheelchair users. It has a very pleasant tea room where hot food is available, shop, information centre and educational rooms. Car parking is free, and entrance for none Wildlife Trust members is not great, as a senior citizen you pay £1.50, there are not many places you can get into for that cheap a price. Brandon is also a superb reserve to visit in the summer, it boasts over 460 wild flowers, including among which are a few orchids. It's butterflies and dragon/damselflies are also worth some effort.

Brandon Marsh's main piece of fame is the fact Cetti's warblers breed here, and there are not many sites in the Midlands with that proud boast, the only other one I can think of is Attenborough. We also have the chance of bittern, one has been reported, and short-eared owls are still being reported regularly, one of the latter would be nice, I have yet to see one this year.

Only 10 of us have made the trip to Brandon, this at least means we can all probably stay together when in the hides. We made our way round to the East Marsh Pool, the largest stretch of water on the reserve, here common tern breed, not today obviously, they have all flown south. We had the Jon Baldwin hide to ourselves, where we quickly picked up a nice flock of lapwing, among which were several golden plover scattered about. I started to count through these when they all took to flight in panic, a male peregrine came flashing across, no wonder they all moved so fast. He did not seem to take anything and quickly vanished from view, this interruption did at least give me a chance to estimate the golden plover numbers and they were in excess of 30.

Peace quickly returned and back in came all the birds. We had four species of gull, black-headed, common, herring and lesser black-backed, teal numbers were very good, and in the bright sunlight the drakes looked magnificent. Shoveler were well represented, as were gadwall and mallard, and a pair of goldeneye gave a good diving display. Time to move on to the Teal Pool Hide.

Things here were very quiet, so we quickly crossed the path to the East Marsh Hide which gave us another angle for viewing East Marsh Pool. Nothing new, except the peregrine gave us another fly past, the effects of which were as previous, so we moved along to the Carlton Hide, the hide from which it is 'rumoured' the bittern may be seen. Needless to say, today it was not, but we did have very nice views of snipe which were feeding just a few metres in front of the hide, and a kestrel gave us a very good performance with it's hovering skills.

On our return journey back to the Visitor Centre we saw a very smart male goldcrest and reed bunting were very active, as were three grey heron hunting in the Grebe Pool. That was until they realised they had an audience, when they promptly flew off.

Time had now caught up with us, four of us decided to visit the tea room for a warm snack, which was most enjoyable, and then homewards we went. Nothing exceptional, but a very pleasant morning birding, and that is what it is all about.

Thursday has dawned brightly, but cold, we had another deep frost last night. I pop down to the Haye and in transit I saw the little egret at Kings Bromley, and spent nearly an hour studying the swan flock at Sittle's Farm, still only mute swans I am afraid, although a good number of Canada geese were also in attendance. I drove slowly back up the rough lane, a few tree sparrow were seen at the feeding station, this time only seven. Stopping at the lake I picked up another little egret feeding along the shore line, but this proved to be the last bird of real interest. I did however get my car cleaned, so I accomplished one thing, mind you how the weather is at present it will not remain clean for long!

Friday has come in damp, with more rain and sleet promised later in the day. I have to visit my physiotherapist this morning when I hope she can do something to ease the discomfort of my shoulder.

Needless to say I called in at Kings Bromley, and I was very sorry to read a notice to the effect that Mr Choppy's mobile kitchen had been stolen, I never fail to be amazed at what thieves can get up to. The little egret was still to be seen, feeding away in the river. A lady nearby was feeding the ducks with her young child, and she was very interested to hear what the bird was, so I spent a few minutes telling her all about it.

As I approached the Haye the sky grew darker, down came more sleet and visibility became very poor. I drove round the rough lane to view the swans but this was almost impossible. Apart from a few which were close in, the bulk were too far distant, and in the current light conditions identification was not on. I continued on my way, stopping near the feeding station, here I was able to count 13 tree sparrows and two reed buntings, so that brightened up a dreary period.

Saturday has come in with little or nothing on the net that is open for us to visit today, so Rocester it will be. We have had another night of persistent rain, which hopefully, it is now 09.30 hours, looks as though it may actually be stopping.

One interesting piece of information gleaned from the net is the fact we have a black stork moving round the county, if we were lucky enough to drop onto that bird we would have something mega, that is for sure. The purists are already claiming it to be an escape from a local collection, although I understand the collection has not reported the loss of the bird. The bird was last reported five miles south east of Leek, so we are travelling in the right direction this morning, we should be so lucky!

Unfortunately the weather has put a right dampener on our plans, we have had nothing but rain and sleet, with just the odd period of dry, and these were few and far between. We never made Rocester, and I salvaged very little in the afternoon, the weather did it's worst and apart from the little egret still showing at Kings Bromley and a small flock of tree sparrow down the rough lane, I saw little else of interest.

Sarah on the other hand went across to Cannock Chase with Martin and was rewarded with seven brambling near to the Marquis Drive feeding station, not a bad little flock that.

I will have a ride over to the Chase today. When Sarah was over here yesterday it was very quiet, not today I am afraid, the car park is almost full, one Blue Badge space left fortunately, and it looks as though the Christmas tree sales are going really well. The feeding station was very busy, I counted seven bullfinch on one table and there were others on the various tables. This area is well known for the number of bullfinch it supports, and today they were certainly well into double figures.

Coal tit were also approaching double figures, with great tit, blue tit and chaffinch also well represented, but hard as I searched, no brambling. I moved from the feeding station to study the trees locally, a small flock of redpoll were actively feeding on the silver birch trees and near to the café nuthatch and chaffinch were feeding on scattered seed. All very nice but not what I had come for, so I decided to pop across to Whitemoor Haye for a few minutes prior to having lunch.

The Haye was very quiet, the large goose flock was still on the shores of the lake, but little else was to be seen. The rough lane had nothing, several dog walkers were out and the small birds were hiding away until peace was restored. I spent several minutes going through the swan flock, still with the same result, only mute swans as far as I could see. That completes a very quiet weekend, but you have to expect a few like this, you cannot win all the time.

Today is our Christmas 'Bash' for the Rosliston Bird Study Group. We have a bit of a party, as mentioned previously, we all have our orders from Heather with regard to what we have to bring, she does a very good job here, and I have a quiz for them which Sarah and Martin have prepared for me. Our 'Bash' was very pleasant, and as well as an exchange of Christmas cards, some good food, and enjoyable quiz (thanks to Sarah and Martin), we were also able to make a few plans for next year.

I understand from Sarah that according to the weather experts, tomorrow, Tuesday, may be a more pleasant day, if that should prove to be the case I will crack on with my duties in the morning and hope to get a couple of hours out birding. A bean goose has been reported from Belvide, a Tundra race specimen, so should it hang about I may well pop over, I have yet to see a bean goose this year.

Tuesday has dawned bright and clear, so let us hope it remains that way, so I may well get out. The bean goose unfortunately has vanished, so I drive across to JCB, Rocester, where Sarah and I failed to make a day or so ago. The lake which normally holds the collection birds was strangely quiet apart from a flock of 20 white duck which dashed across as soon as I got out of my car. A pair of shelduck sat on the weir completely bored with proceedings and a nice drake roseybill sailed past, and that was it, a total of 23 captive birds plus the odd moorhen and coot. I have never known Rocester so deserted, the collection birds must have all sailed off to the northern end of the lake.

I was about to drive off to have a look at the southern lake, which I always consider to be the domain of the wild birds, as a car drove up and out popped a family with two small children and two large bags of bread. The white ducks promptly dashed back, even the shelduck raised their heads to see what was going on, but took no further notice, and two birds came flying in to join in the melee, these were a pair of red-crested pochard, no doubt about their flying abilities. A couple of dozen black-headed gulls joined in, it was simply amazing just how quickly so much bread was consumed, it was probably their first meal of the day!

Now for the southern lake. Here I had to find a suitable spot to pull off the B5030, parking on the road here is not appreciated as a friend of mine once found out. Fortunately the grass verge is more than adequate. Today luck was in my favour, without even having to get out of my car I glanced over the lake and to my surprise I saw seven drake goosander slowly making their way across the surface. They were almost in a straight line, and in the light they really did have a peachy tinge to their plumage. A delightful bird at any time, today they looked especially so.

The 21 December is upon us. I was out and about early this morning as I wished to get my shopping expedition over as painlessly and peacefully as possible, and this I am pleased to say I managed to do. All I now hope is I have bought everything needed, Sarah will soon let me know if not! I quickly completed my odd chore and had time for a quick trip out, only very locally as light conditions were very poor.

On my way down to the Haye via the rough lane I again saw a nice flock of tree sparrow and this time I spotted four corn buntings among them. I parked up on the corner where I could get a decent view of the swans which were well spread out. I was making my way through them when I came across a small group of grey geese, which I initially took to be greylags. Fortunately for me a tractor was very busy going backwards and forwards over the field. The swans did not seem too bothered, they just waddled out of the way, and moved back as soon as it had gone by, the geese, however, were not at all happy. They quickly moved over the field to a quieter location, and luckily for me this brought them a lot closer, and I quickly realised they were not greylags, probably pink-footed geese. It now became a telescope job, and the light conditions were terrible, even though they had moved in closer they were still a good 100 metes away, it was not going to be easy. Pink-footed geese have pink legs, and bean geese have orange, not that you could tell the difference in this light. At least with the telescope I could get a good idea of their size when compared with the mute swans near by, and they were too large to be pink-foots, they just had to be bean geese.

Now a larger problem presented itself, which race of bean goose, tundra or taiga, and in these conditions this was a problem indeed. There was no way I could get any closer to them, a thick hedge was in my way, plus the fact I would have been trespassing. Then luck played a hand, down came the tractor once again and this time the birds took to flight and landed less than 20 metres away from me, as I was behind a hedge they obviously had not twigged my presence. It was now a binocular job, and at this short distance light did not really matter. Three of the birds had a bright orange ring round their bills near to the dark tip, that told me all I wanted to know, as far as I am concerned they are the tundra race, and my first 'Year Tick' for the month, and the way things are shaping up, probably my last for the year. Popping out for an hour this afternoon has turned out very well, and just to put a final gloss on things, the little egret was at the lay-by.

By late Wednesday morning I am off, and it is a lovely clear day. I call in at the lay-by, our friend is still there, so now for the Haye. The lapwing flock seems to be growing by the day, and after carefully scanning through, I locate about 20 golden plover, a nice start. Now for the rough lane and the geese.

The tree sparrow flock is still active in the lane and today we have two male yellowhammers with them, always a lovely bird to see. Stopping on the corner I find the swan flock is well spread out over the field, so it is up telescope and work starts. I spend several minutes and all I can find are mute swans and about 30 Canada geese. It looks very much as though our bean geese had only popped in for a short stay.

Thursday is an absolute shocker, it is now almost 14.00 hours and it is still raining. Sarah and I had things to do this morning, but come early afternoon we both decided to pop out, Sarah with Martin, me for a slow drive round the Haye. I am still hoping to relocate the bean geese, I know my friend Andy would like the chance to photograph these. Stopping to have a glance over the lake I found this fairly quiet, a few pochard, two great crested grebe, 20 or so black-headed gulls, but just as I was about to drive on, a little egret walked round a bend in the lake. I was more than happy with this bird.

Now for the rough lane. I slowly moved along towards the feeding station for the tree sparrows, and stopped a reasonable distance away to study the spot. I have done very well here with the tree sparrows, but today was bonanza day. I actually counted 27 birds and they were constantly flitting in and out of the bushes so I believe it was safe to presume at least 30 birds were out enjoying themselves. The surprising thing was I only saw sparrows, no buntings or finches were among them, they no doubt do not like the rain.

I drove on down to the end in the lane. The field was literally full of birds, Canada geese and swans, I would estimate at least 700 in total, going through all of these in today's conditions to look for the odd bean goose or whooper swan would be well nigh impossible unless they happened to be close in. Driving back the lapwing flock flew overhead, I stopped to look at these, today they were all lapwing, but if I added these birds to the goose/swan flock I reckon I had seen well over 1,200 birds, that in itself is something of note.

In the post I have received a letter from Carolyn Millman, The Pheasant Hotel, with the update information regarding the disabled rooms at the hotel, you will remember I mentioned this last month. The owner is carrying out various improvements including walk-in showers and seated showers, which will make things ideal for both wheelchair and the walking disabled. If you decide to visit, and I certainly recommend the hotel, when you make your reservation make certain you are clear about your requirements. The seated showers are in a shower tray, the type suitable to take a wheelchair will be in a wet room style. If things go to plan, by the time you are reading this the improvements will have been completed.

Christmas Eve has come in a little cooler than of late, but it is a very pleasant morning, I am only too pleased we have completed all of our preparations on the shopping front, and the turkey has cooked nicely. Sarah and Martin decided to pop over to JCB at Rocester, I went for a run locally, intending to call it at Blithfield but it was locked up, and although I have a key it would have meant my opening several locks to drive to my destination and the weather had deteriorated somewhat with rain falling, so I cut my losses and drove onto to the Haye.

I stopped at the lake, a few gulls and pochard were evident and three diving goldeneye caught my attention, all drakes which was a nice little group. Driving down towards the rough lane I located the large lapwing flock I have mentioned previously, and on this occasion they were all lapwings. For a few minutes they gave a marvellous aerial display, I just sat spellbound watching them do so, what a synchronised performance.

As I still had time available I drove round to Croxall to see if any swans had arrived in that area, they had not, but by the Redwood Plantation I had a very pleasant surprise, a woodcock flew over the road in front of me to vanish through the plantation. I have not seen a woodcock since June on Cannock Chase, so this was a rather nice bird to finish up with.

Christmas Day has come in nice and bright, and surprisingly mild, certainly not seasonal weather, not that we should grumble when we think what it was like just 12 months ago. We decided to go for a walk at JCB at Rocester, here, should Sarah and Martin want a nice walk they could, and I for my efforts could quickly find a bench to sit on. We were not the only people out for an afternoon stroll, and one or two new cycles and cameras were to be seen. The usual collection of birds were racing after anyone carrying a plastic bag which looked as though it may contain bread. One of the red-crested pochard caught our attention, and this turned out to be nice free-flying drake, worth the trip out alone. From my viewpoint I saw three paradise shelduck, a pair of eider, a whistling-duck, and a rosybill, not bad if they had all been wild. Upon Sarah and Martin's return they added to this list, hooded merganser, barnacle goose and Egyptian goose, they could not be sure if the last two were free-flying or not, so we will have to presume not.

As we leave JCB we intend to park up for a quick look over the southern lake, we were sure we had seen goosander as we drove by, we had, the seven from a day or so back were still here. Home now for a quiet Christmas Day evening, when I intend to open my bottle of Laphroaig Islay Single Malt Scotch Whisky – Quarter Cask, which Sarah kindly bought me for Christmas.

Boxing Day is upon us, and I have decided to try somewhere new. Sarah and Martin are going out for the day and I intend to visit Albert Village Lake in Leicestershire, just a few miles south of Swadlincote. For about a month or so reports of several of the rarer gulls have been leaking out, glaucous, yellow-legged and Caspian, hardly a day has passed without at least one of the three being reported, on occasion all three were seen.

Need I say it? I pulled in at Kings Bromley, said hello to my little egret, and drove down the Haye. Once again, as far as I can tell, the swans were all mute, and driving back up the rough lane I counted seven tree sparrow, my diversion via Kings Bromley and the Haye proved to be successful thanks to those two species. Now for a quick check on my map for the best route to Albert Village.

As I drove up the B586 I could see the lake below me in a deep hollow, but there was no obvious parking on the road, so I turned off in the village and drove down the opposite side of the lake, or at least were I presumed the lake to lie, where I eventually found a car park. The whole area is riddled with footpaths and is obviously reclaimed land. From the information board near the car park I could see the lake was quite a walk from where I stood, and although I am walking far better, it looked way beyond my present capabilities. The pathways are very good and are ideally suited to wheelchairs, the only proviso I would mention is some of the gradients look quite steep so a motorised chair is suggested, unless you have a friend or relative who possesses strong muscles. I was left with no alternative but to drive back to the B586 to try to find a spot where I could pull off to view the lake. From the amount of aerial activity by gulls it was obvious there must be a good number on the lake.

My luck was in, just past the junction with the B5004, there was an area where you could park up half a dozen cars with care, and it had access to one of the pathways over looking the lake. It was obviously a telescope job due to the distance, but I had come prepared.

Even at midday the lake was covered in gulls, and I do mean covered, several hundred, and gulls were constantly coming in and flying out, so it was an ever-changing scene, just how many gulls I saw I could not even estimate, but it must have been well into four figures. A group of a dozen or so very large gulls flew in directly over my head, all of which I took to be great black-backed, but as they banked to land on the water I realised one of them did not have a black back, it was a very pale grey, and it did not have black primaries. I could not believe my luck, the gull I most wanted to see had just flown in to see me. It was a crisp, full adult, glaucous gull, and a 'Year Tick' to boot. I could now believe all what had been reported about this spot, and to think I had never visited previously, I shall certainly be back.

After several minutes of almost violent bathing, my glaucous took off and vanished in the general direction from whence it first came. I carried on working my way through the roosting gulls on the lake, when an herring gull type caught my attention, this was no herring gull, it was a nice adult yellow-legged gull. I have seen too many of these this year to be confused again, especially by a full adult. I stayed here for nearly an hour, for me that is a very long time to just look at gulls, but they were mesmerising, and on at least two more occasions my glaucous returned, well I presumed it was the same one, we weren't exactly on speaking terms, no one had introduced us. I thought I may have had a Caspian gull, but at this distance I could not be sure, so that one goes down as a 'nearly-bird'.

During the hour or so I spent here I had seen glaucous gull, great black-backed gull, lesser black-backed gull, yellow-legged gull, herring gull, black-headed gull and common gull, seven different species, and who knows it could even have been eight. A return visit come January 2012 will most definitely have to be made. Just one point to raise, there are no facilities available, but 'Conkers' is only a short distance away, this has all the facilities required, and by combining the two you could have a very good day.

After the success of yesterday, I will stay local and pop down to the Haye and call in at Blithfield. The day has come in nice and bright, Sarah and Martin intend to have a day's photography, so I am up to my own devices.

I obviously nipped into the lay-by at Kings Bromley, and once again my friend the little egret was busily going about it's business, and a tidy flock of Canada geese have moved in, at least 50 of them.

On now for the Haye. The main lake looked fairly quiet, the flock of pochard were still in situ, seven great crested grebe could be seen and the wigeon were feeding away on the far bank. Two swans came flying across and I only gave them a casual glance, when I realised I could not hear their wing beat, a closer look was required. My two swans were whooper swans, and I watched them as they slowly vanished over the River Tame, from the direction they were flying in they would not be joining up with the swan flock at Sittle's Farm. Swans in flight, especially the mute swan, are very noisy, a most definite 'Swish, swish' of the wings, the whooper on the other hand is quiet, a very useful bit of information to remember when you next see swans in flight, as long as they are close enough to hear.

Now for the rough lane. There was a lot of activity at the feeding station, so I stopped to study them. A very bight male yellowhammer was easily picked up, a lovely canary yellow this bird. The tree sparrows were up to their usual trick of dashing in and out of the hedge to snatch a bit of seed making an accurate count difficult, but I would estimate at least 15 of them.

I moved on down to the corner to study the swan flock. Although I spent several minutes going though them all I could only locate mute swans once again, still I had seen a couple of whooper a little earlier on. I turned round and drove back up the rough lane and stopped to have a look at the owl tree, and my luck was in. A little owl was sitting at the entrance to an hole, which we believe is the hole the owls nest in, I probably spot the owl sitting in this exact position on 50 per cent of my sightings.

The weather was beginning to look very unsettled, the sun had finished and heavy grey sky was drifting across, not that rain has been forecast, so I continued with my plan and drove across to Blithfield, which turned out to be not very productive. I went to drive along the shore of the reservoir to find a notice barring entry, drove round to the causeway, here apart from mallard and coot, little else was to be seen. The opposite side of the causeway was even quieter, but one thing I did notice was the fact the reservoir had much more water in it than previously seen.

Wednesday has come in rather wet, and to add to the situation we experienced a power cut, the holiday season is over with a vengeance. After just over an hour we were back to normal, so we had only lost a little time. The rain had even stopped and the sky was getting quite blue, although the wind was quite strong. First stop Kings Bromley, and yes, the little egret was still strutting it's stuff, I just hope it hangs on until at least Sunday, be nice to get it on Day 1 of a new year. There were also mallard, teal, wigeon, little grebe, Canada geese, greylag and a heron in attendance, all nice birds if still available come 1 January 2012. Now down to the Haye.

The lake was quiet, just a few black-headed gulls, pochard and wigeon, but the far shore was covered with a larger than ever flock of lapwing and starling, so concentration time was required. As I slowly moved through the flock I started to pick up the odd brownish bird, we had golden plover here. Time to start counting, we certainly had at least 50 of them. While counting away a large mixed flock of Canada and greylag flew in and landed on the water, scattering what few birds there were there.

Time for the rough lane. Only mute swans once again, I am beginning the think the reports of whooper among them is a figment of someone's imagination. Further round for the tree sparrows, and they did not disappoint, in excess of 20, these look almost guaranteed for the start of the year. Three dumpy birds flew down to join them, corn buntings, I hope they hang around, and the male yellowhammer who was still to be seen. Not a bad little group of birds, and I had a buzzard fly past as I drove home.

Thursday is very wet and the local forecast is for frequent and heavy showers, not the weather for birding by the sound of things. I would try an hour down the Haye.

The large lapwing flock was on the far shore, but light conditions were so poor it was impossible to see what else was hidden among them. The lake itself was very quiet, just a few pochard and black-headed gulls. Next stop the rough lane.

The swans were well spread and although I spent several minutes going through these it was only mutes for me. On now to the tree sparrow spot. I was not to be disappointed here, at least 15 birds were flitting in and out of the hedgerow as they landed on the verge for seed, of which there looked a very abundant supply, they were not going to go hungry today that was for sure.

December 30th is now with us, and a very damp morning it is too. Not that I could have done much this morning as I have a physiotherapy appointment at 12.30 hours, which has rather limited time available. My visit went fine, my shoulder appears to be back to normal, she gave me some ultra sound treatment to my knees to see if it would help, and basically signed me off. She has kept my name on record for a further month so I can 'phone in at anytime to book an appointment if I feel I need to. My other problem is gout, and she cannot do anything about that, if it persists I shall have to visit my doctor, growing old is lovely!

After my appointment I pop up to Branston Water Park, I have not been here for some time so it will be rather nice to check up on the waterfowl situation as a starter for 2012. I was the only person there, the rain was very heavy, but I saw enough to convince me I would start my next years birding from here. Waterfowl were in double figures, and when you add on the other resident birds you could knock off 20 or so in the matter of minutes. The 'tame' ducks were not very pleased with me, they had come running up for food to find I had none, but their luck was in, just as I was about to drive off a family party came in with bag of food, I just hope they could cope with the mad rush that took place.

As I had time on hand I drove home via the Haye, I still have not given up on the wild swans, but as I arrived wild swans became secondary in my thoughts. Near to Roddige Farm is a pig farm, and gliding across this came a dark brown bird with long, slender wings, a harrier, but which one? I drove on as quickly as possible to get a clearer view, and the bird turned out to be a hen harrier, a ringtail, the female of the species. You will remember we saw one of these a few days ago, Sarah found it. Hen harriers are so rare it is safe to presume this is the same bird and has stayed in the area, if we were fortunate enough to see this bird on Day 1, what a start to the year that would be. We live in hope I hasten to add.

The lake was very quiet, only three birds to be seen on the water, these were coot. There did appear to be a lot of people at the leisure activities centre, I wondered if they had been out on the water and disturbed all the birds. Should this happen on a regular basis, and I believe it will, the lake at Whitemoor Haye will lose all of it's charm, but Croxall Lakes NR may take it all on, so it need not become a disaster.

I have just returned from my trip out and found my garden under siege from long-tailed tits, there were at least double figures at my various feeders, and they were more than welcome.

New Year's Eve is upon us, and as with all the best laid plans of mice and men, it has gone astray. The weather is continuing where it left of yesterday, grey, wet and horrible, so any thoughts of going further afield have bitten the dust. I have a few things I can do at home so I will concentrate on those and then pop out this afternoon for a bit of local reconnaissance work. My current thoughts are to visit the permissive footpath area at Blithfield with particular emphasis on the feeding station, in the past I have had woodpecker, nuthatch, treecreeper and siskin here, they would be nice birds to get on Day 1.

As it stands at present my plan for tomorrow or 'Day 1' is as follows. I will obviously start off at home, could be good for a dozen or so birds, then on to Branston Water Park, here I could easily knock up a further 20 or so. Across into Leicestershire for the gulls at the Albert Village Lake, the glaucous gull and yellow-legged gulls are still being reported. Back via Whitemoor Haye, Kings Bromley and finish off at Blithfield. If all goes to plan I could end the day with 50 or more species which would be a nice start to the year. However, for some, 50 on the day is small fry, many will be out after their first 100, and will have been up before dawn in their attempt, those days are over for me I am afraid. I have spent a full 24 hours on occasion when partaking in a charity bird race, and on one magical day we knocked up 99 and that race took place within the county boundaries of Staffordshire, not some bird watching heaven such as Norfolk.

A definite improvement in the weather has occurred, and the sun is actually out, so Blithfield it will be. I drove off via Kings Bromley, needless to say, no egret but I did see a superb grey wagtail, a super male, this more than compensated for the missing egret. I just hope the wagtail hangs around until tomorrow, they have been very thin on the ground this year.

Nothing of great note was seen as I drove across to Blithfield, and due to the improved weather there were several cars parked up on the car park, whether they were birders or walkers I do not know. I made my way to the first view point and as I approached this I could hear the calls of golden plover, and out in Tad Bay they were assembled, along with a few hundred lapwing. The lapwings numbers this year seem to have been very good. At Whitemoor Haye the flock is at least 400, and I would not think it is much less here at Blithfield, they obviously are unlikely to be British birds in this volume, so we must have had a good number of migrants from northern Europe. I was very pleased to see that the water levels was quite high and the birds were much closer than I had anticipated they could be. Going through the birds I estimate there were at least 50 golden plover moving among the lapwings, it is amazing the volume of sound just a few birds could emit. As I was enjoying the lapwings and the plovers a pair of duck flew in, they were goosander, always a nice bird to see, and another bird I hope hangs around for at least another day, along with the plover.

I had the hide to myself, all the feeders were full, and a fair amount of activity was going on. Titmice were plentiful, great, blue and coal, a nuthatch kept popping in, another one I hope hangs on until the 'morrow, and a great spotted woodpecker could be heard calling, but did not visit the feeders. Pheasant were feeding on the fallen seed under the feeders, and a buzzard could be heard calling from overhead. All of this looks very good for the start of the year.

As I type this up it is late in the evening of 31 December, the world outside is black, I think I can safely say my year's birding is now over, and I close on 233 for the year, which includes a 'Lifer. In view of various circumstances I am more than happy with that total. I am even more happy with what I have accomplished.

Firstly, and most important to me, I kept my word made to my dying wife, Dorothy, when I promised her I would write my book, well here I have, good, bad or indifferent, this is my result. Secondly, I have seen some magnificent birds, thirdly, shared the experience with some wonderful people, and finally, I hope, introduced the hobby to many others who will now be able to share the pleasure and companionship such a hobby brings in.

Never again say the words 'I can't because of.......'. If you are able to get into a car then you can, even if you are unable to drive the car, as long as someone else can, you too can enjoy this wonderful world. Remember, I have not walked all that far, I appreciate to do some of the things I have you had to be able to walk with the aid of sticks, but much could have been accomplished from a wheelchair, and finally, probably over 50 per cent was either done from my car or from close proximity to it.

Map references:
Brandon Marsh NR: SP 386761.
Croxall Redwood Plantation: SK 196144.
Albert Village Lake – Car Park: SK 299174.
Albert Village Lake –View Point from B586: SK 309174.

Epilogue

The year is over, I trust you enjoyed the journey as much as I did, and thank you for your company. I hope the intention of introducing you to the pleasures of birding and the ease in doing so has set you up for many a year ahead. I find that when I am sharing my life with birds, I may be on my own, but I am never alone. I have my memories and I am surrounded by exquisite creatures who share this planet with us. As mentioned, many a time, there is a wonderful world out there, full of beautiful riches, and you do not have to travel miles to see them, you just have to keep your eyes open and be patient.

I have been fortunate in having many friends to share this adventure with, they may not realise it but they have helped me through many a painful moment, for which I will always be grateful. I had thought of listing them all, but there is no real need, they know who they are only too well, many have been mentioned through these pages. Three people, however, do require a mention, firstly my daughter Sarah for her support and company, Andy Toman for his marvellous photographs which have enhanced this book, and finally my publishers who took a gamble on an unknown, I just hope it worked out for them.

Back now to the present. We managed to see some very interesting and unusual species during the year, just to remind you of a few: waxwing, mealy redpoll, hawfinch, great northern diver, Caspian gull, great white egret, spoonbill, Ross's goose, wood duck, black-throated diver, honey buzzard, Temminck's stint, Slavonian grebe, American wigeon, rough-legged buzzard, pectoral sandpiper, long-billed dowitcher, red-throated pipit, white-rumped sandpiper, great grey shrike, jack snipe, melodious warbler, little auk, crane, Tundra bean goose, ending up with the glaucous gull, to mention just a few. Before you started out on this journey, how many of those had you heard of?

This journey now ends, but do not let it be the end. Get yourselves a new note book, sharpen your pencil, get your warm clothing ready, and set off on another years birding, you never know what is lying round the corner, it could even be me.

All it remains to say now is have a look at the sequential listing, which follows, and I hope this brings back memories of some of the birds seen.

Once again, thank you for your company, hope to see you in the future.

Sequential Listing 2011

1 January

Home: 1. Carrion Crow, 2. Blackbird, 3. Blue Tit, 4. Robin, 5. Jackdaw, 6. Rook, 7. Magpie, 8. Chaffinch, 9. Great Spotted Woodpecker, 10. Woodpigeon, 11. Starling, 12. Long-tailed Tit, 13. Great Tit, 14. Collared Dove, 15. Waxwing, 16. Sparrowhawk, 17. Canada Goose, 18. Bullfinch, 19. Coal Tit, 20. Dunnock, 21. Lesser Black-backed Gull.

Kings Bromley: 22. Mallard, 23. Barnacle Goose, 24. Wigeon. 25. Moorhen, 26. Greylag Goose, 27. Goosander.

Whitemoor Haye: 28. Song Thrush, 29. Mute Swan, 30. Black-headed Gull.

Stubby Leas: 31. Fieldfare, 32. Redwing, 33. Kestrel, 34. Bewick's Swan.

Tamworth: 35. Tufted Duck, 36. Mistle Thrush.

Coton Lakes: 37. Great Crested Grebe, 38. Coot, 39. Pochard, 40. Little Grebe, 41. Cormorant, 42. Buzzard.

Middleton Hall: 43. Herring Gull, 44. Shelduck, 45. Common Gull.

Whitemoor Haye: 46. Lapwing.

Croxall: 47. Goldeneye, 48. Pheasant.

Home: 49. Greenfinch.

2 January

Home: 50. Blackcap.

Yoxall: 51. Pied Wagtail.

Cannock Chase: 52. Crossbill.

Blithfield Reservoir: 53. Grey Heron, 54. Teal.

Home: 55. Nuthatch, 56. Wren.

3 January

Home: 57. Siskin, 58. Goldfinch.

Park Hall Country Park: 59. Marsh Tit, 60. Long-eared Owl.

Axe Edge Moor: 61. Red Grouse.

4 January

Home: 62. Great Black-backed Gull.

7 January

Kings Bromley – Prince's Farm: 63. House Sparrow.

Home: 64. Reed Bunting.

8 January

Home: 65. Goldcrest.

9 January

Carsington Water: 66. Tree Sparrow.

JCB Rocester: 67. Egyptian Goose, 68. Red-crested Pochard.
Croxall: 69. Whooper Swan, 70. Pink-footed Goose.

11 January
Whitemoor Haye: 71. Golden Plover.
Walton-on-Trent: 72. Raven.

12 January
Blithfield Reservoir: 73. Linnet.

13 January
Chasewater: 74. Smew.

15 January
Chasewater: 75. Iceland Gull.

16 January
Kings Bromley: 76. Little Egret.
Croxall Lakes NR: 77. Redshank.

17 January
Home: 78. Tawny Owl.
Branston Water Park: 79. Gadwall, 80. Shoveler, 81. Lesser Redpoll.

21 January
Orgreave: 82. Stock Dove.

22 January
Park Hall Country Park: 83. Willow Tit.
Cannock Chase – Penkridge Bank: 84. Green Woodpecker.

23 January
Blithfield Reservoir: 85. Ruddy Duck, 86. Treecreeper.

24 January
Whitemoor Haye Main Lake: 87. Curlew.

26 January
Sittle's Farm: 88. Corn Bunting.

29 January
Whitemoor Haye: 89. Yellowhammer.

30 January
Cromford: 90. Hawfinch, 91. Mealy Redpoll, 92. Dipper.
Bradley: 93. Mandarin.

31 January
Cannock Chase, near quarry entrance: 94. Lesser Spotted Woodpecker.

4 February
Croxall Lakes NR: 95. Pintail.

5 February
Croxall Lakes NR: 96. Oystercatcher, 97. Cormorant (Sinensis).

6 February
Carsington Water: 98. Great Northern Diver, 99. Yellow-legged Gull.

7 February
Kingsbury Water Park: 100. Snipe.

8 February
Whitemoor Haye, rough lane: 101. Green Sandpiper.
Walton: 102. Red-legged Partridge.

9 February
Cannock Chase Marquis Drive: 103. Brambling.

10 February
Park Hall Country Park: 104. Jay.

11 February
Whitemoor Haye, rough lane: 105. Merlin.

13 February
Blithfield Reservoir: 106. Mediterranean Gull.

16 February
Whitemoor Haye: 107. Grey Partridge.

21 February
Carsington Water – Sheepwash Hide: 108. Caspian Gull.

24 February
Croxall Lakes NR, West Side: 109. Ringed Plover.

6 March
Blithfield Reservoir, Tad Bay: 110. Great White Egret.

12 March
Croxall Lakes NR, West Side: 111. Stonechat.

13 March
Whitemoor Haye, the rough lane: 112. Skylark.

15 March
Titchwell: 113. Avocet, 114. Dunlin, 115. Ruff, 116. Black-tailed Godwit, 117. Brent
  Goose.

16 March
Salthouse: 118. Turnstone, 119. Meadow Pipit.
Cley: 120. Shorelark, 121. Grey Plover, 122. Spoonbill.

17 March
Cley: 123. Marsh Harrier, 124. Barn Owl.

18 March
Titchwell: 125. Cetti's Warbler, 126. Twite, 127. Red-breasted Merganser, 128. Long-
  tailed Duck, 129. Common Scoter, 130. Sanderling, 131. Bar-tailed Godwit, 132.
  Water Pipit, 133. Chiffchaff.

19 March
Thornham: 134. Rock Pipit.
Hunstanton: 135. Fulmar.
Holme: 136. Peregrine Falcon.
Snettisham: 137. Knot.

20 March
Cley – Sea Watch: 138. Kittiwake, 139. Eider, 140. Little Gull.
Cley Reserve: 141. Ross's Goose.
Stiffkey: 142. Sand Martin.

21 March
Titchwell: 143. Spotted Redshank.

22 March
Thrapston (Northants): 144. Red Kite.

27 March
Whitemoor Haye: 145. Little Owl.

1 April
Yoxall: 146. Swallow.
Blithfield Reservoir, Nr Angling Club: 147 White Wagtail.

3 April
Wolseley Bridge, SWT – HQ: 148. Wood Duck, 149. Kingfisher.

6 April
Blithfield Reservoir – Dam Wall: 150. Yellow Wagtail.

8 April
Blithfield Reservoir – Dam Wall: 151. Wheatear.
Blithfield Reservoir – Admaston Reach: 152: Little Ringed Plover.
Croxall Lakes NR: 153. Common Tern.

12 April
Rangemoor: 154. House Martin

14 April
Yoxall Meadow Woods: 155. Willow Warbler.

17 April
Croxall Lakes NR: 156. Sedge Warbler, 157. Whitethroat.

18 April
Chasewater: 158. Whinchat.

21 April
Cannock Chase – Seven Springs: 159. Garden Warbler, 160. Wood Warbler.
Cannock Chase – between Seven Springs and The Stepping Stones: 161. Tree Pipit.

22 April
Croxall Lakes NR: 162. Reed Warbler.

23 April
Croxall Lakes NR: 163. Grasshopper Warbler, 164. Common Sandpiper.

24 April
Croxall Lakes NR: 165. Ring Ouzel.

25 April
Croxall Lakes NR: 166. Cuckoo.

27 April
Rosliston Forestry Centre Flight Pond: 167. Pied Flycatcher.

29 April
Tittesworth reservoir: 168. Hobby.

30 April
Whitemoor Haye: 169. Arctic Tern, 170. Swift.
Alrewas National Memorial Arboretum: 171. Lesser Whitethroat.

1 May
Whitemoor Haye: 172. Greenshank.

3 May
Blithfield Reservoir – Blythe Bay: 173. Black Tern.

9 May
Flamborough Head – North Landing: 174. Guillemot, 175. Razorbill, 176. Puffin, 177. Gannet.
Bempton Cliffs RSPB: 178. Feral Pigeon, 179. Rock Dove.

12 May
Whitemoor Haye, rough lane: 180. Quail.

14 May
Whitemoor Haye: 181. Little Tern.
Shustoke Reservoir: 182: Black-throated Diver.

16 May
Whisby Nature Park: 183. Nightingale, 184. Turtle Dove.

19 May
Croxall Lakes NR: 185. Temminck's Stint.

22 May
Tittesworth Reservoir – River Churnet: 186. Spotted Flycatcher, 187. Redstart, 188. Grey Wagtail.

27 May
Staunton Harold Reservoir – Dam: 189. Osprey.
Staunton Harold Reservoir – Calke Viewpoint: 190. Goshawk.
Cannock Chase – Sherbrook Valley: 191. Woodcock.

29 May
Croxall Lakes NR: 192. Little Stint.

5 June
Blithfield Reservoir – Tad Bay: 193. Wood Sandpiper.
Hoar Cross: 194. Honey Buzzard.

14 June
Lichfield: 195. Harris Hawk.

17 June
Cannock Chase: 196. Nightjar.

18 June
Alrewas Aboretum: 197. Hen Harrier.

19 June
Blithfield Reservoir: 198. Sandwich Tern.

3 July
Blithfield Reservoir : 199. Garganey.

!0 July
Pitsford Reservoir: 200. Slavonian Grebe, 201. American Wigeon.

15 July
Blacktoft RSPB: 202. Marsh Sandpiper, 203. Bearded Tit.

20 August
Rocester – JCB: 204. Swan Goose/Chinese Goose.

22 September
Blithfield Reservoir: 205. Curlew Sandpiper.

23 September
King's Mill Reservoir, Mansfield: 206. Black-necked Grebe.

27 September
Blithfield Reservoir: 207. Greater Scaup.

29 September
Blithfield Reservoir: 208. Rough-legged Buzzard.

30 September
Frampton Marsh RSPB, Lincs: 209. Pectoral Sandpiper.
Freiston Shore RSPB, Lincs: 210. Long-billed Dowitcher, 211. Red-throated Pipit.

16 October
Daventry Reservoir Country Park: 212. Grey Phalarope.

21 October
Old Moor RSPB Reserve: 213. Water Rail.

23 October
Rutland Water – Lapwing Hide: 214. White-rumped Sandpiper.

24 October
Whitemoor Haye: 215. Hybrid Pochard/Tufted Duck.

28 October
Cannock Chase Quarry: 216. Great Grey Shrike.

30 October
Croxall Lakes NR – Main Lake: 217. Jack Snipe.

31 October
Attenborough NR: 218. Squacco Heron.

7 November, Norfolk Week
Blakeney – Norfolk: 219. Cattle Egret.

8 November
Kelling Heath: 220. Dartford Warbler – audible.
Glandford: 221. Black Redstart.
Cley Beach – Sea Watch: 222. Red-throated Diver, 223. Velvet Scoter, 224. Little Auk,
  225. Pomerine Skua.

9 November
Strumpshaw Fen RSPB: 226. Bittern.
Happisburgh: 227. Melodious Warbler – 'Lifer'.

10 November
Titchwell RSPB: 228. Yellow-browed Warbler – audible.

12 November
Holme NR: 229. Desert Wheatear.

13 November
Cley Marsh NR: 230. Lapland Bunting.

14 November
Guyhirn: 231. Crane.

21 December
Whitemoor Haye, Sittle's Farm: 232. Bean Goose (Tundra Race).

26 December
Albert Village Lake, Leics: 233. Glaucous Gull.